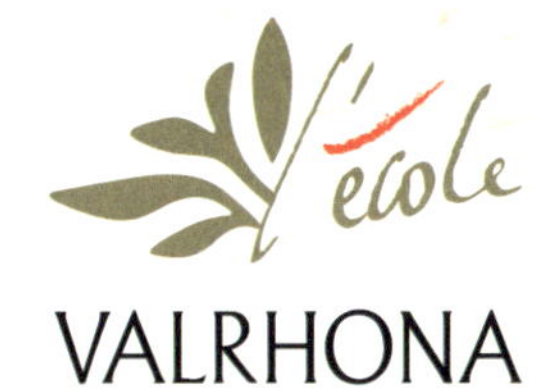

L'ÉCOLE VALRHONA BROOKLYN
2018 PROFESSIONAL CLASS SCHEDULE

We invite you to share in our taste for excellence at L'École Valrhona's newest, state-of-the-art location in Brooklyn, New York, with training courses designed to meet the needs of today's pastry professionals.

ARTISTIC CHOCOLATE SHOWPIECES
FEBRUARY 26-28
Chef Stéphane Tréand

WEDDING CAKES ✲
FEBRUARY 26-28
Chef Ron Ben-Israel

MODERN BUFFET
MARCH 6-7
Chef Sarah Tibbetts

FRAMED CHOCOLATE BONBONS WITH THEORY
MARCH 19-21
Chef Nicolas Botomisy

ALL ABOUT PRALINÉ
JULY 24-25
Chef Ginger Elizabeth Hahn

PANNING AND CHOCOLATE TREATS
APRIL 23-25
Chef Derek Poirier

MOLDED CHOCOLATE BONBONS
MAY 21-23
Chef Nicolas Botomisy

TASTES AND VARIATIONS ON VIENNOISERIE
JUNE 5-6
Chef Greg Mindel

PETITS GÂTEAUX AND PLATED DESSERTS
JUNE 11-13
Chef Patrice Demers

ARTISTIC CHOCOLATE SHOWPIECES
JUNE 18-20
Chef Stéphane Tréand

A COLLABORATION ON ENTREMETS AND PETITS GÂTEAUX
JULY 9-11
Chef Antonio Bachour and Chef Carles Mampel

WEDDING CAKES ✲
JULY 16-18
Chef Ron Ben-Israel

MOLDED CHOCOLATE BONBONS
JULY 16-18
Chef Derek Poirier

MODERN BUFFET
AUGUST 7-8
Chef Sarah Tibbetts

ENTREMETS AND TRAVEL CAKES
AUGUST 21–22
Chef Nathaniel Reid

PLATED DESSERTS ACCORDING TO LINCOLN
AUGUST 28–30
Chef Lincoln Carson

FRAMED CHOCOLATE BONBONS WITH THEORY
SEPTEMBER 10-12
Chef Derek Poirier

PANNING AND CHOCOLATE TREATS
SEPTEMBER 17-19
Chef Nicolas Botomisy

INTRODUCTION TO CHOCOLATE
SEPTEMBER 25-26
Chef to be announced

TASTES AND VARIATIONS ON VIENNOISERIE
OCTOBER 2-3
Chef Greg Mindel

PLATED DESSERTS
OCTOBER 16-17
Chef Philippe Givre

UNVEILING MODERN PÂTISSERIE
OCTOBER 23-25
Chef William Werner

A MODERN TWIST ON TARTS
NOVEMBER 5-7
Chef Gianluca Fusto

✲ *Off-site course. Please visit www.us.valrhona.com for details.*

To learn more about L'École Valrhona Brooklyn's 2018 schedule or to register, visit *http://bit.ly/ecolevalrhona* **or** *us.valrhona.com*

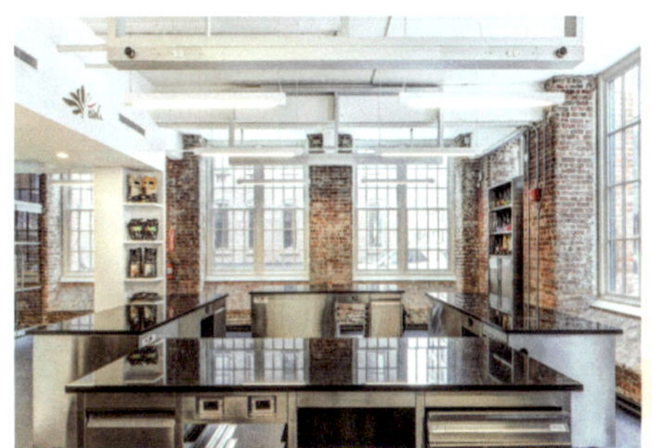

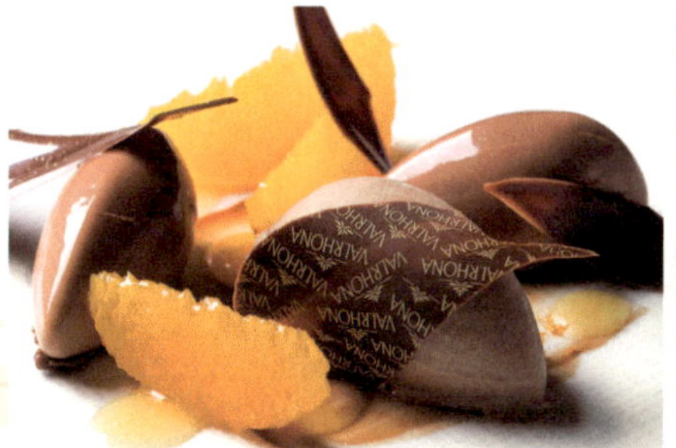

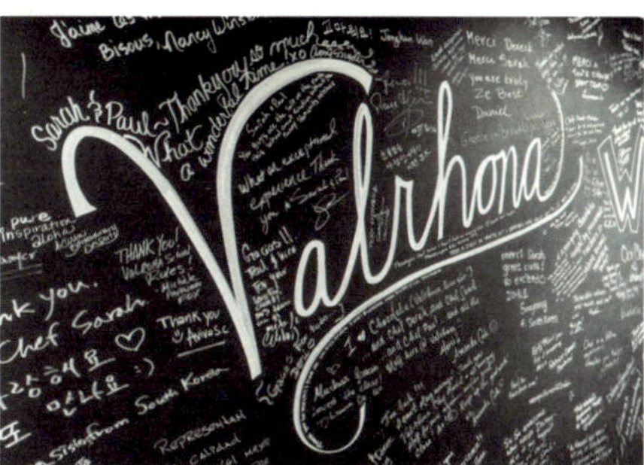

Classes and Dates are subject to change. Please check ***http://bit.ly/ecolevalrhona*** *or* ***us.valrhona.com*** *for up-to-date information.*

VALRHONA INC • 222 Water Street, Brooklyn, NY 11201 • 718-522-7001 • us.valrhona.com • ecolebrooklyn@valrhona.com
@valrhonausa #EcoleValrhonaBK #ValrhonaUSA

Nick Muncy LLC
San Francisco, CA

WEB
www.toothachemagazine.com

CONTACT
For inquires about advertising, distribution, or collaborations:
nickm@toothachemagazine.com

Printed in Canada

First Printing, 2018

ISBN: 978-0-9988640-2-0

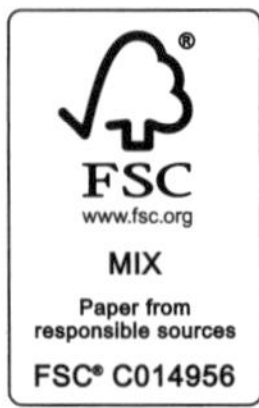

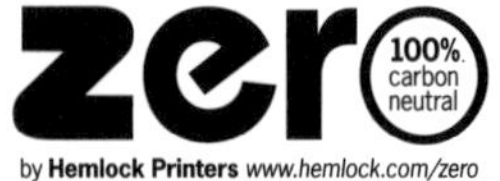

"The man with a toothache thinks everyone happy whose teeth are sound. The poverty-stricken man makes the same mistake about the rich man."
- Bernard Shaw

ISSUE NUMBER THREE:

Toothache issue three is here! The magazine has survived its first year, and because of your support and love, Toothache forges on. When I started this magazine, I never thought this would become my full-time job. Doing something that you have no experience with can be fun and exhilarating, but also incredibly stressful.

Our last issue received a considerable amount of attention and press, and I'm excited to see the magazine reach people across the country and world. After getting many requests, I'm also pleased to have finally started subscriptions, despite complicating the job for such a small team.

Each chef controls their own content, so I never know what the magazine is going to end up looking like until its done. This issue happens to have a ton of interviews and recipes that feature old friends, new friends, and chefs that are my culinary idols (of which I would very much like to be friends with). Some chefs spoke about creativity, influences, and tradition. Some chefs wrote about managing their restaurants, and others talked about their plans and dreams for the future.

Lastly, this issue's cover features an octopus for absolutely no reason, except that it looks neat.

Toothache is for chefs, by chefs. I hope you enjoy it.

Nick Muncy - *editor and creator*

editor & creator:

nick muncy

contributers:

albert adrià
erik anderson
gabriela càmara
melissa coppel
melissa king
belinda leong
gabriele riva
miles thompson
aitor zabala
mike zakowski

editorial assistants:

michelle matvey
ben rosenberg

photography & art:

nick muncy
patrick sean gibson
jill paider
alan shortall
bonjwing lee

printer:

Hemlock Printers Ltd.
7050 Buller Ave.
Burnaby BC Canada VSJ 454

instagram & twitter:

@toothache_mag

thank you:

austin muncy
charlotte randolph

CONTENTS

CONTENTS

TICKETS

BODEGA
1900
BARCELONA

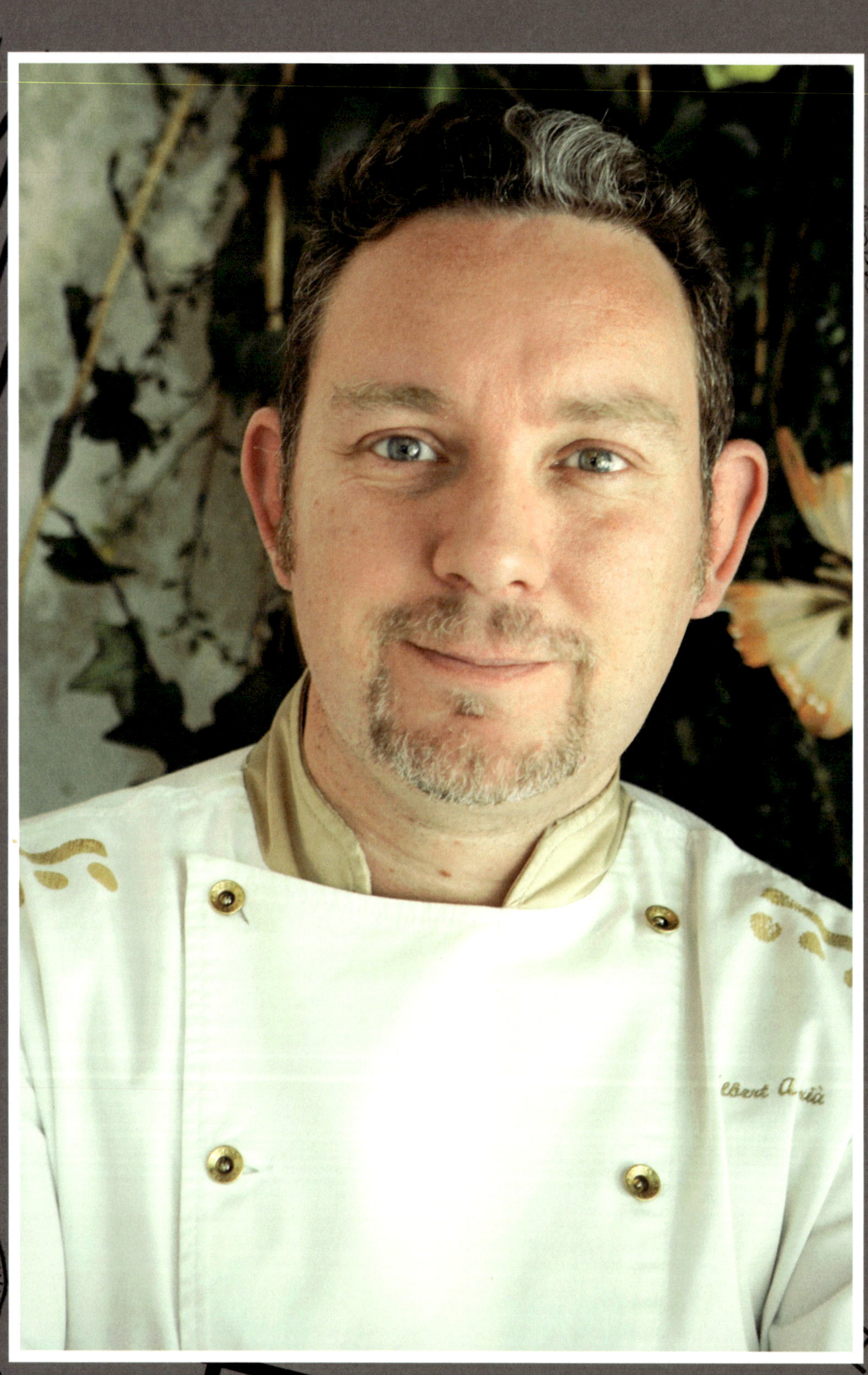

NIÑO VIEJO

HOJA S

PAKTA

albert adrià

elBarri
barcelona, spain

Porque decidió abrir un grupo de restaurantes en vez de uno solo?

No fue un acto premeditado, sencillamente me di cuenta de lo interesante que era tener un restaurante cerca de otro para aprovechar sinergías e incluso provocar cierta competividad entre estos, para ser mejores en el conjunto.

Como eligió cada uno de los diferentes conceptos en los restaurantes? Usted crea un restaurante para un jefe de cocina, o viceversa, busca a un jefe de cocina para un concepto?

Un poco de todo: en el caso de Tickets, Bodega 1900 y Enigma, son conceptos creados en los que poco a poco se ha ido asentando un jefe de cocina. En el caso de Enigma específicamnte, este jefe ya trabajó conmigo en el desaparecido 41°. En el caso del Pakta y Hoja Santa, los jefes de cocina ya trabajaban conmigo y luego creamos los restaurantes, ya que como es obvio, mis conocimientos de cocina Peruana o Mexicana son limitados.

Why did you decide to open a group of restaurants instead of a single restaurant?

It was not a premeditated act. I simply realized how interesting it was to have one restaurant near another. To take advantage of synergies and even provoke some competition among them, to be better in the whole.

How do you choose your different restaurant concepts? Do you create the restaurant for a chef, or do you find the chef for a concept?

It's a bit of everything: in the case of Tickets, Bodega 1900 and Enigma, these were concepts created in which little by little, a chef has settled. In the case of Enigma specifically, the chef had worked with me at the now-closed 41 Degrees. In the case of Pakta and Hoja Santa, the chefs already worked with me, and we then created the restaurants, since as is obvious, my knowledge of Peruvian or Mexican cuisine is limited.

Que tan involucrado está en cada uno de los conceptos? Está en todos o en uno más que en otros?

Absolutamente a partes iguales, con mi equipo les dedicamos el mismo tiempo y esfuerzo a cada uno.

Los cocineros en USA a veces mencionan que hoy en día hay falta de cocineros, especialmente de cocineros buenos. Es un problema también en Barcelona?

Por suerte no tenemos el problema de conseguir cocineros, el problema lo tenemos con la sala y encontrar camareros.

Cuando usted se decide en hacer un restaurante que sirva algo como es la cocina mexicana, Con cuanto tiempo de antelación trabaja sobre el concepto y el menu?

Trabajamos con mi equipo y los chefs de cada restaurante para implementar platos nuevos, pero en el caso de los mexicanos, Paco Méndez es mi socio y uno de los mejores cocineros que conozco, en su caso apenas intervenimos en la creación de los platos más allá de algún consejo.

Le dedica mucho tiempo a viajar y probar recetas?

Viajar es importantísimo para ver cosas nuevas, productos, estilos o conceptos pero hay que encontrar el equilibrio, porque si estás mucho tiempo fuera no es bueno para tu negocio.

Los clientes de su restaurante se esperan platos de elBulli?

elBulli es historia y la cocina sigue evolucionando, lo que hace 10 años era novedoso hoy te lo comes en diferentes restaurantes de todo el mundo, entiendo que nunca se ha comido tan bien como ahora, en España seguro y que cada vez más hay una madurez para buscar la buena cocina, sea o no creativa.

How involved are you with each concept? Are you at any single one more than the others?

Absolutely in equal parts. With my team, we dedicate the same time and effort to each one.

Chefs in the US sometimes mention that nowadays there is a lack of cooks, especially good ones. Is that an issue for you in Barcelona?

Luckily, we do not have the problem of getting cooks. The problem we have is with the dining room and finding waiters.

When you decide to do a restaurant serving something like Mexican food, how long do you work on the concept and menu?

My team and I work alongside the chefs of each restaurant to implement new dishes, but in the case of our Mexican dishes, Paco Méndez is my partner and one of the best chefs I know. In his case, we hardly intervene in the creation of the dishes beyond some advice.

Is there a lot of time traveling and testing recipes when working on a restaurant concept and menu?

Traveling is extremely important to see new things, products, styles or concepts, but you have to find the balance. If you are out for a long time, it's not good for your business.

Do customers expect elBulli dishes at your restaurants?

elBulli is history, and cuisine continues to evolve. What was novel 10 years ago today you eat in different restaurants around the world. I believe that we have never eaten so well as now, in Spain definitely, and that more and more, there is the maturity to look for good cuisine, whether it is creative or not.

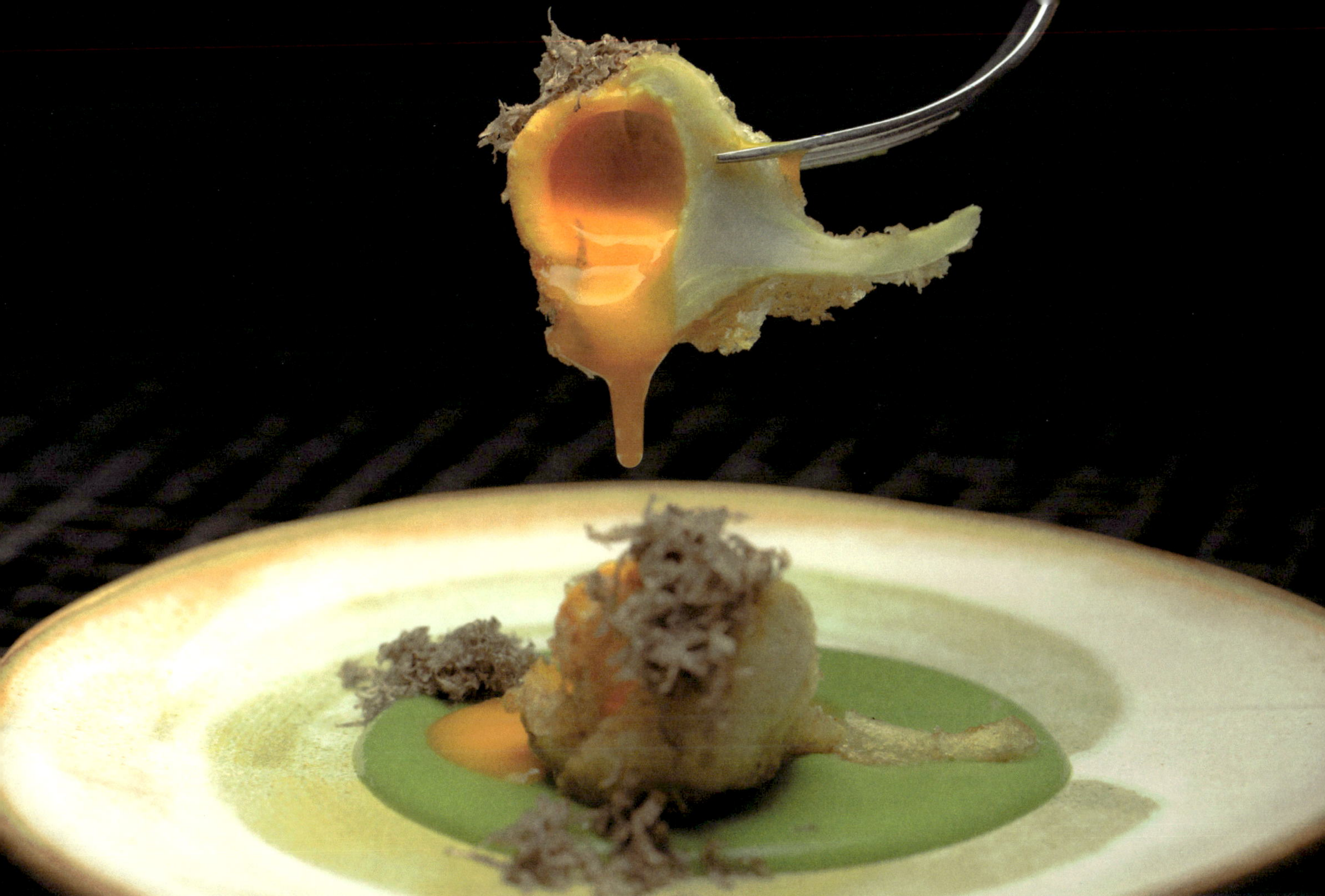

Cleaned Artichokes

Ingredients:

1000 g	artichokes
1000 g	mineral water
3 g	ascorbic acid

Method:

Combine the water and ascorbic acid. Peel the artichokes and scoop out the heart (trying to leave it as big as possible), and cut the top to 3 cm. Empty the center of the artichoke with the help of a #22 scoop. Peel the stem of the artichoke, and place the cleaned artichokes into a vacuum bag. Add 150 g of the acidified water and vacuum to 100%. Cook in a steam oven at 100 C for 17 minutes, and then cool them in an ice bath. Reserve 10 pieces for frying.

Spinach Puree

Ingredients:

100 g	baby spinach

Method:

Blanch the spinach for 15 seconds and then submerge in ice water to cool. Blend the spinach with the same amount of ice water and then pass. Keep cold.

Chicken Stock

Ingredients:

2.5 kg	chicken carcasses
750 g	chicken
3,75 L	water
13 g	salt
25 g	cilantro
25 g	mint

Method:

In a large pot, boil the water, chicken bones, chicken meat, and salt. Once it reaches a boil, turn the heat to low and let cook for 4 hours. Remove the impurities formed on the surface, then strain. Add the cilantro and mint and let it infuse until the stock cools.

Assembly

Toss a cleaned artichoke in flour and shake off the excess. Place an egg yolk in the center and sprinkle flour over the yolk with the help of a small sieve. Dust off excess flour and then submerge the yolk-filled artichoke into 190 C oil and fry for 55 seconds. Once fried, take the artichoke out of the oil, dry on a paper towel, and sprinkle with red chihuacle powder. Place 40 g of artichoke mole on a hot plate, and place the fried artichoke in the center. Microplane 2 g of black truffle over the top and serve.

Su trabajo es copiado por muchos chefs alrededor del mundo, eso le molesta, especialmente cuando están mal ejecutados?

Es cierto, cuando copian o se inspiran en tu trabajo no deja de se un homenaje, otra cosa es que cuando van a un congreso y lo hacen público debería comentar la autoria o quedan en evidencia, como el que ejecuta mal algunas técnicas, las técnicas no son ni buenas ni malas, es el chef con su criterio y sentido común el que puede hacer un buen plato o una copia.

Your work is copied by other chefs around the world. Does that bother you, especially when done poorly?

It's true, when they copy or are inspired by your work, it does not stop being a tribute. It is another thing when they go out and make it public; they should comment on the authorship, or they remain at fault. For the one who executes techniques badly, the techniques are neither good or bad, it is the chef. It is up to their skill and common sense that can make a good dish or a copy.

Que tipo de consejo le daría a jóvenes cocineros que quieran abrir su propio restaurante?

Muchos. Pasión entendiéndola por trabajar 12 horas al día y humildad entendiendo que te levantas cada día sin saber nada y te queda todo por aprender... Por otro lado, personalmente no les recomendaría tener su propio restaurante hasta los 30 años, antes deben viajar y conocer muchas de las verdades que existen en este oficio.

What advice would you give a young chef who wants to open their restaurant?

Lots. Passion for understanding it by working 12 hours a day, and humility in understanding that you get up everyday without knowing anything and still have everything to learn. On the other hand, personally I would not recommend having your own restaurant until you are 30 years old. Before, you should travel and learn many of the truths that exist in this trade.

Como se imagina el futuro de la cocina española?

Brillante, cada vez se come mejor y mejor, al final es una cuestión de honestidad porque los que lo hacen mal, ya saben generalmente que lo hacen mal. En España tenemos cientos de cocineros jovencísimos que están haciendo cosas muy interesantes y restaurantes donde se come realmente bien.

What do you imagine the future will look like for Spanish Cuisine?

Brilliant, we are eating better and better. In the end it is a matter of honesty, because those who do it poorly, generally know that they do it poorly. In Spain we have hundreds of very young chefs who are doing very interesting things and creating restaurants where you can truly eat well.

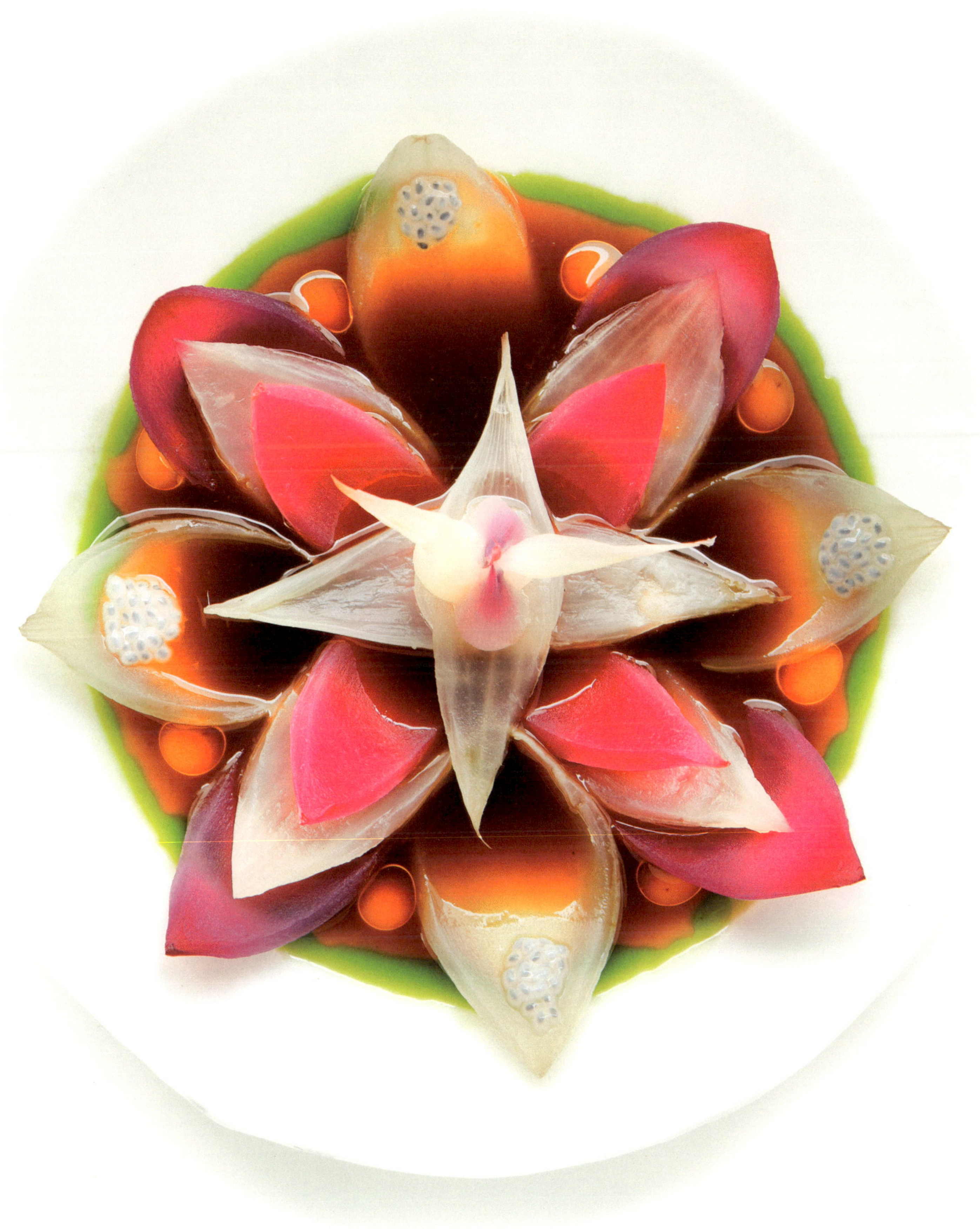

Onion Water Lily

Xnipek Salsa

Ingredients:

100 g	purple onion
25 g	habanero chili
70 g	lime juice
20 g	orange juice
.5 g	dried oregano
2 g	salt

Method:

Cut the onion into a fine julienne. Clean the habanero and cut into cubes as small as possible. In a bowl, combine the salt and onion and squeeze the onions until they are translucent and soft. Add the habanero pepper, lemon juice, orange juice, and oregano. Mix well and leave to marinate for 3 hours. Reserve in a sealed container in the refrigerator overnight. Drain and reserve the liquid.

Purple Onion Petals

Ingredients:

1 ea	purple onion, 90 g
150 g	Xnipek salsa (recipe above)
to taste	fine salt

Method:

Peel the whole onion and put it in a vacuum bag with salt and salsa. Compress and seal at 100 % vacuum, and then cook in a steam oven for 30 minutes at 100 C. Remove from the oven, and cool in an ice bath. Let the onion sit in a refrigerator for 12 hours, then cut into quarters and reserve.

White Onion Petals

Ingredients:

1 ea	white onion, whole 150 g
to taste	salt
to taste	black pepper
10 g	Worcestershire sauce

Method:

In a rectangle of foil, place the onion with salt, pepper and Worcestershire sauce. Wrap and cook in a 180 C oven for approximately 50 minutes. Allow to cool to room temperature before cutting into quarters.

To Build the Water Lily

Ingredients:

purple onion petals

white onion petals

Method:

Arrange the petals with the larger on the outside and smaller on the inside to make the shape of a water lily. Reserve for service.

Xanthan Gum Base

Ingredients:

1 lt	mineral water
12 g	xanthan gum

Method:

Blend the water and xanthan to hydrate the gum. Reserve in an air-tight container in the refrigerator.

Onion Broth

Ingredients:

2 kg	onion
500 g	water
20 g	aji amarillo pepper paste
50 g	rice vinegar
25 g	xanthan gum base (recipe above)

Method:

Peel and cut the onion into a julienne. Sauté in a sauce-pan with a little bit of olive oil until well cooked. Add the water and cook for 30 minutes over low heat. Once cooked, cool down over an ice bath. Strain the broth before blending in the rice vinegar, aji amarillo paste and xanthan gum base.

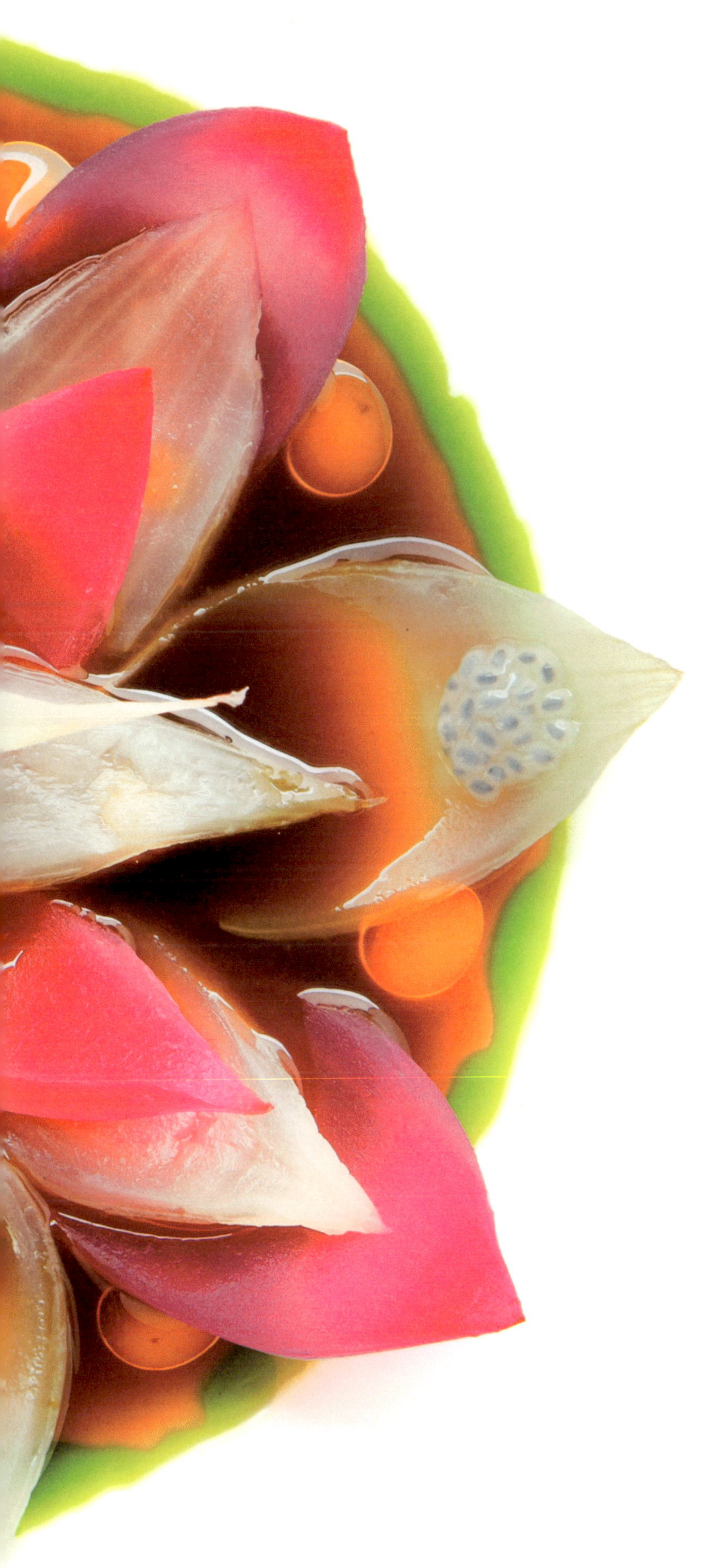

Cilantro Oil

Ingredients:

300 g	fresh cilantro
125 g	sunflower oil

Method:

Remove the leaves from the stem and blend with the oil at 80 C for 5 minutes. Pass through a fine strainer and then through a coffee filter. Allow the oil to cool and reserve in a pipette for service.

Chili Oil

Ingredients:

1 ea	dried chili
10 g	olive oil
to taste	salt

Method:

Put the oil, crushed pepper, and salt in a small pot and cook over low heat. Cook for 10 minutes and then remove from the heat. Put in a bottle and reserve.

To Hydrate the Basil Seeds

Ingredients:

20 g	basil seeds
20 g	mineral water

Method:

Soak the basil seeds in the water and reserve in an airtight container.

Assembly

Heat the onion broth in a saucepan. Place the water lily plate under the salamander to warm it slightly. Once hot, add the onion broth. Make a line of cilantro oil around the outside of the dish. Between each petal, add a drop of chili oil. On the tip of four outside white petals, add a small spoon of basil seeds. Serve.

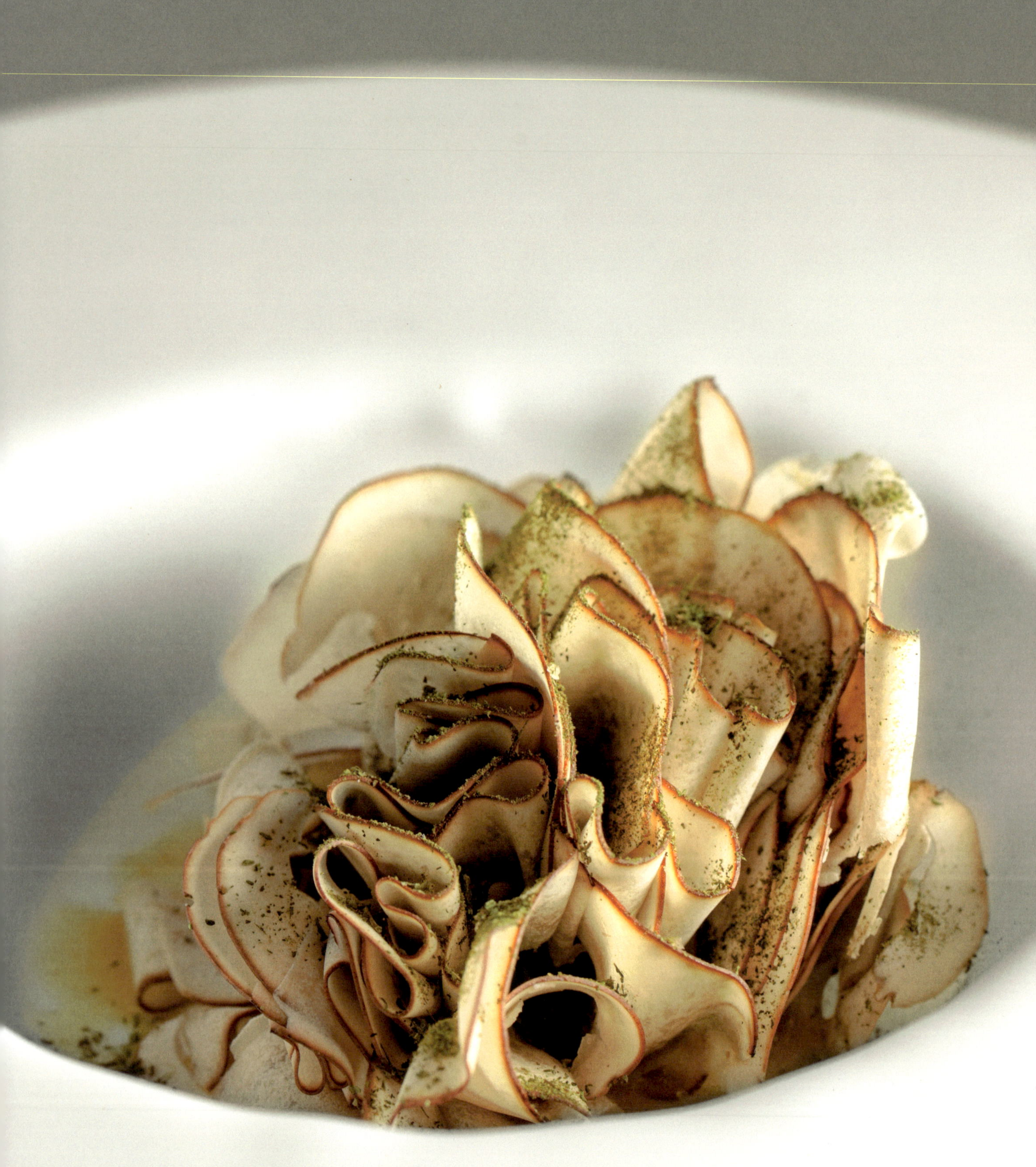

Cloud of Ceps

Parmesan Cream

Ingredients:

100 g	Parmesan cheese
200 g	cream

Method:

Cut the Parmesan into cubes. Place them in a thermomix, and start blending. Boil the cream and then pour it over the blending cheese. Let blend for 2 minutes before straining and reserving in a container. Cover the top with plastic wrap to keep a skin from forming.

Garlic Oil

Ingredients:

100 g	olive oil
50 g	garlic

Method:

In a sauce-pan, arrange the garlic and oil, and lightly brown the garlic. Place in a vacuum bag and cook at 80 C for 4 hours. Cool.

Cep Broth

Ingredients:

1000 g	ceps
1 L	mineral water
100 g	garlic oil (recipe above)
4 g	rosemary
2 g	lemon thyme
60 g	white wine vinegar

Method:

Cut the ceps into sheets. Brown the sheets of mushroom in the garlic oil in a large sauce-pot. Once the mushrooms are golden, add the water and deglaze the pot. Cook over low heat for 30 minutes and then add the aromatic herbs and the vinegar. Let stand for 30 minutes and then strain. Season with salt to taste and cool down.

Cep Cloud

Ingredients:

24 ea	ceps

Method:

Clean the mushrooms with a damp paper towel and a peeler. Shave the mushrooms with a truffle slicer in your hand, until you get a flower shape. Reserve in a small container.

Lemon Thyme Powder

Ingredients:

1 bunch	lemon thyme

Method:

Place the lemon thyme on sheets in the dehydrator and let dry for 24 hours. After it has fully dehydrated, remove the leaves from the stems. Using a thermomix, blend the leaves into a fine powder, and pass through a sieve. Reserve.

Assembly

Put 7 g of Parmesan cream in the bottom of the bowl. Place the cloud of ceps on top and season with a little powdered salt. At the table, sprinkle the thyme powder and finish with 20 g of cep broth. Serve.

Humita

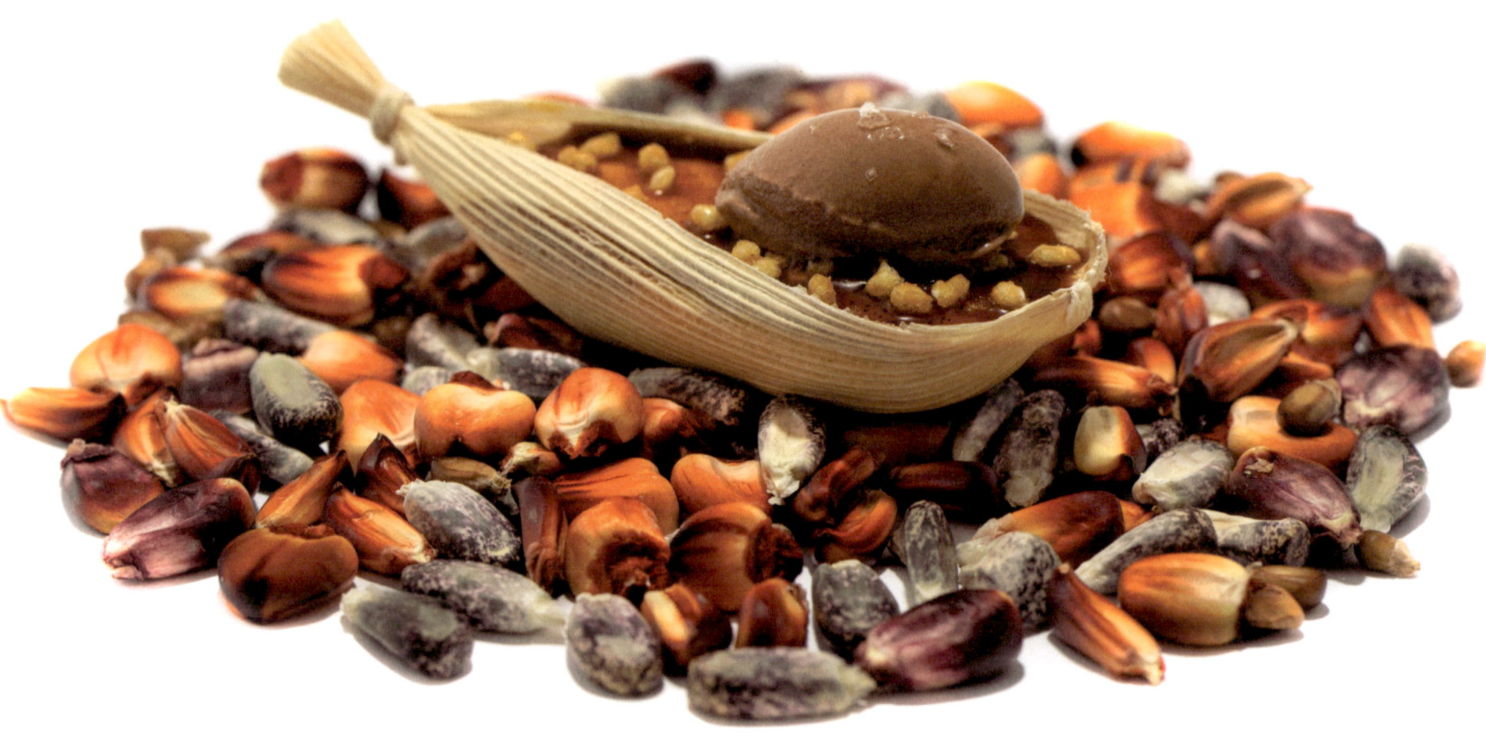

Corn Water

Ingredients:

660 g canned corn, Bonduelle brand

Method:

Blitz the corn in a robot coup. Squeeze the corn through cheesecloth to get the liquid. Reserve in the refrigerator.

Corn Puree

Ingredients:

1000 g canned corn, Bonduelle brand

Method:

Blend the corn and pass through a fine sieve. Cook the strained mixture in a saucepan until it thickens. Reserve in an airtight container in the refrigerator.

Corn Cream

Ingredients:

250 g milk
250 g corn puree (recipe above)
160 g egg yolk
125 g sugar
50 g cornstarch
110 g butter

Method:

In a saucepan, heat the milk and corn puree. Add the yolks, sugar, and cornstarch and heat until it reaches 84 C, then remove from the heat. Cool over an ice bath until it reaches 30 C, and then add then blend in the butter. Once the cream is made, reserve in a container in the refrigerator.

Clarified Brown Butter

Ingredients:

100 g butter

Method:

Clarify the butter and separate it from the milk solids. Leave on the stove until it turns tan.

Cinnamon Candy Powder

Ingredients:

500 g white sugar

30 g cinnamon stick

Method:

Place the sugar and cinnamon in a pot and cook until the sugar is a caramel color. Pour onto a silpat lined tray and let cool. Once the caramel is set up and cooled, blend in a food processor and reserve in a bag or airtight container. Grind only what is needed for the recipe.

Cinnamon Ice Cream

Ingredients:

374 g milk

20 g skim milk powder

36 g trimoline

2.4 g ice cream stabilizer

72 g chocolate, guanaja

24 g white sugar

24 g cinnamon candy powder (recipe above)

12 g glucose powder

47 g cream

Method:

In a sauce-pot, combine the milk, trimoline, and glucose and bring to 40 C. Sprinkle in the rest of the dry ingredients, and heat the base to 82 C. One it has reached 82 C, strain the base over the chocolate and blend it with a hand blender. Finally, blend in the cream and leave to mature 24 hours.

For the Humita

Ingredients:

400 g corn puree (recipe above)

400 g corn water (recipe above)

400 g corn cream (recipe above)

3.2 g agar agar

80 g clarified brown butter (recipe above)

Method:

Place the corn water, butter, and agar in a saucepan and bring to a boil to activate the agar. In a separate saucepan, heat the corn cream and puree. With the help of a hand blender, mix all the ingredients until a homogeneous mix is obtained. Fill each corn husk with 25 g of the base. Let it set up in the refrigerator.

Coffee Toffee

Ingredients:

50 g white sugar

40 g cream

20 g espresso coffee

4 g ground coffee beans

Method:

Make a dry caramel. Heat the cream with the espresso and add the cream little by little into the caramel. Take off the heat and add the ground coffee. Let cool and reserve in a piping bag.

Caramelized Quinoa

Ingredients:

50 g white quinoa

50 g sugar

Method:

Boil the quinoa for 12 minutes, until it is well cooked. Drain and let dry on trays at room temperature for 48 hours. Fry the dried quinoa in 180 C oil for 10 seconds and inflates. Season and dry well on paper towels. Cook the sugar with a little water until it reaches 118 C. Then stir in the quinoa until the sugar coats them and crystallizes.

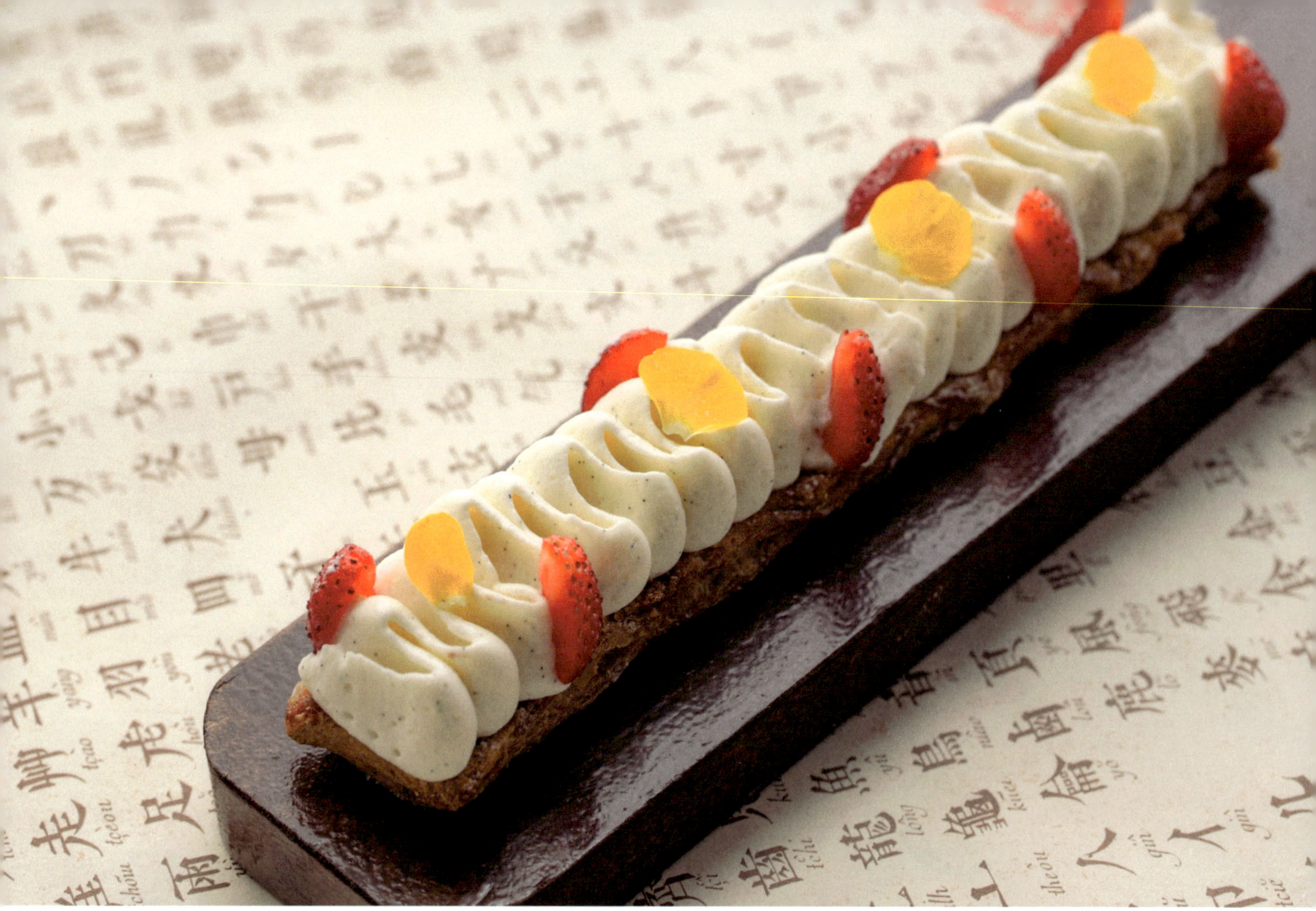

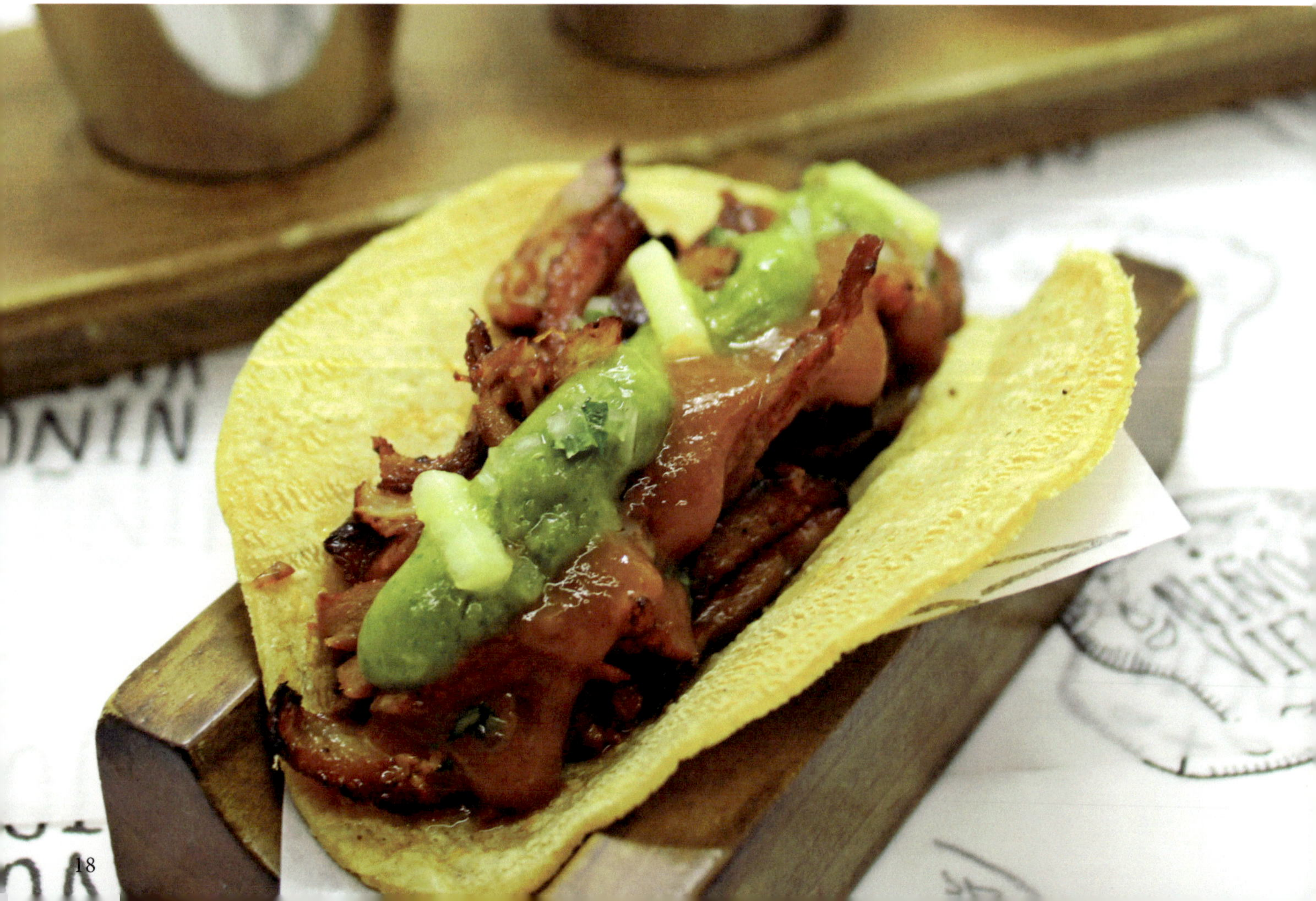

Vilaplana Puff Pastry with Burnt Cream

Pastry Cream

Ingredients:

250 g	milk
50 g	sugar
4.5 ea	egg yolks
22.5 g	cornstarch
1/4	lemon peel
1/4	cinnamon stick
1/4	vanilla bean

Method:

Boil the milk with the vanilla, cinnamon, and lemon peel. Infuse for 10 minutes. Combine the eggs, sugar, and cornstarch, and then temper in the strained milk. Stir well and cook to 85 C. Cool the cream and cover the surface with plastic wrap so keep a skin from forming. Reserve.

Vilaplana Puff Pastry

Ingredients:

1 ea	puff pastry, 80 g
1/2	puff pastry, 40 g

Method:

Look at the color of the puff pastry and see if you need to bake a little more. Store the puff pastry, with silica gel, in a tightly covered airtight container.

Burnt Cream

Ingredients:

sugar glass

sugar

Method:

Put the cream on the puff pastry. Burn the cream. Cover the top part of the puff pastry. Sprinkle the top of the puff pastry with icing sugar.

Tacos Al Pastor

Pastor Salsa

Ingredients:

40 g	green salsa
2 g	salt
1.5 g	lime juice
1.5 g	oil 0.4
3 g	cilantro juice (recipe below)
15 g	avocado

Method:

Combine all of the ingredients and mix. Store in a bottle in the refrigerator.

Tortillas

Ingredients:

1 kg	masa harina
110 g	corn flour, Maseca
200 g	mineral water
	fine salt

Method:

Boil the water and mix with the other ingredients. Knead the dough until the masa is fully mixed. Keep the fridge covered with a damp cloth. Portion into 16 g balls and flatten in a press to 2mm.

Pork Trompo

Ingredients:

150 g	duroc pork neck
50 g	duroc pork jowl
2 g	Nomu spice mix
15 g	guajillo chili
3 g	ancho chile
41 g	pineapple juice
33 g	achiote
13 g	apple vinegar
17 g	salt

Method:

Combine all of the ingredients, minus the meat, and crush together. Marinate the jowl and neck fillets for 24 hours. Take a skewer and at the base put a 2 cm piece of a pineapple bottom and follow with alternating pieces of neck and jowl meat. Cook in a rotary oven for 30 minutes before thinly cutting the meat.

Cilantro Juice

Ingredients:

100 g	cilantro leaves
1200 g	mineral water
100 g	ice
.4 g	zanthan gum
18 g	fine salt

Method:

Boil 1000 g of the water with 15 g of the salt. In a bowl, combine the remaining 200 g of water and 3 grams of salt. Blanch the cilantro for 15 seconds and then cool it in the seasoned ice water. Once cool, blend the blanched cilantro and 100 g of ice water and then strain. Take 100 g of cilantro juice and blend in the zanthan gum.

Others

50 g fresh pineapple, 20 g chopped onion, 5 g chopped cilantro, 5 corn tortillas.

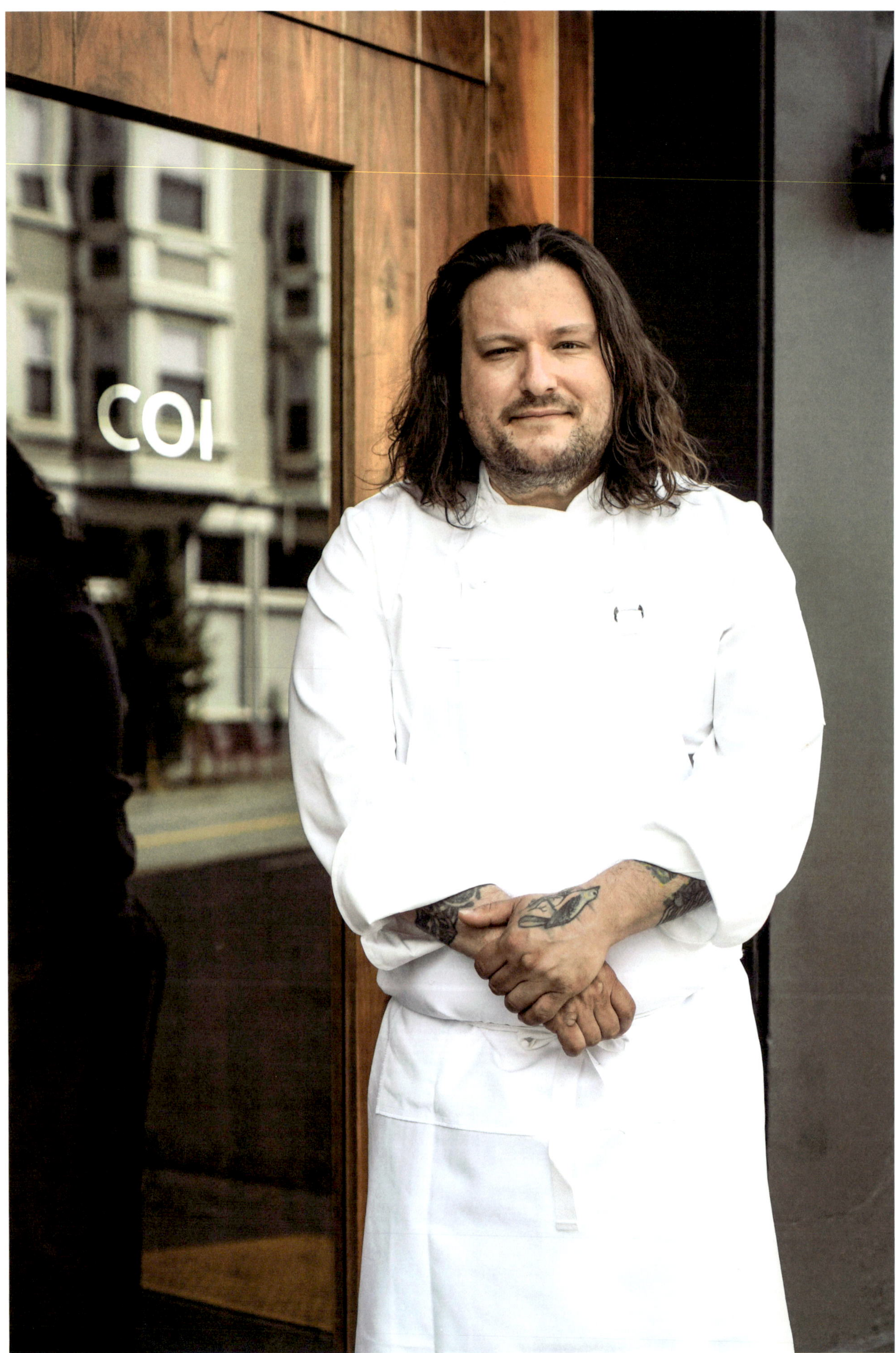

Portrait by Bonjwing Lee

erik anderson

cooking with birds and a duck press

COI

san francisco, california

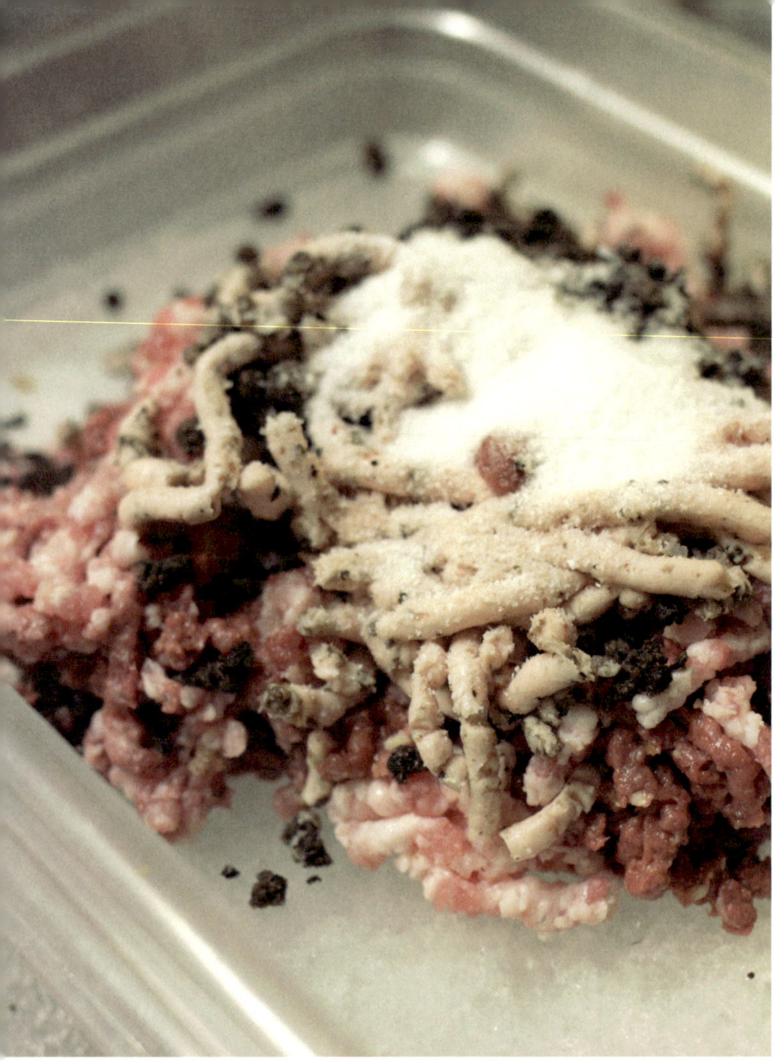

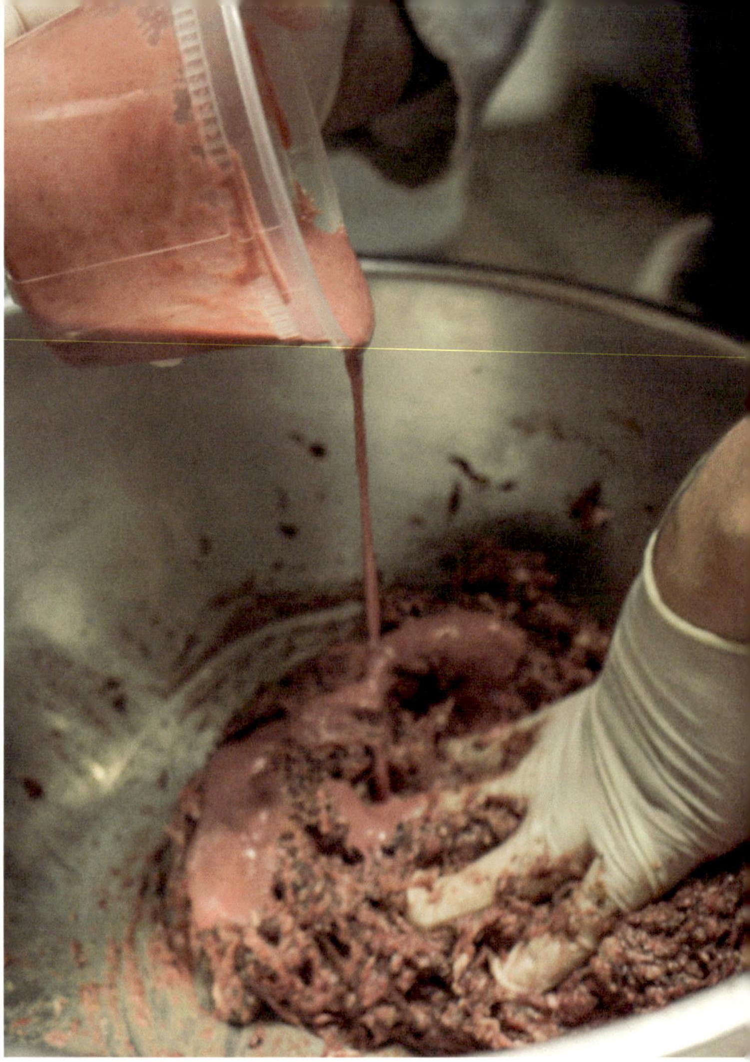

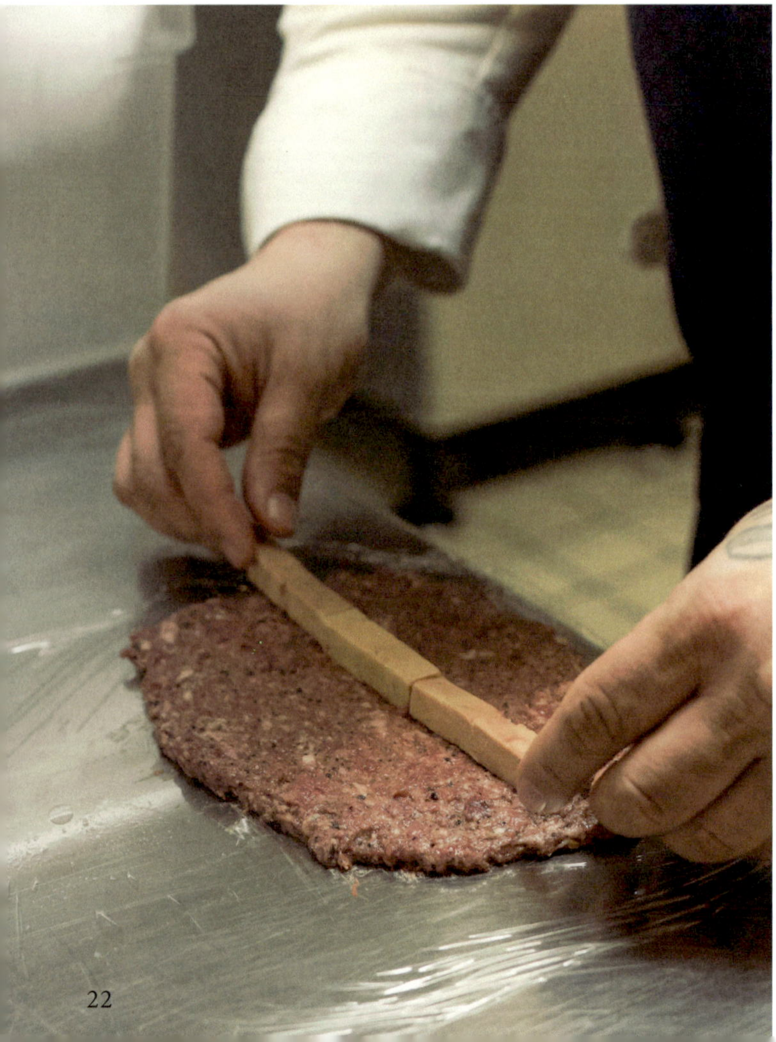

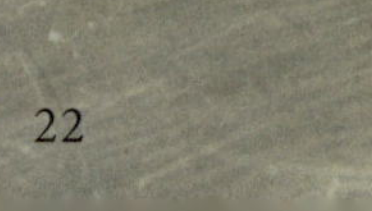

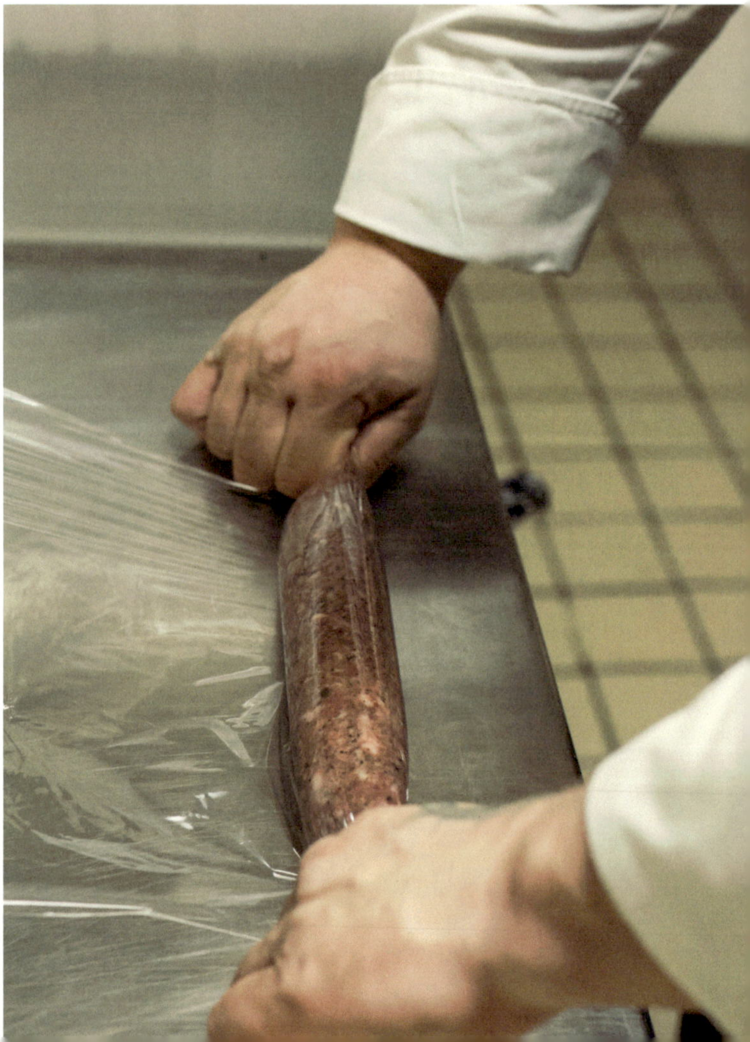

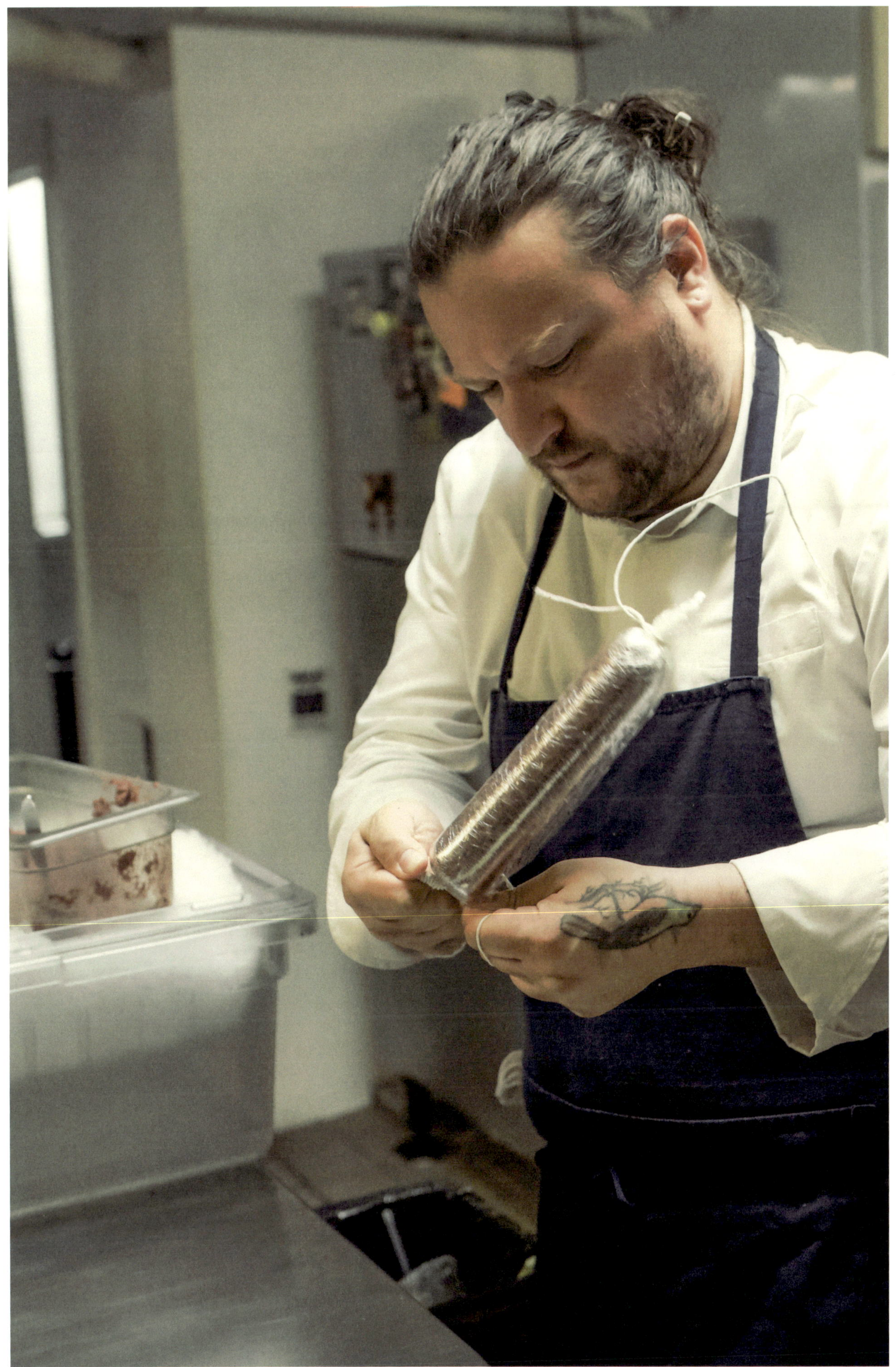

Tell us about your background in cooking. How did you get started?

During the 60's and 70's my father was a sous chef at a place called the Drake Hotel in Chicago. At that time, the Drake was a very opulent and over the top experience. A time when hotels were all about extravagance. When I was born, my father left the Drake and was working full time as a fireman. He eventually purchased a small diner with my mother and worked there every day off from the firehouse. I don't think the guy ever had a day off! I grew up washing dishes at that diner. It was me and a triple sink, and as a 12-year-old I remember being stuck washing dishes on Saturdays while all my friends were out screwing off and having fun. It taught me a lesson that I carry through to this day - you can't be afraid to get your hands dirty and work hard. Fast forward years and years later, after spending far too much time babysitting musicians in the music industry, I finally decided to return to cooking. After a stint at culinary school and an externship at The French Laundry, I was back in the kitchen. That was almost 15 years ago.

Tell us about the duck press. What's the story behind this tool?

The dish itself, although not created at Tour d'Argent, was popularized there. Each diner received a card with their duck's number on it as a keepsake, and each duck was raised on a farm specifically for the restaurant. The idea is that the duck is roasted rare and the carcass is pressed, extracting all the blood and marrow from the bones. This liquid is then used to thicken the sauce. For me, this dish is truly about the sauce and less about the meat.

How does it compare to modern day preparations?

I like to imagine how things were back in the days of Careme. Back before electricity, before robot coupes and vita mixes, back when finesse came from brute strength. You were forcing fish through a tamis to produce a mousseline; there was no machine to help you beat the hell out of it with except your two hands. I like the idea of breaking a sweat to create something delicious. As cooks, we get lazy, and we need to remember how hard the people before us had it.

Why the duck press? What's your interest in using it?

For me, the press is all about the extraction of flavor. Flavor is something that has gone a bit by the wayside in the world of modern cuisine. Unfortunately, people emphasize the way a dish looks rather than the way it tastes. There is also a unique kind of barbaric beauty in crushing bones using something that seems so elegant.

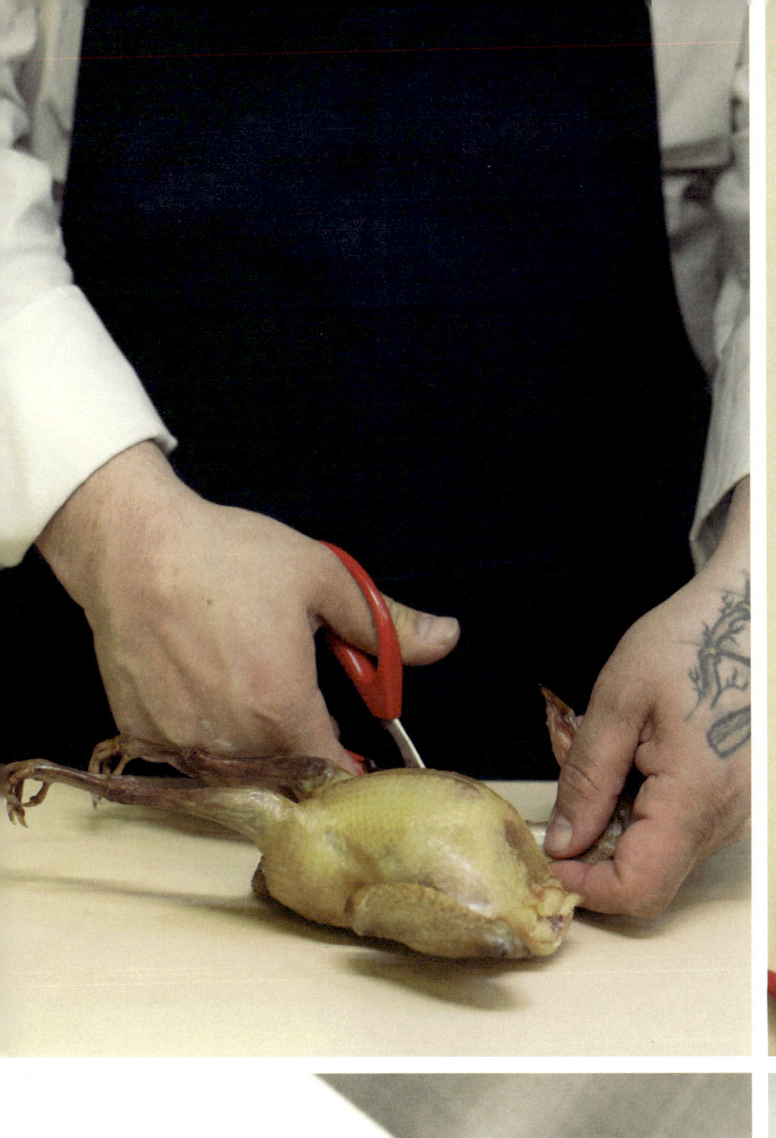
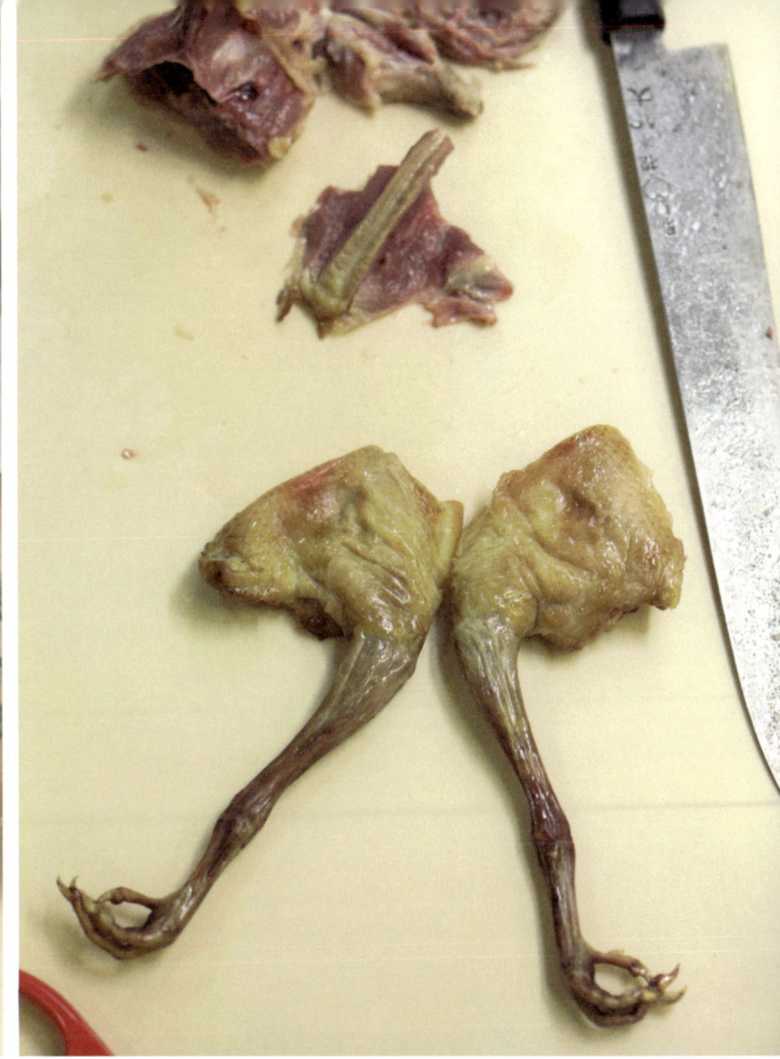
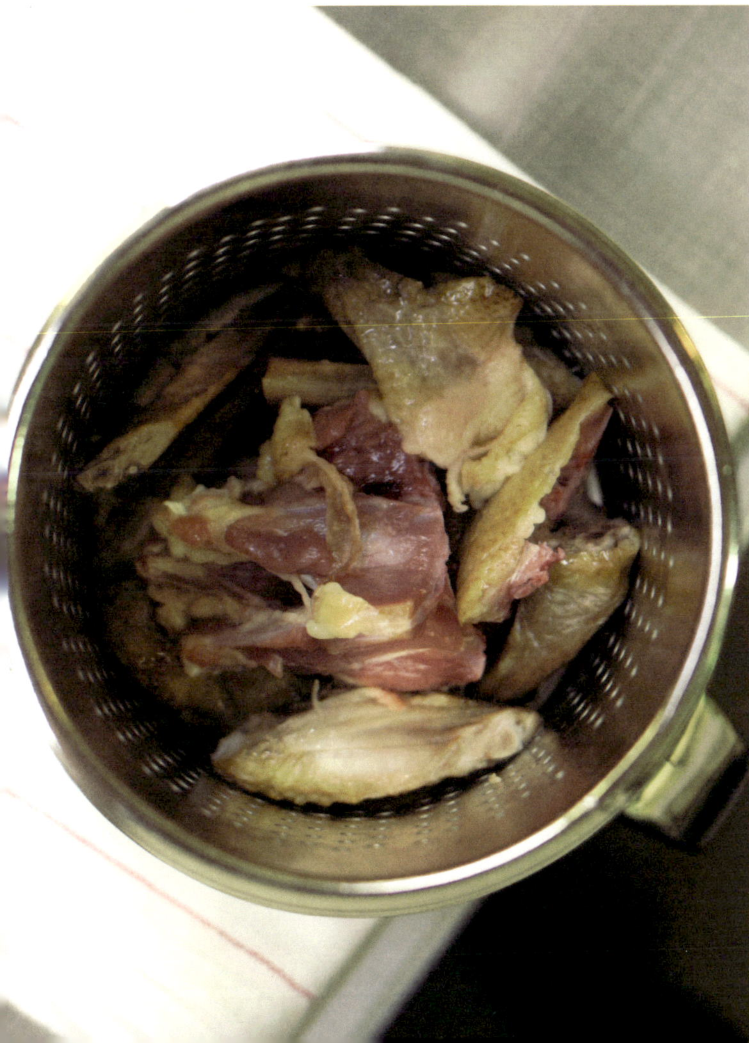
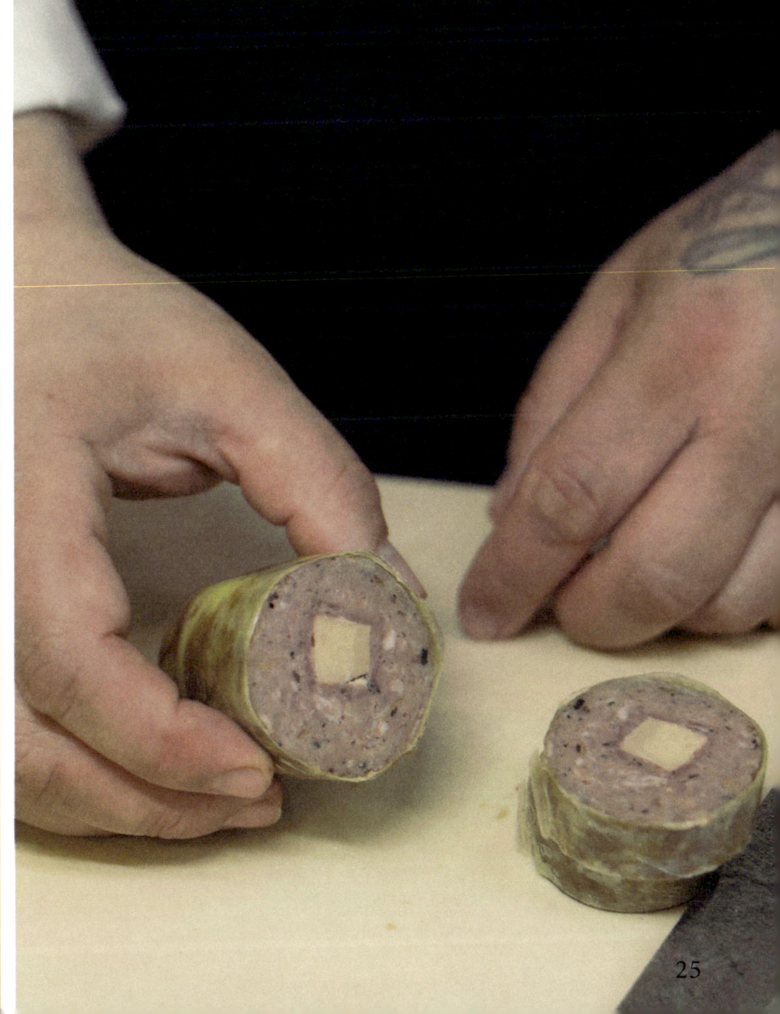

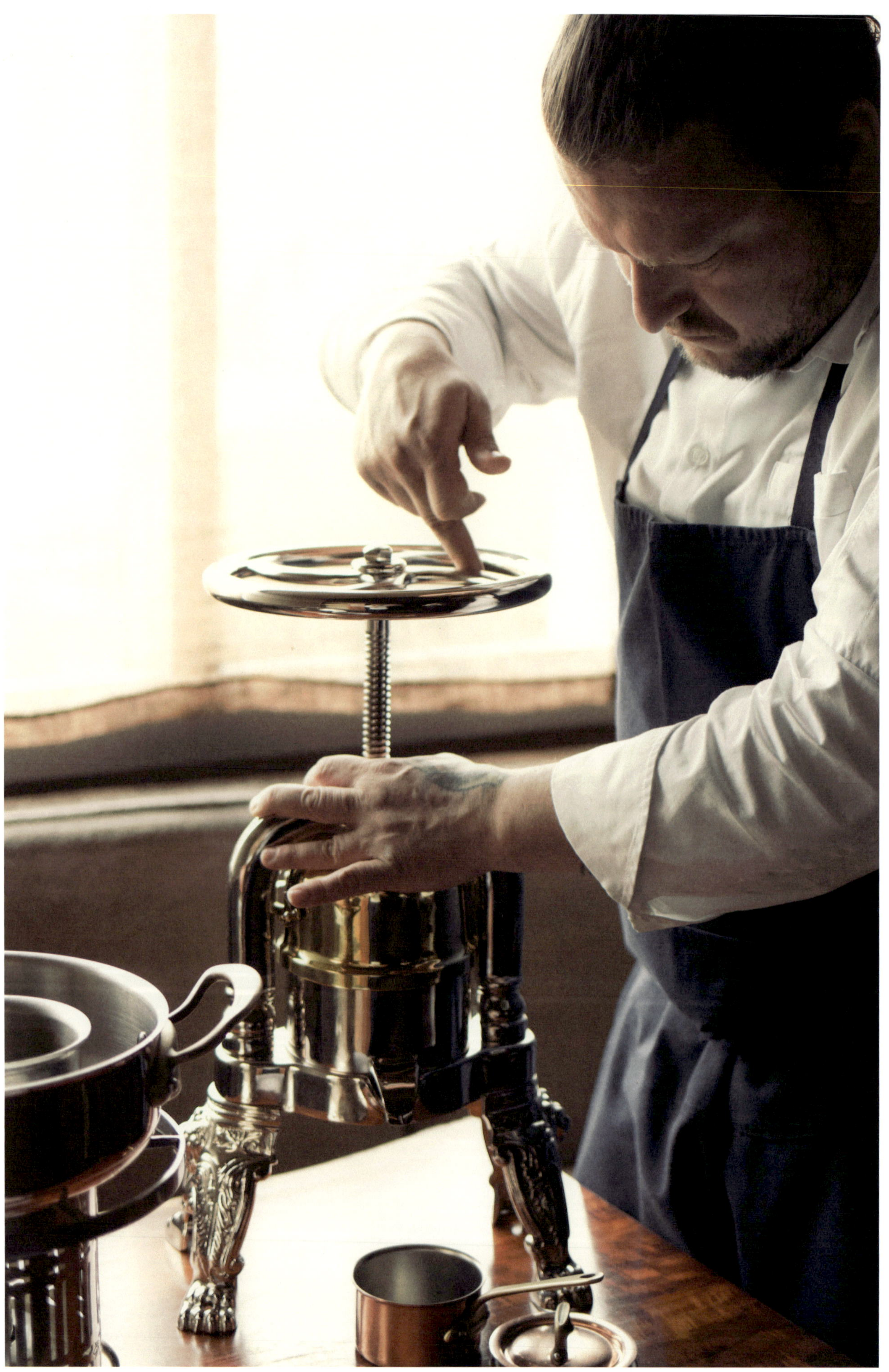

What inspires your food?

I wish I were one of those guys who say they get inspired by a walk in the woods or some BS like that. But I'm not. Inspiration comes to me from the people I surround myself with, the cooks, and my peers.

How has it been moving and cooking in San Francisco?

Obviously, the product is superb, but the city is also very vibrant. I relish the early morning walks to work with just myself, my headphones, the smells, and the sounds. It's an incredible way to start the day. Plus I love being by the water, and I feel fortunate to live by the ocean for the first time.

A lot of people think of Coi as either Daniel Patterson's vegetable-centric food or Matthew Kirkley's super technical seafood. What style of food are you focusing on? Have you changed your style of cooking at all for Coi?

I think myself and Matt both have a love of old French classics and French, three-star dining. Matt focuses on seafood, and I focus a bit more on things that fly. Daniel is very vegetable-centric, and I was fortunate enough to spend a bit of time with him in the COI kitchen before I took over. During that time he was doing a kind of "greatest hits" menu, and that had a tremendous impact on the way I taste food now, the subtle things to look for, and how to correct things. He has an incredible palate, and I have consciously been trying to lighten my food up a bit.

What is it like taking over a newly 3 star restaurant?

I like to lie and tell people I don't think about it much, but the truth is it is pretty nerve-wracking. In my mind, Matt Kirkley is without a doubt one of the two greatest chefs in this country at the moment. They're huge shoes to fill.

What are your goals for the future?

My goal has always remained the same. To be able to cook the food I want to cook, no matter where I have to go to do it.

Textures you're digging:

Chewy.

Flavor profiles you're into:

Bitter, floral, citrus.

Ingredients you're excited to work with:

Wolfe Ranch Quail.

Best bite in recent memory:

Beef Shumai at Good Mong Kok Bakery.

Where to eat in SF:

I'm late to the party on this one, but State Bird Provisions is killer! I think SingleThread is simply amazing. And I'm super excited about Rodney Wages' new place, Avery.

next page: royal with white asparagus

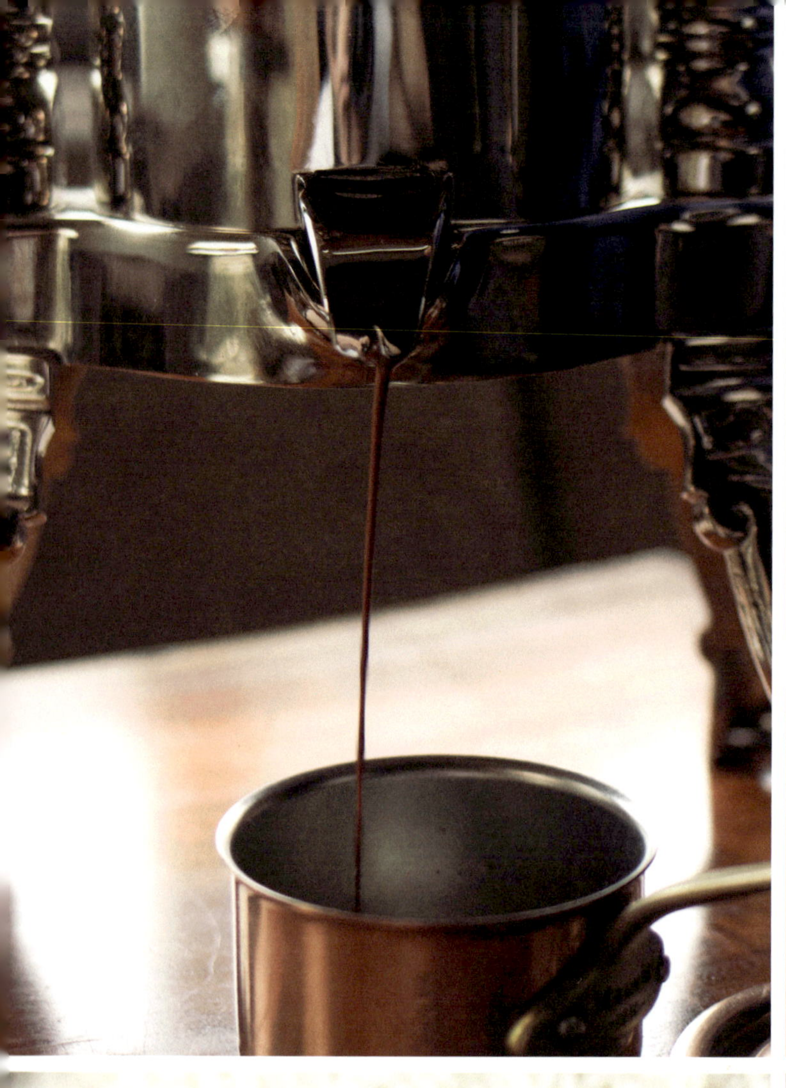
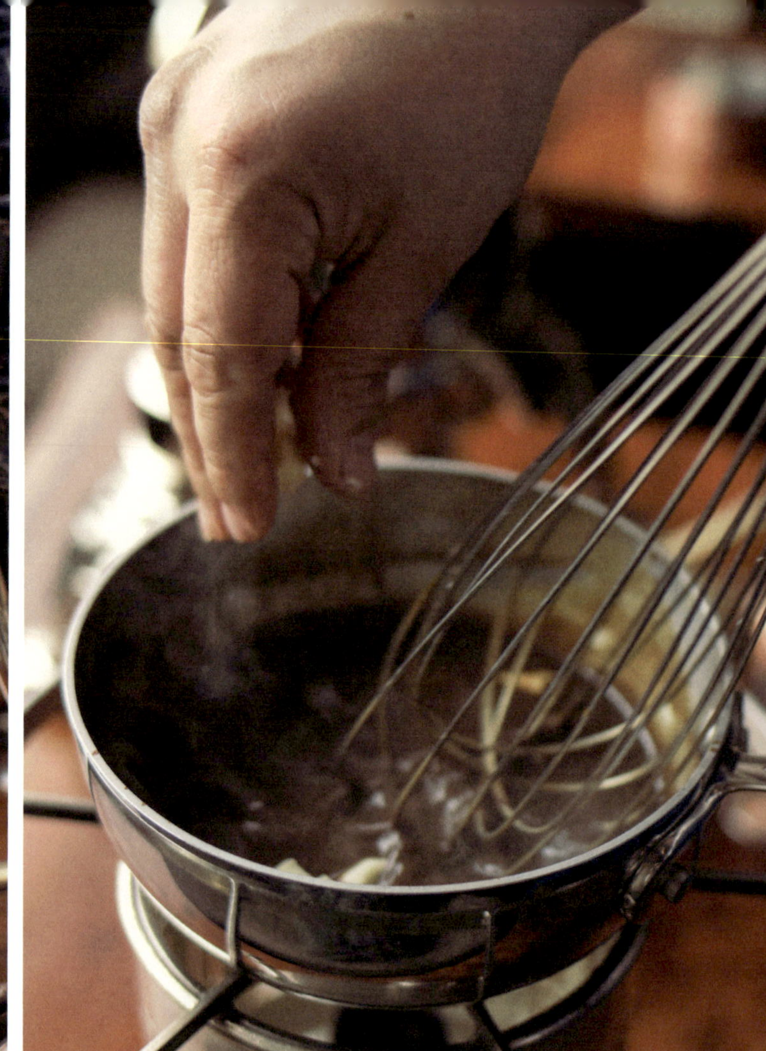
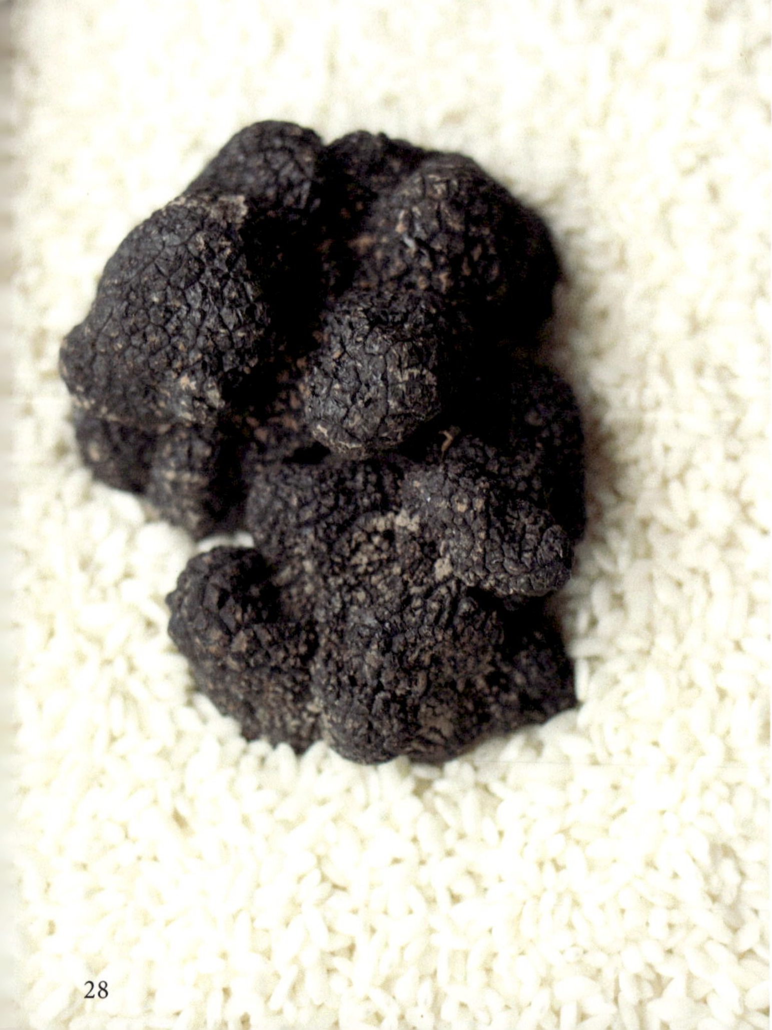
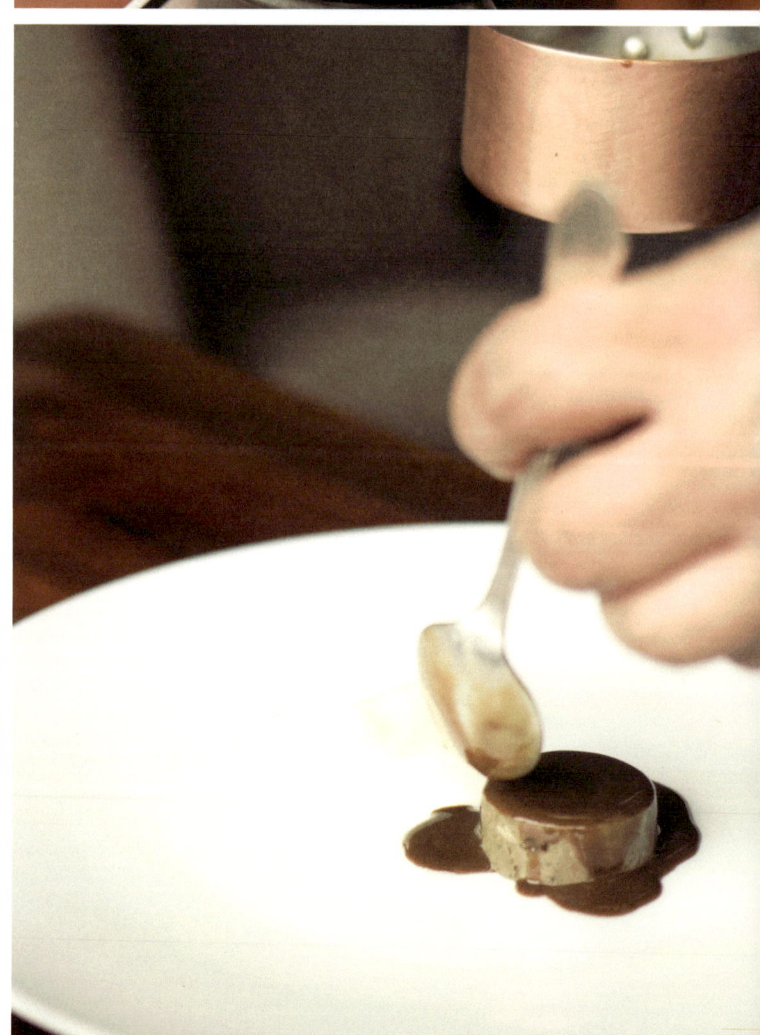

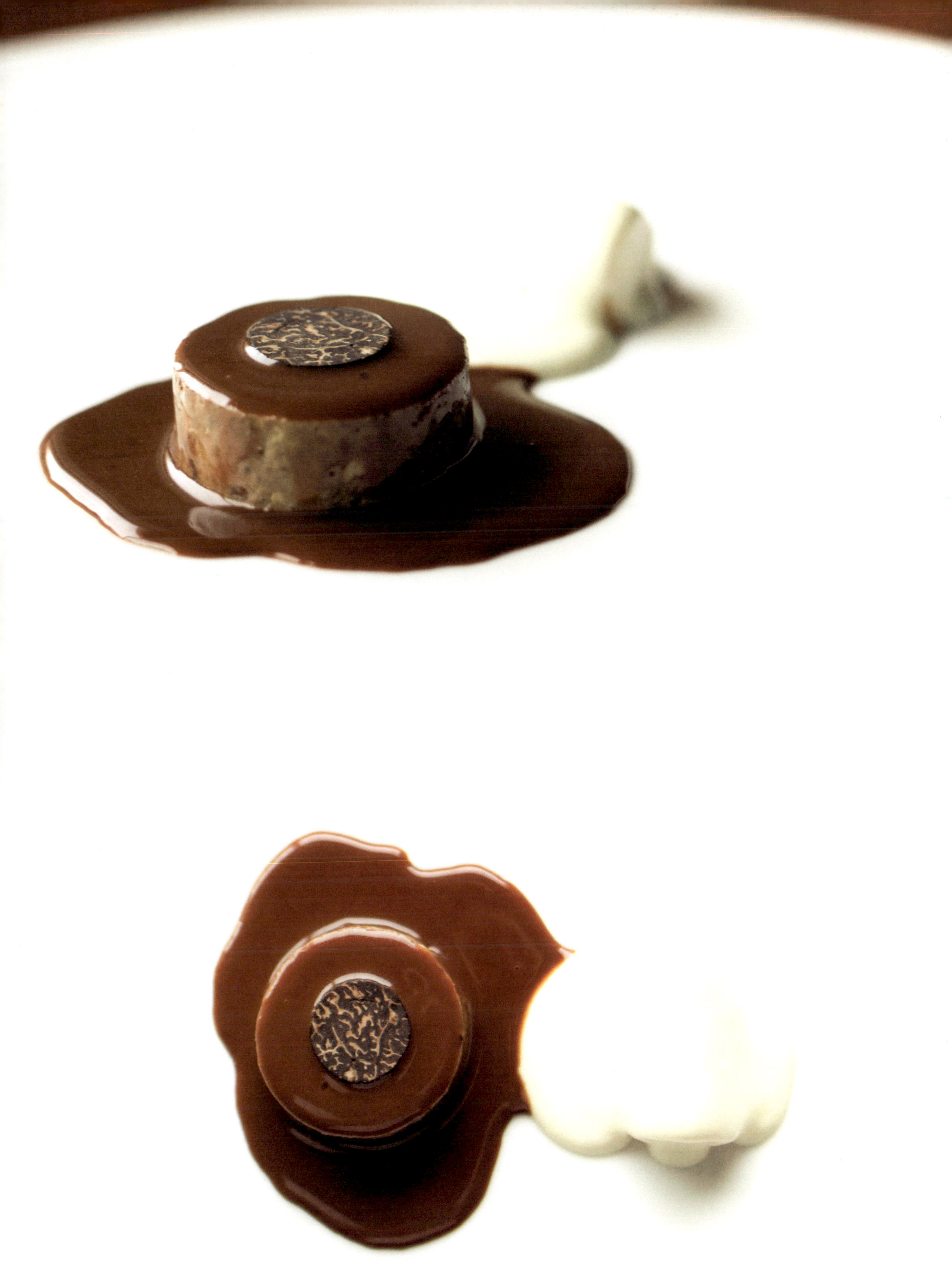

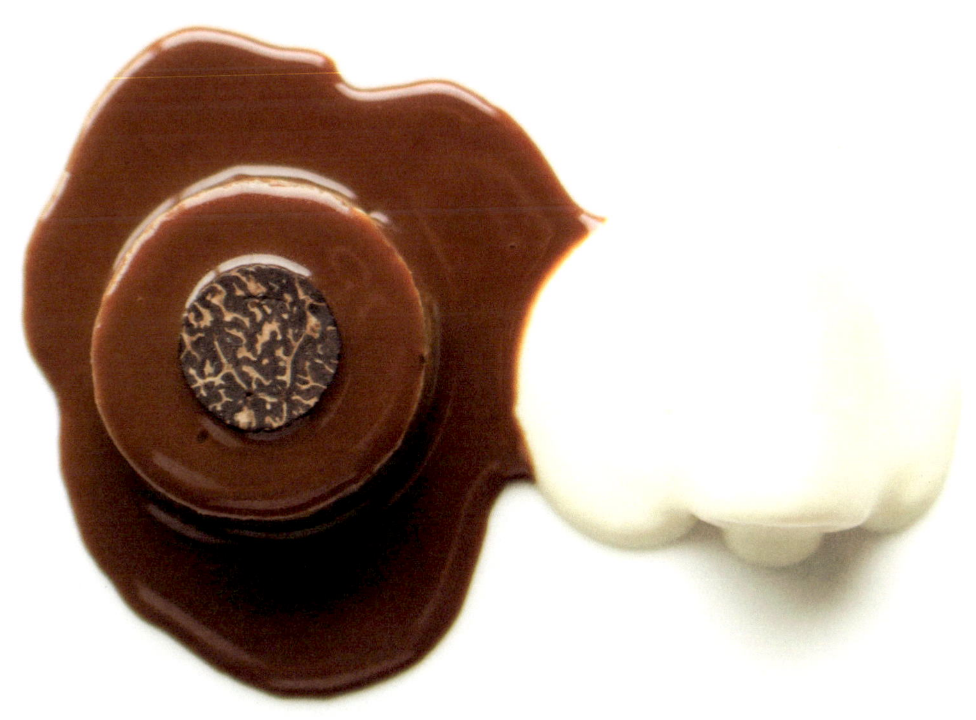

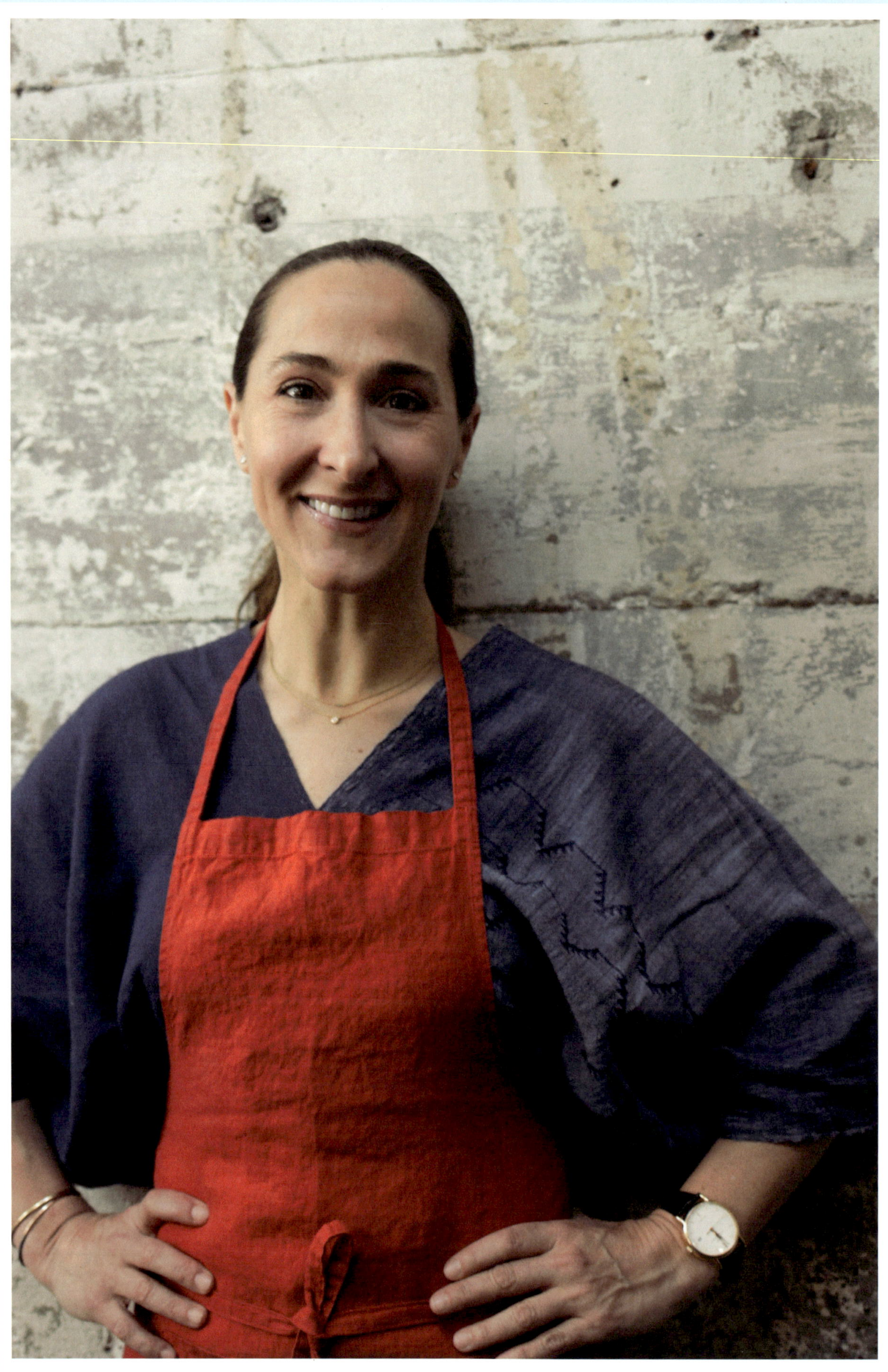

gabriela cámara

cooking in mexico city and san francisco

cala, san francisco, california

contramar, mexico city, mexico

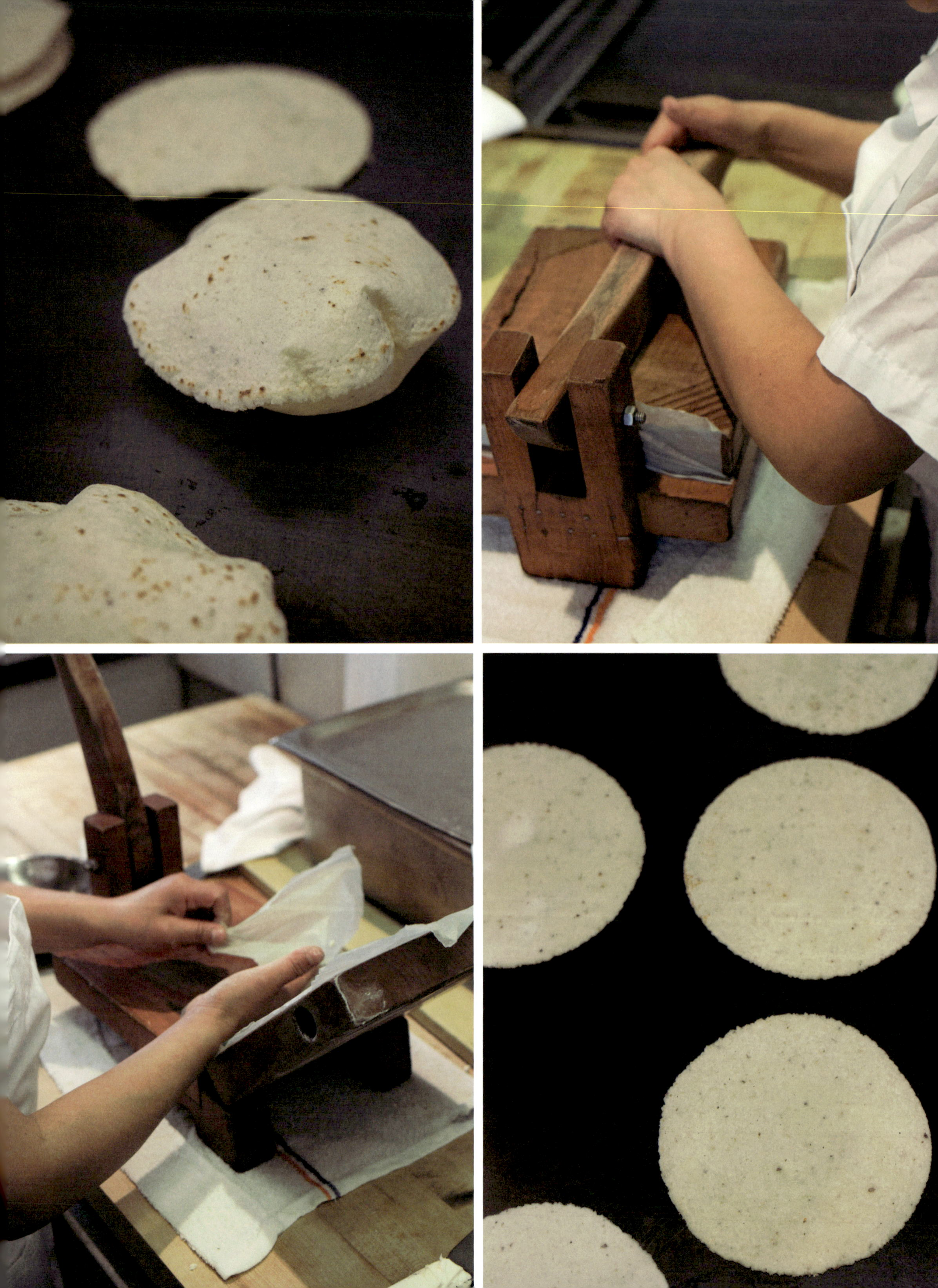

I've been cooking since I can remember. I always loved eating, and I come from a family where food is very important. I have early memories of it being a communal event where we all enjoyed preparing and cooking food together, so I'm very comfortable in the kitchen, even if I didn't formally train as a chef. When I was choosing what to study after high school, I had a tough time deciding. In Mexico, you select a single school subject, so that means four and a half years of whatever you choose, and only that. People would suggest I go to cooking school, but I didn't think I wanted to be a professional chef at the time. I just enjoyed cooking casually as I always had, until I opened Contramar. Even then I wasn't cooking every day. I was still finishing my undergraduate studies and interning at the National Museum of Art in downtown Mexico City, so I didn´t really have the bandwidth to be on the line daily. In Mexico, cooking is very convivial, and family gatherings often include more than fifty people. Fortunately, as I finished my studies and had more time for the restaurant, I used that experience of cooking for my family. In a way, growing up I had learned large-scale cooking without even knowing I would one day put it to professional use.

I've always loved the ocean and eating fish, which in general is a difficult ingredient if you're not familiar with it. Most people in cities haven't had good, fresh fish. So why would they like it if they've only had the frozen stuff from the supermarket? I loved fishing with my grandfather who would take us often. The whole point of fishing was to cook what we caught, so I guess that's where I learned that there is nothing like fresh fish. This is how we started Contramar. A group of friends, all on vacation in Zihuatanejo, off the coast of Guerrero, wondering how we could get that kind of fish in Mexico City. The city has a big Spanish influence of seafood, especially at fancy restaurants. But usually, you would get great fish from Spain, which had been frozen or not as fresh as the local fish you could find at the Mercado de la Viga in Mexico City. So as great as the fish was, it didn't possess what I had learned was the most important quality: freshness. Mexico City is only 4 hours away from either coast, east and west. So in 1998, we opened Contramar as an experiment of offering fresh fish cooked on the grill and in simple ceviches and tostadas that were easy to eat for everybody. There was no restaurant like that in the city. Also, I never imagined I'd be cooking or working in a restaurant every day. It was never part of the plan, but I loved it from day one. With time I discovered the social and political act of professionally feeding and taking care of people. I still love it and enjoy doing it with the most extraordinary products available, and the best people that I know.

Mexican cuisine is starting to become a pretty popular food trend.

I think it's because we're generally re-appreciating everyday food. Mexican food is close to many Americans' hearts in a curious way. It's comfort food.

I had taco night pretty often at my house growing up. But it was store bought tortillas with ground beef and bagged taco seasoning.

Yeah, but isn't that funny? That taco Tuesday or taco night is a popular thing in the US...?

Do you feel the cultural relationship to food differs between the United States and Mexico?

I think in Mexico we have a longer history of food being important and sophisticated, and there is much pride around it. It's been considered part of our cultural heritage. Food in Mexico is complex. There are centuries of tradition in a dish, and you can't beat that. It has been influenced by pre-hispanic, colonial, and later French cuisine; so you have layers and layers of history in our food.

In the US it´s different. There is a lot of pride in regional food like the South, for example. But the new appreciation of food in general terms is more recent. Now we're trying to go back to the way it used to be, with fermenting and preserving, and anything that we were doing before TV dinners and all of that industrialization of food. Even though it is still an elitist trend for the most part, unfortunately, I think it's wonderful that people are looking beyond.

Why did you choose San Francisco to open Cala?

I love San Francisco and this whole area of the world for so many reasons, but opening Cala was more of a coincidence of many things and not a very well planned business decision. The ingredients and incredible produce you have access to here are out of this world, and I thought I could make a restaurant here that would be different from anything else that was here when I came. Cala is the result of my experience with Mexican food, in the context of Northern California food and ingredients. I wanted to bring my little piece of Mexico City here, and I like to make restaurants I would want to go to myself, so this is how Cala came about.

Is cooking Mexican food in America different from cooking Mexican food in Mexico?

I cook depending on what I have, and when you cook like that, it is always different.

But, do you change the level of spice or anything?

No. Contramar is not particularly spicy. If someone can really not eat spice at all, then you can't even do a dish with chipotle, so I always try to have spice free options. My food is not spicy for the sake of spiciness; it´s spicy for the sake of flavor. Chiles have a wide range of flavors, and they add a lot to other ingredients.

How involved are you at your restaurants, especially with them being in two different countries? Are you still active in creating the menu? Or does your focus shift more into management?

I am in charge, but since I cannot be everywhere at once, I have others that execute everyday operations. I'm there for menu development and guiding, of course. The restaurants are what I imagine and want them to be, and I am involved with every important decision taken. That´s my job. But also there is a lot that the great team I work with figures out daily. Here in San Francisco, Kenny, who is an amazing creative mind, leads the day-to-day kitchen activities and I trust him to go the market and guide the way. His taste is very in tune with mine, and it's a pleasure when you have that. We are on the same page of what we want and the style of the food. I think that's the challenge. When you have a team, you need to be aligned, because whatever is created has to make sense.

What I basically do is to imagine possibilities of food and how to best do what we need to do. There are a lot of decisions to be taken in restaurants. I thought I

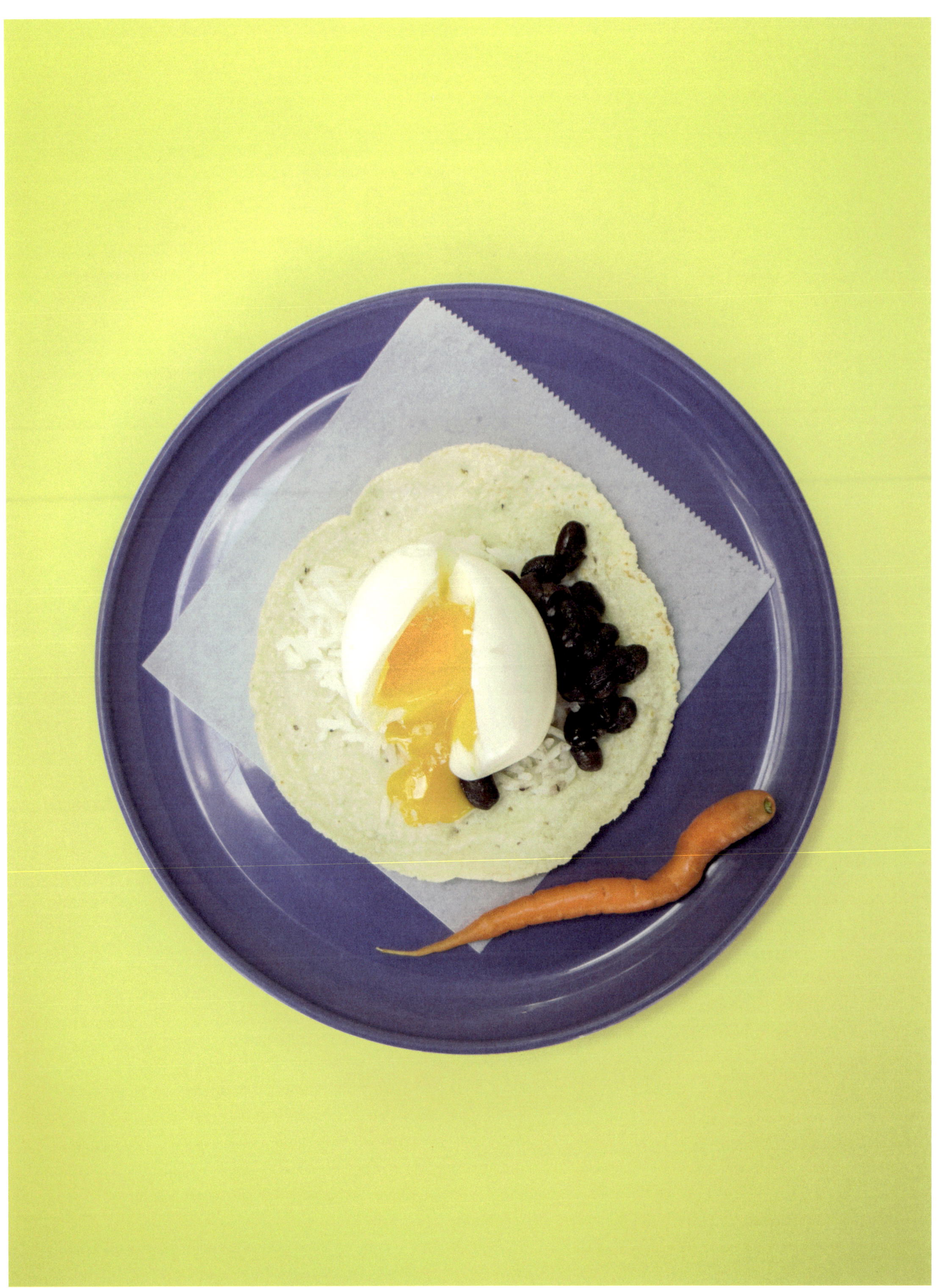

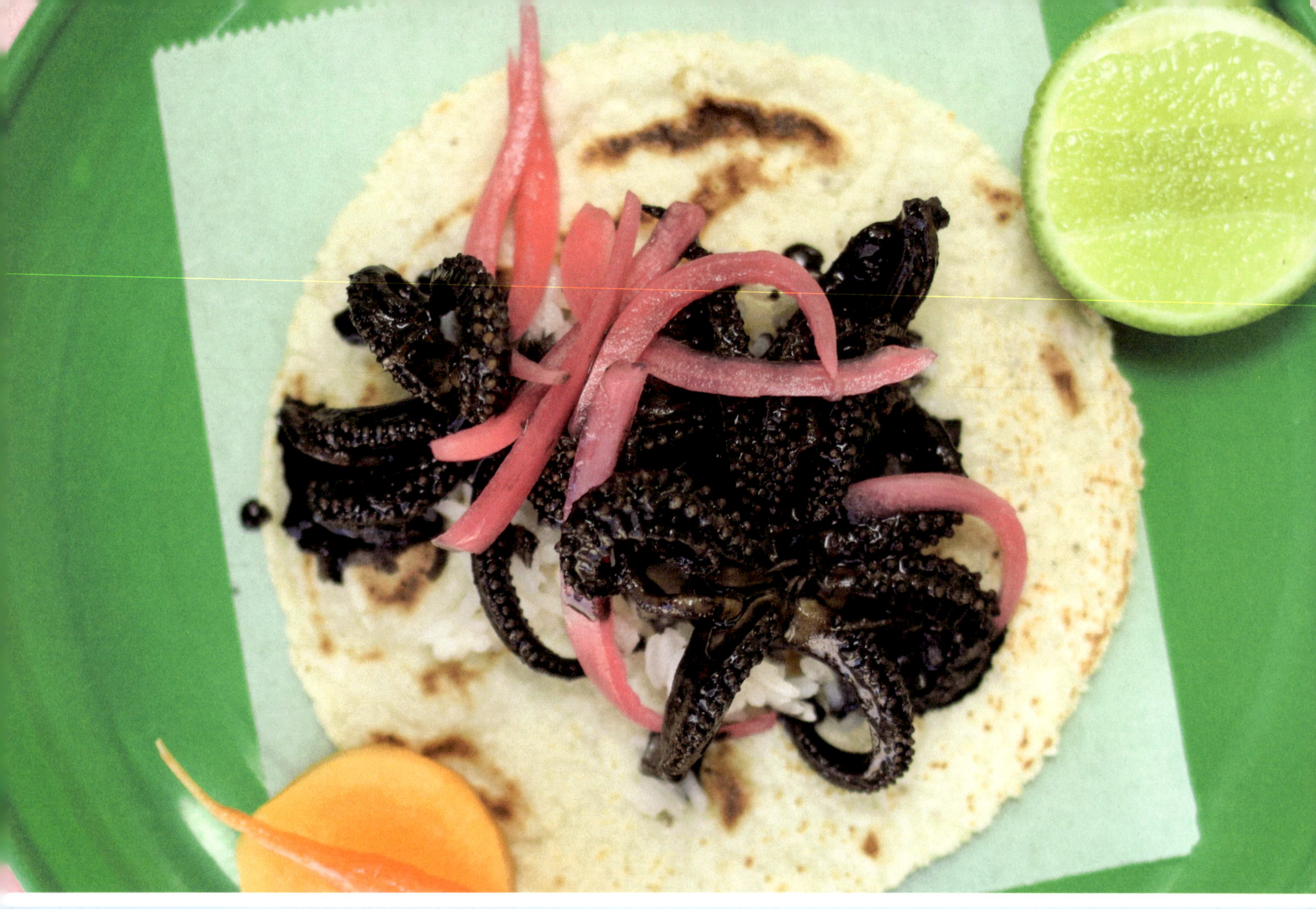

would be a curator of contemporary art, and instead, I ended up being the "curator" of my restaurants, or the person in charge for whatever goes on in them. It's like an editorial job. So I'm a curator and editor, but of food, the team, and décor. That's what being a restaurateur means. And of course, you have to know how to cook and eat. But you can't be doing it all, or else there isn't a person to see the bigger picture.

So what drives and inspires your food?

Ingredients. At Cala, I've been super neurotic about focusing on just what we have on the Pacific coast. We do get things from Baja California, but we don't get anything from the East Coast, the Gulf of Mexico, Europe or Asia. When it comes to fish, I try to keep it as close as I can. We get amazing trout from McFarland Farms, for example, and that's why I don't do the tuna tostada here, and instead do a trout one. I have made it a point to make it super local, and it´s something I am extremely proud of. Here it´s easy with all the bounty there is, and the changes in season only make it more fun.

Do you cook seasonally in Mexico?

The thing is the Mexican climate, in general, is pretty uniform and you can get things year round. But then you have corn shoots and things at certain times, which do make for special dishes. And of course, we have a lot of rotation in the fish and seafood that we use, depending on what is available.

Mexico City is declared the place to be by many artists. How do you feel about Mexico City becoming the global stage for art, cooking, and culture? What makes Mexico City so special?

It always has been a very central place, geographically speaking. It has close access to both the Pacific and Atlantic oceans, which is pretty amazing. It is close to the equator and between Asia and Europe. Can you imagine what that meant for the Spanish Empire? That newly discovered access to China and India? It's always been a center of many things, and culturally, it has always been a very rich city. There are all these accounts of when Europeans arrived at the Americas in the 16th century,

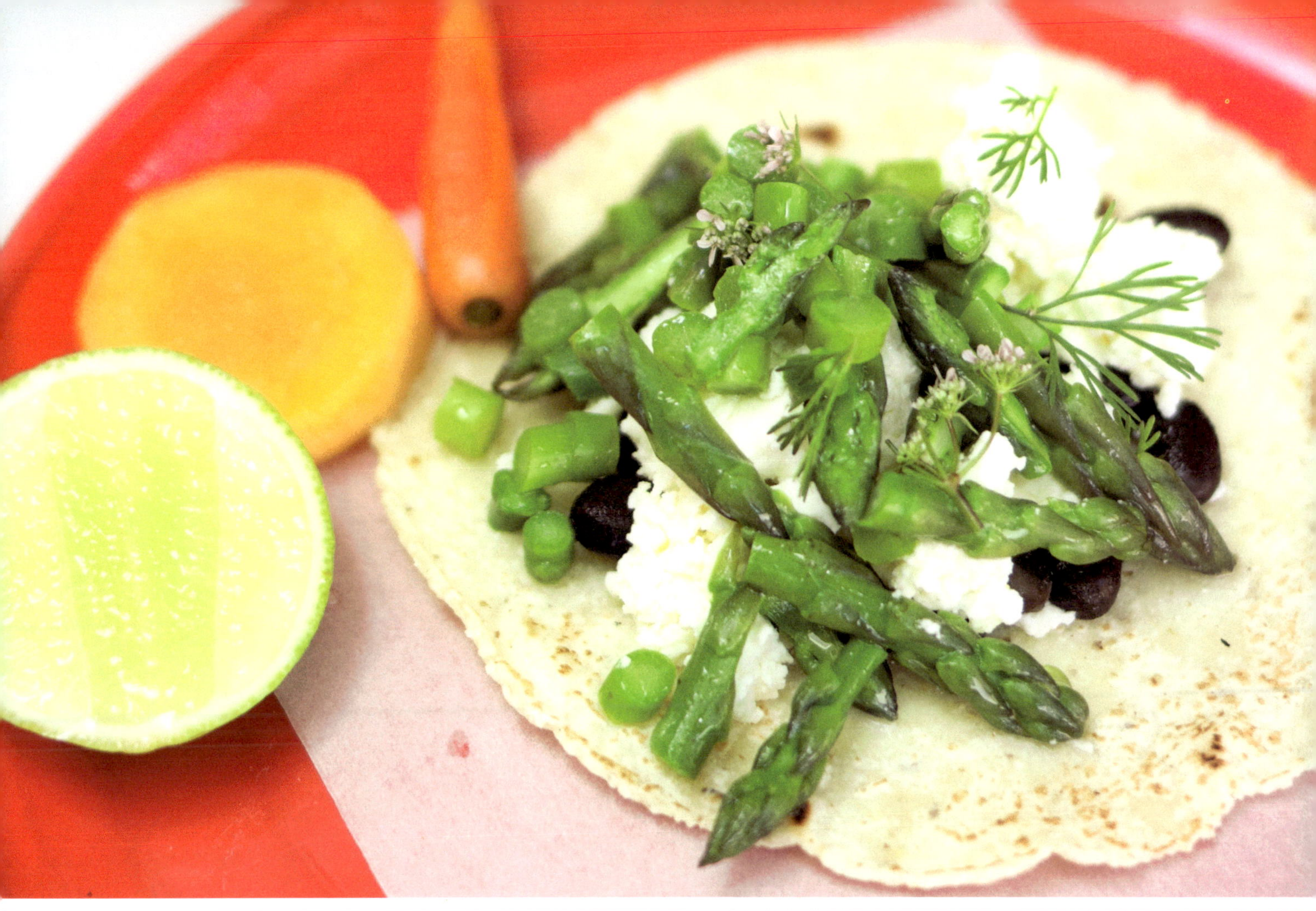

and they wrote of Tenochtitlán (where Mexico City now is) as the biggest city they'd ever seen, because it was and still is huge. It has always been a grand place.

I think it's funny that young hipster Americans interested in food and culture are visiting it now. There are certain neighborhoods where you can hear a lot of English on the streets. But then, again, Mexico City has always been a very cosmopolitan place, and it always was a place that interested artists because it is so culturally rich. It has such an amazing gastronomic culture, also, and now that people are so into food, it makes even more sense that it's become important.

What is contemporary Mexican cuisine to you?

For me, there is a sort of frequency or wavelength of Mexican cuisine that is the balance of acid, spicy, salt, and fat. There is high acidity and deep flavor, because of the balance of these elements. I kind of think of it as a musical composition, and it's a very bright one, regarding how flavors come together.

But it is also very, very complex. There are many moles, for example. And the words traditional and authentic are so blotchy to me and nothing and everything at the same time. Sometimes I'm concerned about traditional food disappearing, but that is sort of evolution and how we've come to be where we're at as humans. I do think it's important for people to know about the history of a recipe, but the food is always something that is evolving. It's always hanging between tradition and innovation. Every time you make a recipe, you might alter it a little. And is that innovation, or is that a mistake? It gets messy. I think the important thing is that it's good. And then that's the most difficult thing to define. Except for in restaurants it's easy because people either like it or they don't. I love that concreteness of restaurants.

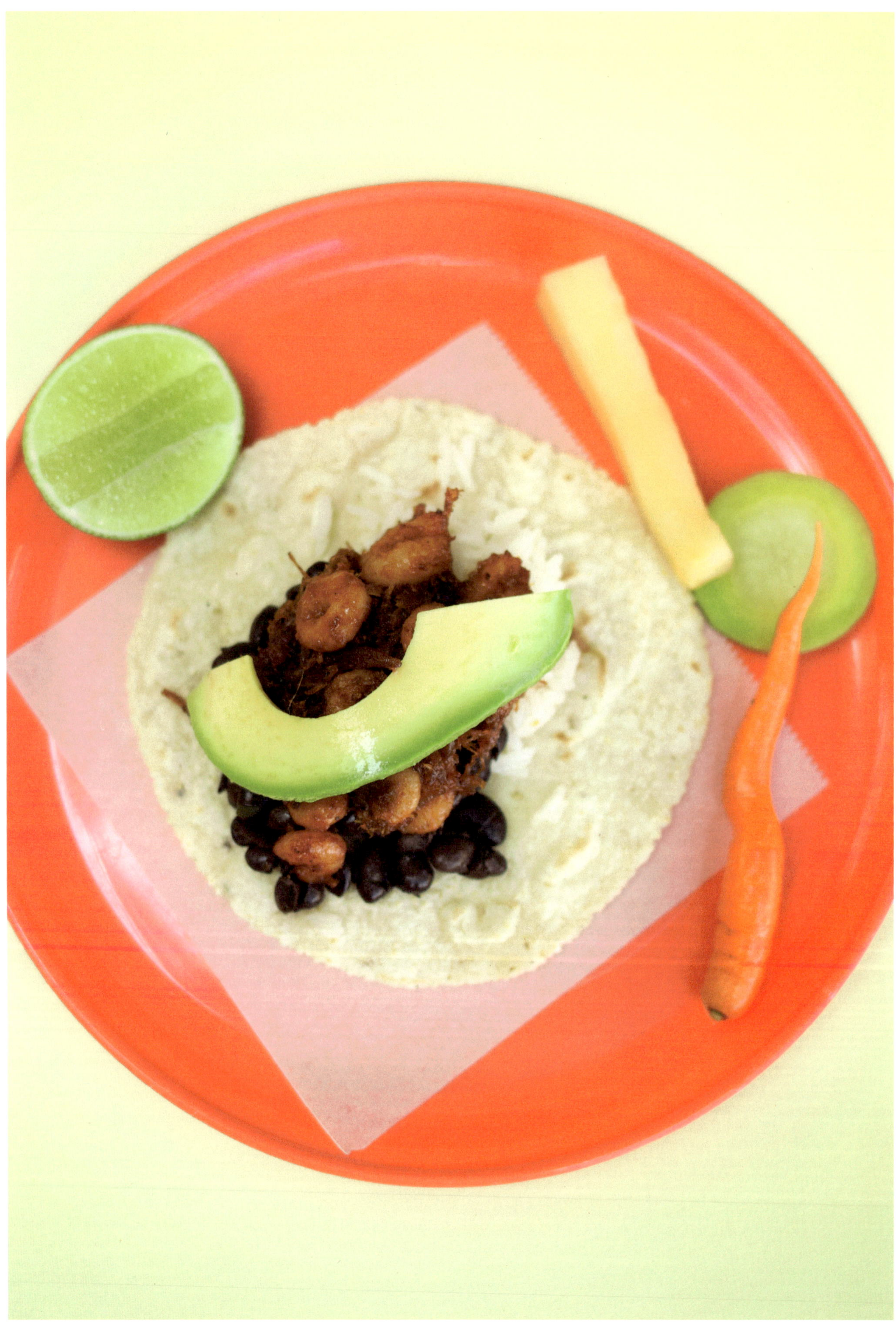

Bay Shrimp and Pork Carnitas Tacos

Recipe by Gabriela Cámara

Bay Shrimp and Pork Carnitas Tacos

Ingredients:

1 lb	bay shrimp
1 lb	pork carnitas (cut small, without bones)
1/4 cup	lard
1 lb	roma tomatoes
1 cup	adobo salsa (see below recipe)
3 cups	leeks, sliced thinly
1 pinch	oregano
	salt to taste
6 ea	corn tortillas
1 ea	avocado, sliced
4 cups	black beans
4 cups	white rice

Method:

Heat the lard in a large pot and sauté the leeks. Add the carnitas and cook until golden. Take them out of the pan and reserve them. In the same pan, start cooking the shrimp and add the adobo until it's well integrated. Add the Carnitas to the shrimp. Add a pinch of oregano and salt to taste. Serve over rice and beans on corn tortillas. Top with sliced avocado.

Adobo Salsa

Ingredients:

2 ea	garlic cloves
1 ea	white onion
5 ea	roma tomatoes
2 ea	ancho chiles, dried
2 ea	cascabel chiles, dried
2 ea	guajillo chiles, dried
1/2 oz	achiote paste, dissolved in 1 T of water
1 cup	rice oil
1 T	salt
1 cup	water

Method:

Remove the stems from the chiles and put them in a bowl with the water for 10 minutes to soften. Blend everything together until you obtain a smooth consistency. Strain.

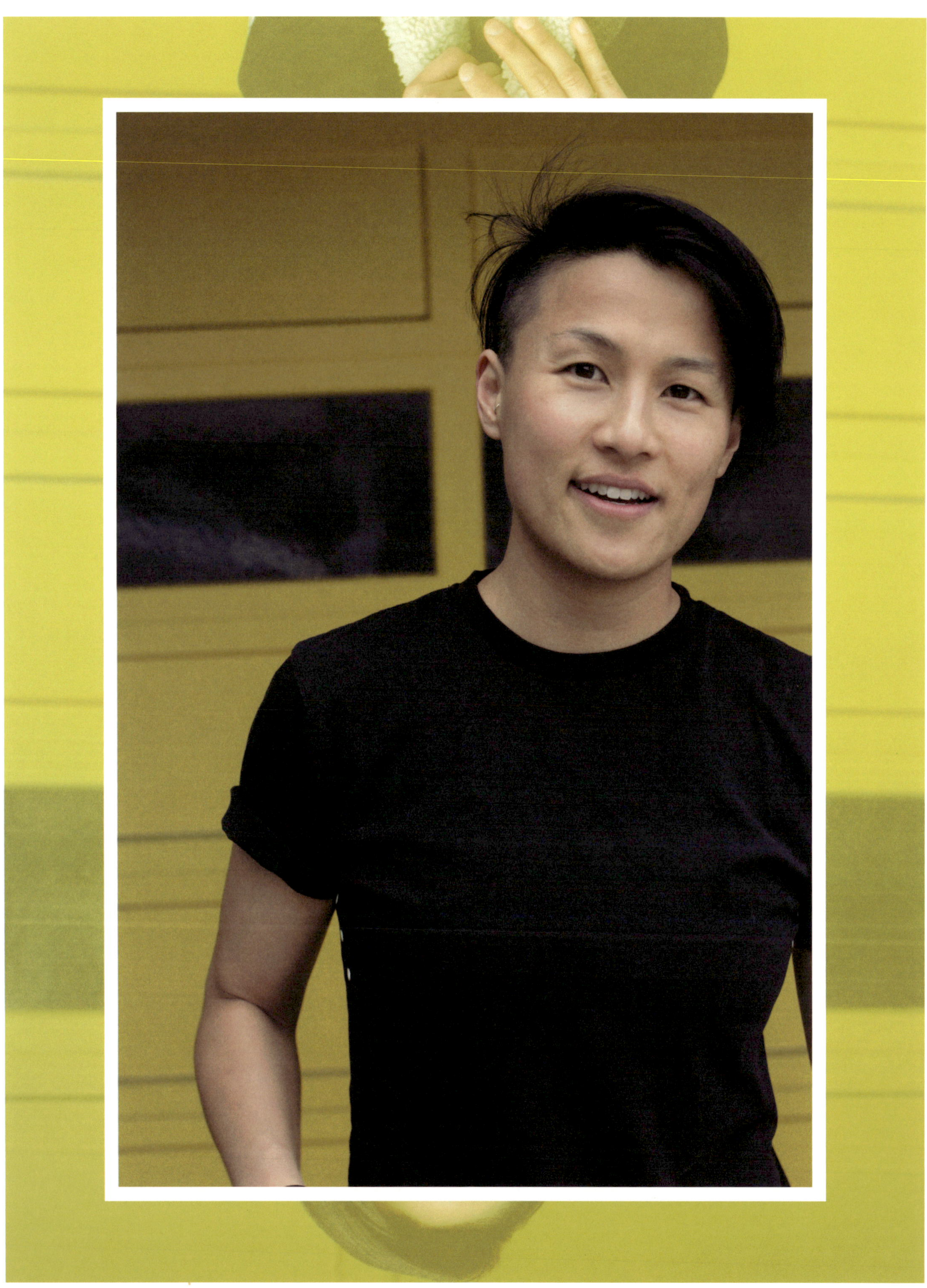

melissa king

san francisco, california

I started helping my mom put dinner on the table around age 5 or 6 — standing on a stool, prepping bok choy with a Chinese meat cleaver and frying eggs in a giant wok. I always knew I wanted to cook, but my parents fought hard for me to attend college to "get a real degree". At age 17, I picked up my first professional job in the kitchen at the Getty Museum in Los Angeles as a pastry assistant and catering cook. I made minimum wage and woke up at 4am to drive through hours of LA traffic while juggling my full-time undergrad schedule, to see if professional cooking was really something I wanted to dedicate my life to. After I graduated from UC Irvine with my bachelor's in cognitive science, I jetted off to culinary school at the Culinary Institute of America in Hyde Park and never looked back.

During culinary school, I interned at Campton Place in San Francisco and got my first taste for fine dining kitchens. I went through a dramatic learning curve – I scrubbed every surface of that kitchen daily before being allowed to touch a vegetable, it took me hours to correctly brunoise something with my dull-ass knife, and multitasking was definitely not in my vocabulary yet. During those 7 months, I went from clueless intern to garde manger, and graduated to the hot line on entremetier. It was a humbling and validating moment, but it was only the beginning.

After culinary school, I moved to San Francisco and returned to Campton Place, trained with Dominique Crenn for a few years, ran the pasta station at Delfina, and trained with Ron Siegel at the Ritz Carlton Dining Room for close to 4 years. I was the in-house butcher at Luce, and spent time instructing and hosting private events. Shortly after, I went on Top Chef Season 12 and placed as a finalist.

If you asked me a few years ago, I would have told you I'd never be caught dead on a competitive TV cooking show. I was pretty shy and completely content with my head down, tucked away behind a Michelin kitchen door. But I'm also the type of person that doesn't like to turn away an opportunity once the door opens.

Who would you say your biggest mentor has been?

My biggest mentor is Chef Ron Siegel. I have immense respect for him, his philosophy of life and cooking, and the way he leads his kitchens. He opened my eyes to Californian seasonality and supporting local farmers and artisans. He always slowed down to work side by side and show me how to be a stronger cook — how to butcher a pig for the first time, how to properly layer and infuse flavors with the right technique, and how to utilize every part of a product. He would actively participate on the line if he saw a moment where help was needed. He would run circles around you. You would even catch him hand-washing dishes at the dish-pit when the machine went down — he was that kind of leader. His was the one kitchen I trained in where everyone on the team, from the sous chefs to the dishwashers, were always treated with respect and equality. I hope to carry on his philosophy in my own restaurants.

What inspires your food?

I'm a total Californian. I'm inspired by nature, what's growing around me, and direct sourcing. I have friends that hunt, fish, free-dive, and forage around Northern California – sometimes I get incredibly fresh dungeness crabs or salmon caught that morning from Half Moon Bay, sea urchins from the Mendocino coast, or wild boar from Anderson Valley. I feel inspired to create dishes that respect every part of the product.

I'm also inspired by my experiences, global flavors, food memories, and cultural traditions. When I travel, I go straight to the outdoor markets to see what's growing in that area, and I try to experience as many of the traditional foods that each culture has to offer. I often dissect traditional Chinese dishes or the Asian flavors I grew up on. I try to absorb these techniques or flavors from my experiences, and bridge them with ingredients I find in San Francisco.

above: hamachi collar, kumquat, ponzu brown butter

below: scallop, mandarin, purple daikon, nasturtium

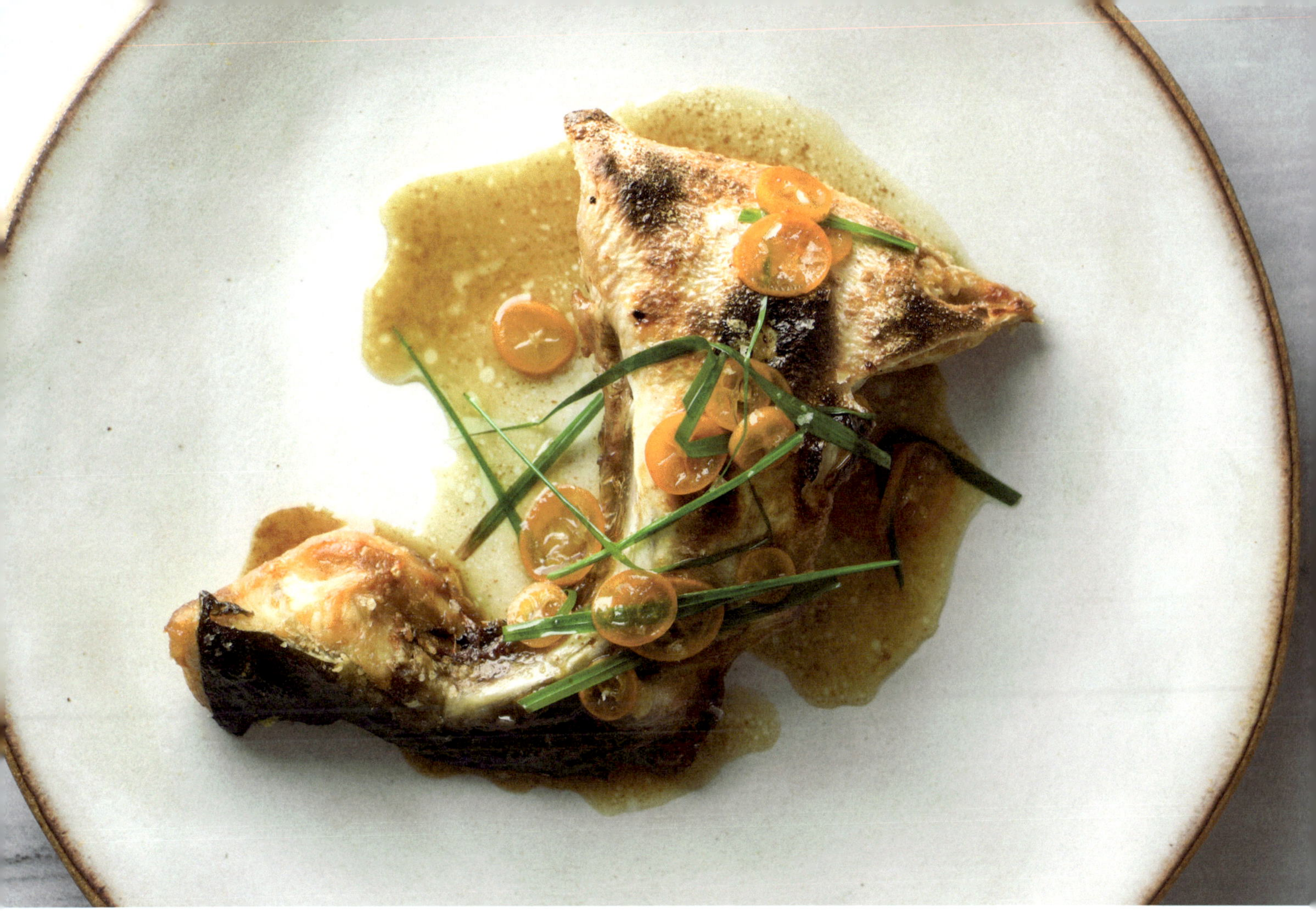

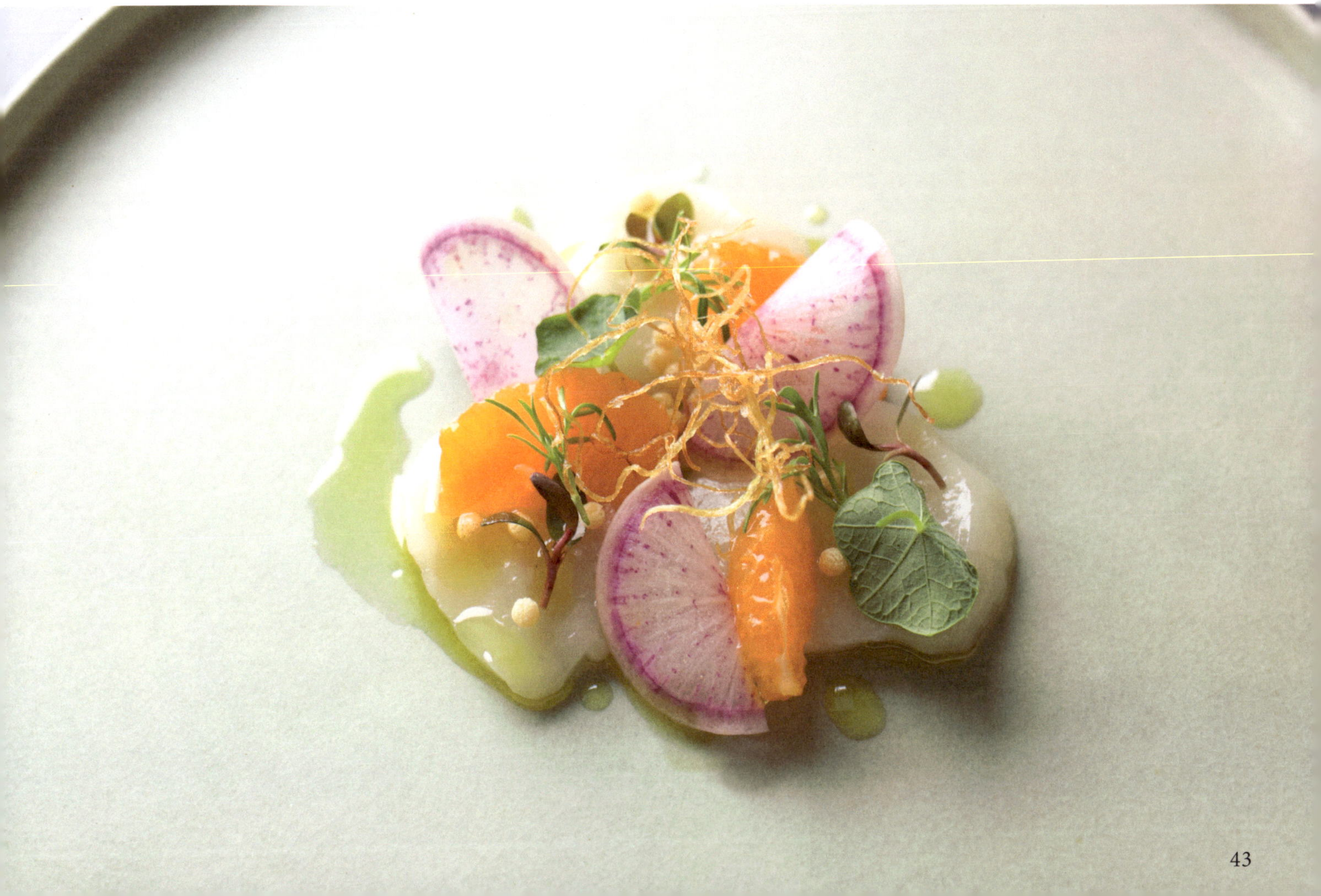

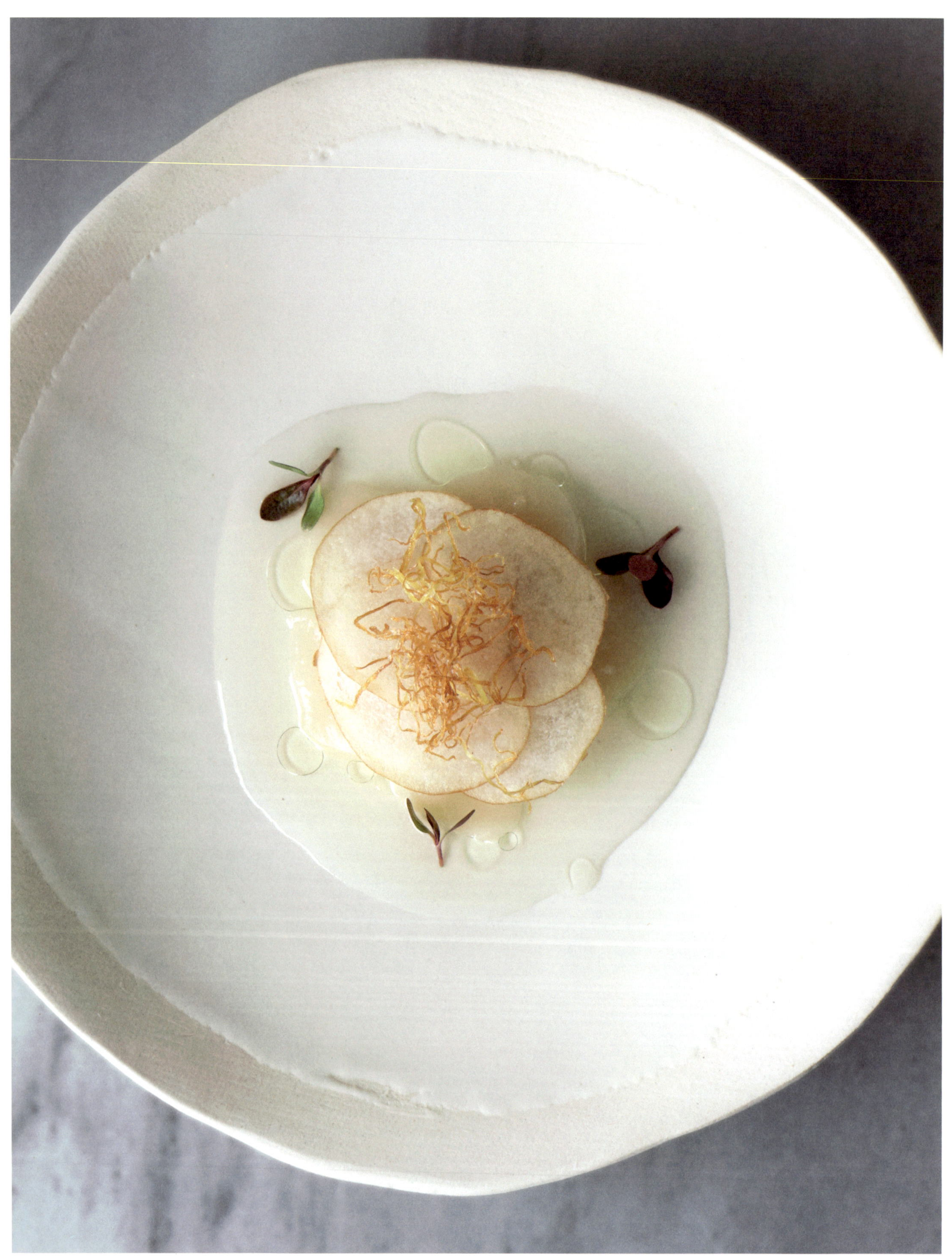

raw scallop, asain pear, ginger, hazelnut oil

You are currently out of the restaurant game. What do you miss most about being away from restaurants?

I miss staff meals. I miss the salt crystals on my face and the high I'd get after an intense service. I miss drinking water out of deli cups. I miss having a kitchen family. When you freelance, you're often working solo or with a traveling sous chef or two. I'm usually jumping in and out of different kitchens with different teams. It's fun in it's own way, but I do miss seeing, working with, and laughing with the same group of people everyday.

What do you think of the restaurant scene in SF, and the crazy prices of starting a new restaurant right now?

It's been a bit crazy here, and it's all triggered by the rise in real estate. Chefs and other artists struggle to afford the cost of living in SF and have to travel from hours away to a job that makes minimum wage or move away all together to another city. Meanwhile, restaurants struggle to be able to pay higher wages when hit with a rise in expenses, like rent. I've definitely noticed a lull in new restaurants opening around the bay, but I hope to find a way to build a sustainable restaurant concept that can improve the happiness and quality of life for our community.

What are you currently up to?

I started my own company a few years ago — you'll find me demoing at food festivals, hanging out in kitchens, curating pop-up dinners, designing ice cream flavors, and using food as a tool to speak about other areas that I'm passionate about -- women's empowerment, LGBTQ, Asian American communities, food education, and entrepreneurship.

I'm also focusing my time this year on getting my ducks in a row for a restaurant. It's always something I'm working on. I have my business plans ready to go, and at this point, it's just a matter of the other pieces falling into place.

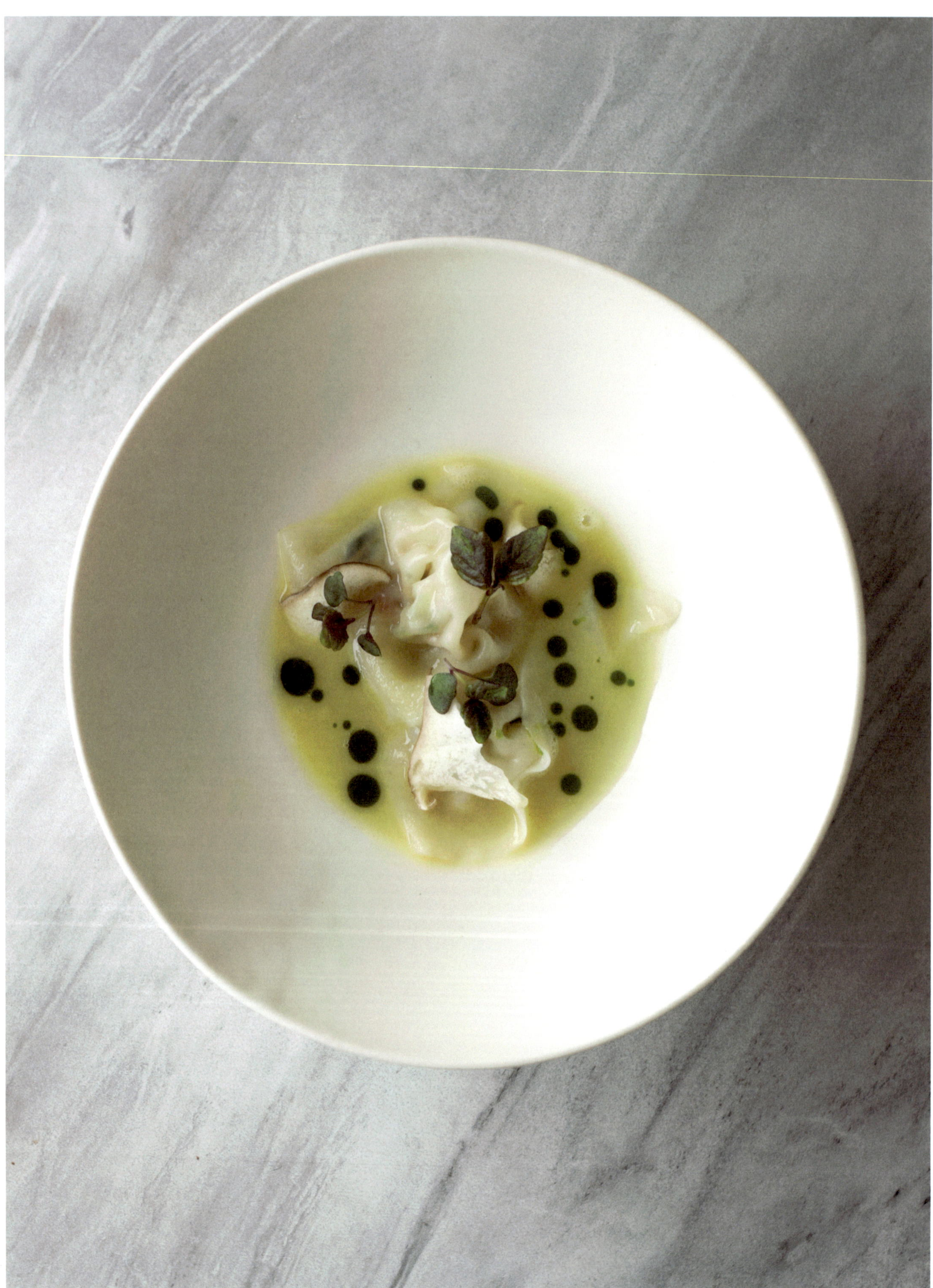

Lobster Wonton, Alliums, Yuzu Broth

Recipe by Melissa King

Lobster Wontons

Ingredients:

450 g	lobster meat, de-shelled, deveined (or shrimp)
25 g	water
15 g	agrumato lemon oil
2 g	salt
2 g	lime leaves, fine julienne
1 g	lemon zest
	ginger, grated on microplane
	white pepper
	wonton wrappers (thin, square)

Method:

Rough cut the lobster into pieces. Place into a kitchen aid mixer with the paddle attachment and whip on low with water, lemon oil, salt, lime leaves, zest, ginger, and white pepper until slightly emulsified. Wrap wontons into bundles. Boil the wontons for 1-2 minutes, or until they start floating.

Yuzu Broth

Ingredients:

1000 g	filtered water
4 g	kombu
2 g	ginger, peeled and sliced
10 ea	shiitake mushroom stems
30 g	katsuoboshi
25 g	white shoyu
25 g	mirin
15 g	yuzu juice
	salt
	butter

Method:

Place the filtered water, kombu, ginger, and mushroom stems into a pot and bring to a very gentle simmer. Add the katsuoboshi and turn off the heat. Keep the pot over a pilot light for 1 hour, and then strain through a cheesecloth. Season with white shoyu, mirin, yuzu juice, and salt until there is a balanced flavor. On the pick-up, emulsify with cold butter to give the broth a little richness and body.

Allium Oil

Ingredients:

300 g	green garlic, green tops (or leeks or scallions)
	grapeseed oil

Method:

Blend with only enough grapeseed oil to create a vortex and emulsify. Do not over oil or it will dilute the color and flavor of the oil. Heat a very hot sauté pan, and add the puree to the pan. Use a rubber spatula to stir it quickly. The oil will separate and turn bright green. After 1-2 minutes, strain and hang with cheesecloth to get a very dark green oil. This can be kept in the freezer.

Assembly

For the plate:

Boil the wontons. Emulsify the butter into the yuzu broth. Garnish with allium oil, micro shiso, and shaved raw mushrooms such as matsutake.

Yellowtail, Melon "Aguachile", Chicharron

Recipe by Melissa King

Melon "Aguachile"

Ingredients:

500 g	green melon, ripe
100 g	cucumber, peeled
20 g	cilantro stems
1 g	serrano chili
1 g	ginger
1 g	garlic
10 g	lime juice
	salt
	agrumato lemon oil

Method:

Juice the melon, cucumber, cilantro, chili, ginger, and garlic in a juicer. Mix in fresh lime juice and salt to taste. Strain through chinois then strain through a coffee filter. Chill over an ice bath.

Assembly

Add the melon broth to the bowl. Layer sliced yellow tail and season with finishing sea salt. Garnish with shaved radishes, cucumber leaves, petite cucumber, herbs, flowers, chicharron, and agrumato lemon oil.

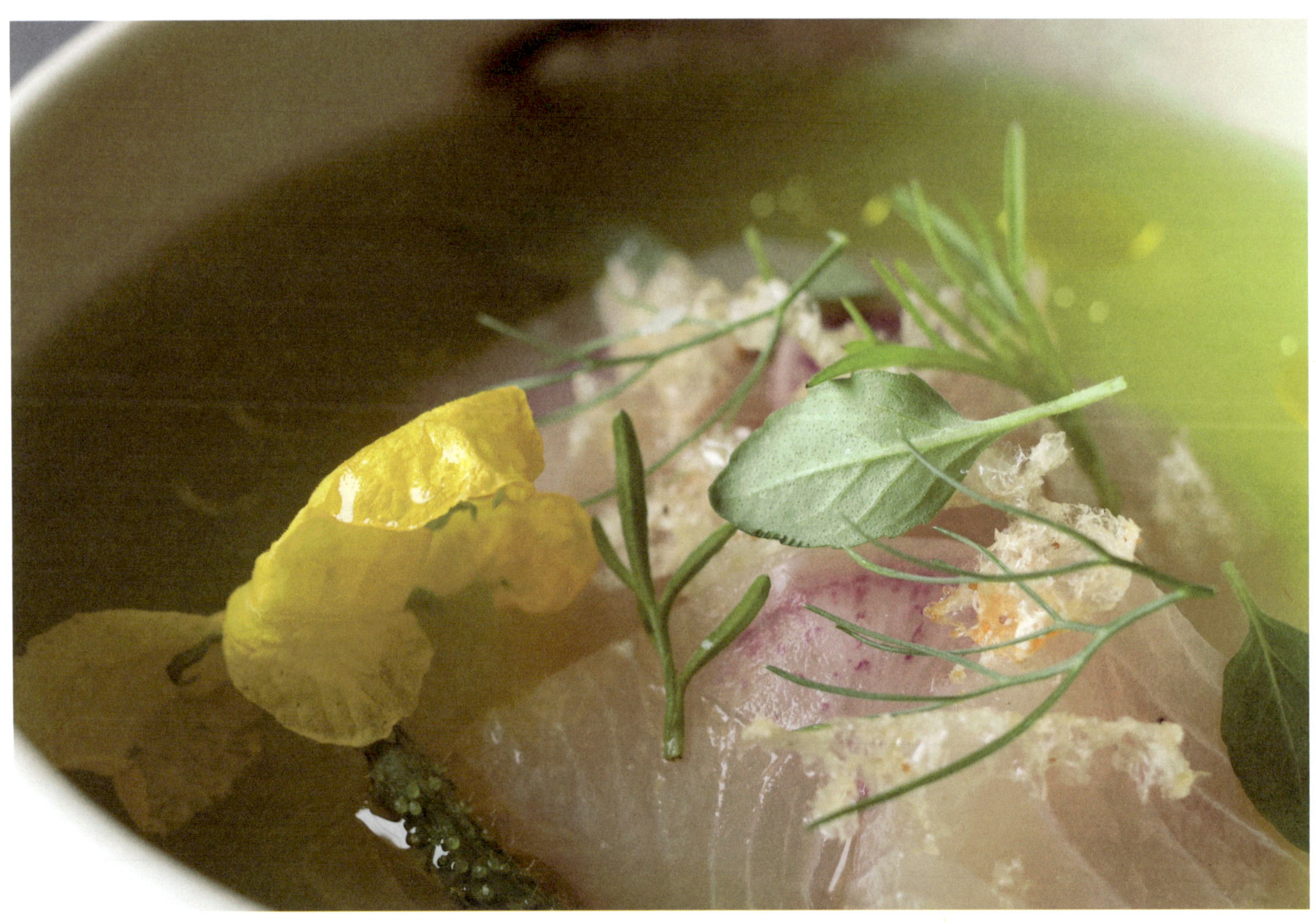

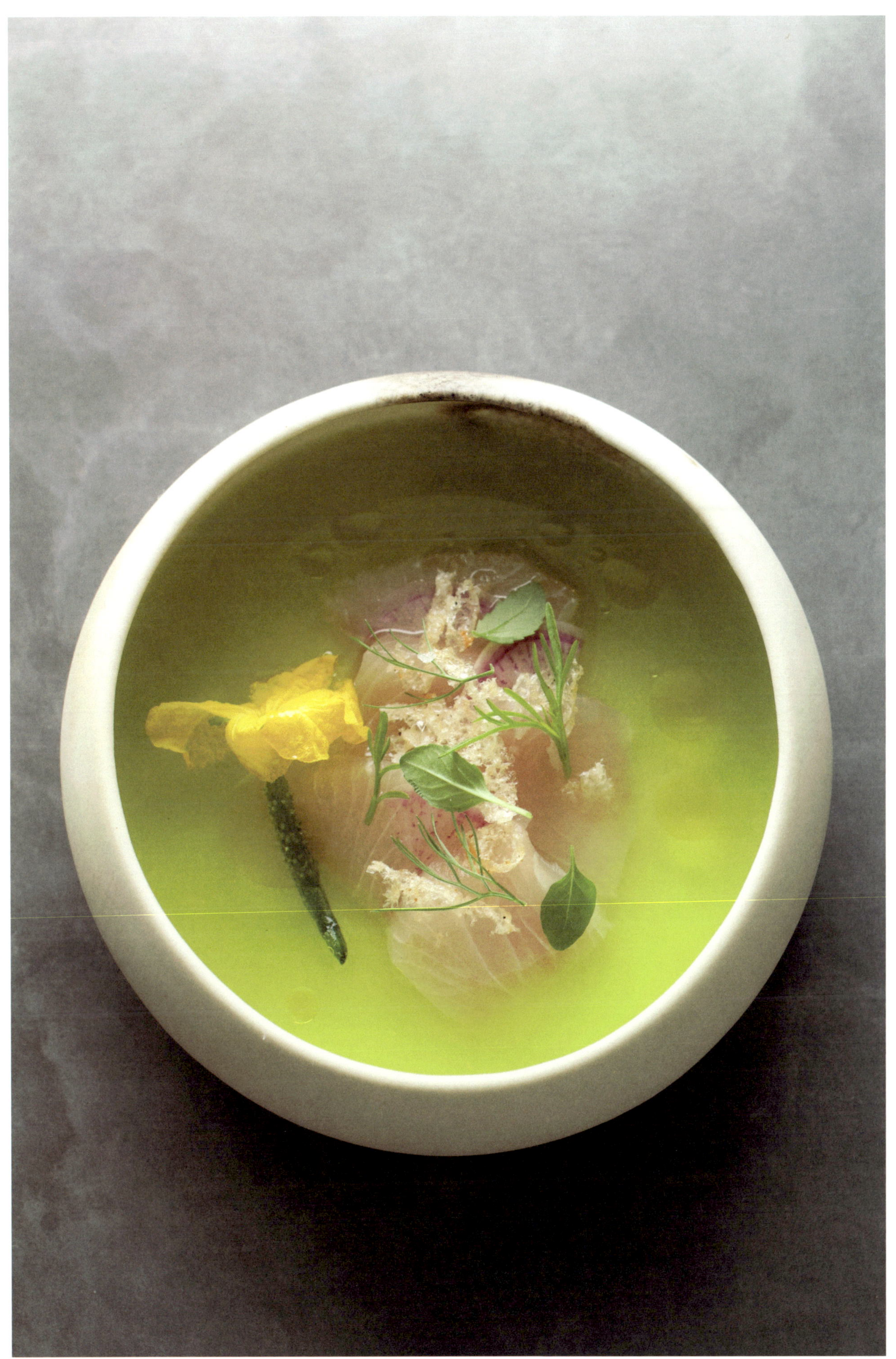

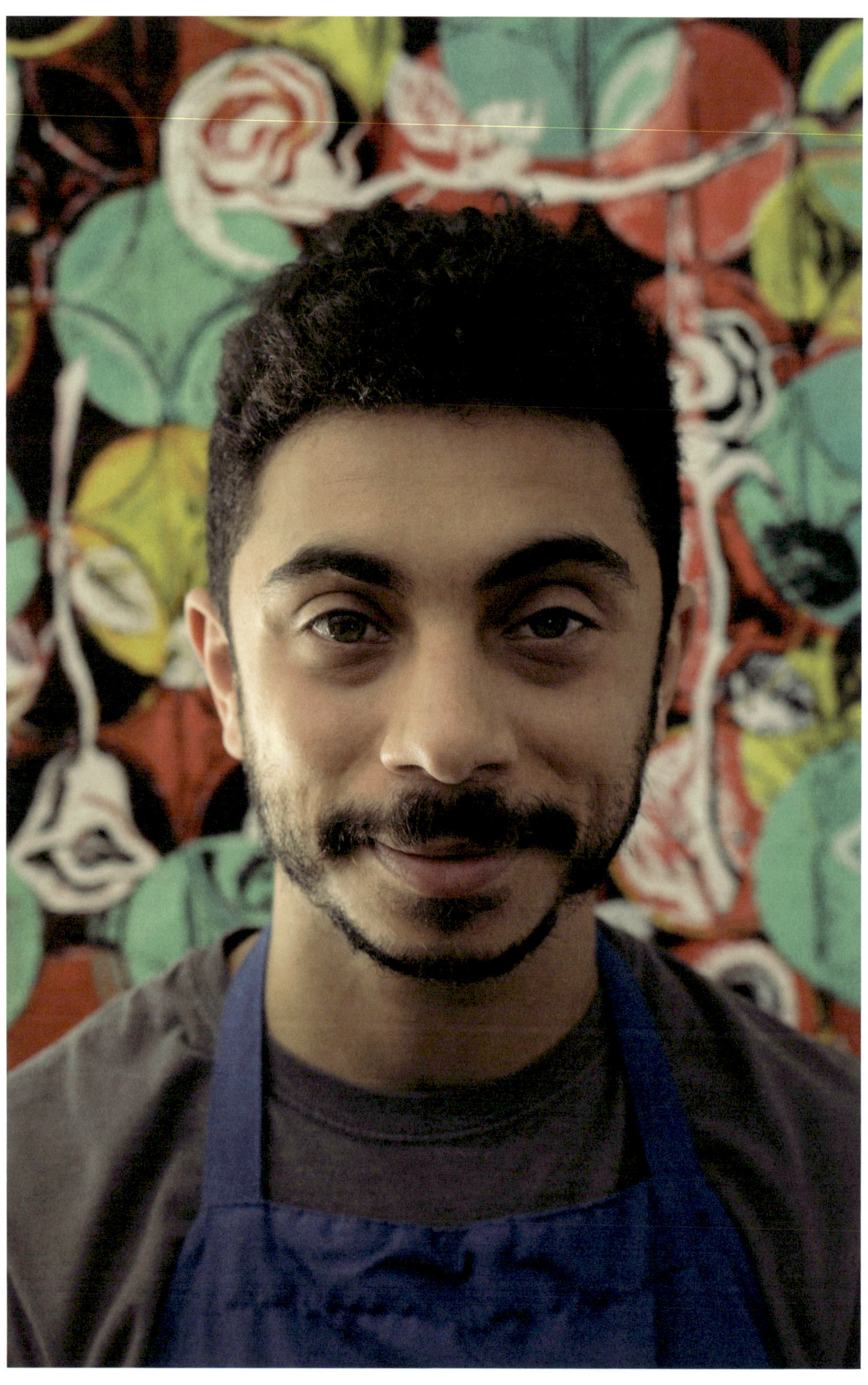

miles thompson

michael's
santa monica, california

Why did you get into cooking?

When I was 13, I went to a party catered by the friend of a family friend and was absolutely blown away by the food – I immediately wanted to learn how to make food taste like that. I was introduced to the chef, Charlotte Berwind, and asked for a job. I was given one as a dishwasher and ended up working for Charlotte for six years, in all capacities.

What were some of your crucial formative experiences with food?

Food has always been very important to my family. We cooked dinner at home nearly every night for the entirety of my childhood. Understanding and seeing food come to fruition from birth gave me a deep respect and love for the process of cooking.

As a young teenager, I watched a lot of cooking shows and read the congruent cookbooks, trying all of the recipes that looked interesting to me. I have no formal training, but I look at this, along with the time that I spent with Charlotte, as the beginning of my education.

I remember the first time that I ate a tasting menu alone – I was 19 – at Providence in Los Angeles. I still have the menu tucked away with all of the handwritten recipes that I have collected over the years. I remember smiling, crying, and being in awe of a level of food and execution that I had only read about, over the course of that meal. Certainly I had eaten alone before that experience, but it was the first time I really 'dined' alone, a remarkable thing to do and still one of the most enjoyable things that I do in my life.

The first time that I tried sayori when I worked at NOBU sticks out to me - it being braided and shimmering atop the bullet of rice. It was astonishing to me. So pure and perfect.

When I was taught how to cook and compose the veal brain dish at animal by chef Vinny Dotolo, in the middle of a busy service, really pops out to me. I had picked that dish up several times before at the instruction of the senior line cook, but that was the first time I saw it made properly, by its creator. There was a radiant difference in the structure, form and execution of the dish that really has never left me.

What inspires your food? When you reach creative blocks, what are ways you get passed those?

The products we use, my history as a student of various art forms, and the people around me inspire the food that I cook. To the first point, I am very lucky to cook in California and work with a bevy of stunning farms and ranches supplying us with impeccable products – that alone is inspiring. As a younger person I practiced and studied martial arts, poetry, classical and jazz music, and theatre – in all of those arts, there are common themes and techniques that are easily translated to cooking, such as improvisation, discipline, repetition, and economy of motion. Certain dishes are poems for people, some are songs of various types and forms of love, and others are simply reflections of nights caught in conversation.

When I reach a creative block, I return to what I know. I return to the volumes of recipes and books that I have amassed over the years and become a vigorous student of. I also eat at places and in forms of restaurants or styles of cuisine that I am un-/less familiar with. I feel that blocks happen when you are not feeding your mind with enough new information and experiences. We can't rely on creativity to create. We have to strengthen it as a daily practice.

How would you describe your relationship with food? Is it one of love, obsession, or passion? All three? Is it something else?

I would describe my relationship with food as a passionate and obsessive love. It is also a place of safety; in it, I know there will always be moments of happiness, failure, frustration, giddiness, loss, and memory. Food provides life, but it also lives.

What is your understanding of balance in cooking when creating a new dish? In terms of textures and flavors?

I approach balance based upon the building blocks of the products' basic flavor and how they may be augmented or masked (at times for effect) by salt, sweetness, acidity, bitterness, umami, and spice. I am a fan of multi-textural foods, and at times tend to push for surprising juxtapositions when creating dishes. At other times, I am more interested in gradations of the same texture – such as a dish with multiple creamy elements. Some may be soft, some may be sticky, and some may be slippery, but all are creamy at the core.

Ultimately, the dish must strike a balance with the other dishes on the menu. You cannot have too many salt or sugar forward dishes at the same time, or too many crunchy dishes. It makes for a less dynamic and enjoyable experience for the diner.

Do you think of cooking as more of craftsmanship or artistry?

I think that cooking is an art. However as with any art form, the artistry will only emerge once the basic craft has been honed, understood, and digested. Then when utilizing the skills taught by the craft, one can progress to artistry. You are afforded the freedom of creativity supported by a strong technical basis.

How much of your cooking relies on experiments and how much is based in classical technique?

I would say that there really is a 50/50 split between experimentation and classical technique in my cooking currently.

Michael's is a Los Angeles institution whose kitchen has produced many influential chefs. Nancy Silverton and Sang Yoon to name a few. How do you see yourself as part of this tradition?

I see myself as very lucky to be among those chefs. I still have trouble grasping the concept of being 'among' them, as they have influenced my career and way of thinking as a cook and a chef. However, I see myself as being tasked with upholding and pushing the standards that they set as chefs in this city and hopefully cooking in a manner that helps to evolve and grow California/Angeleno Cuisine - to a place that not only has a hand in creating, but also in putting that style of cooking on the map.

Do you feel the need to continue any of the restaurant's traditions? How do you balance serving your food in such an iconic restaurant?

I feel the need to continue the tradition (and for me the luxury) of using the most impeccable and interesting ingredients that the Farmers Markets of Southern California have to offer. In doing so I am able to serve whatever is most inspiring and delicious. However I do want to honor the history of the restaurant. For example, Michael's is known for its preparations of Duck and Chicken, so we always have one of those proteins on the menu.

Do you feel a responsibility to stick to 'California Cuisine'? What does that term mean to you in 2018?

I do not feel a responsibility to stick to 'California Cuisine.' However I am drawn to it, or more so, what I have started to call 'Angeleno Cuisine'. This to me is food rooted deeply in the agricultural bounty of California, but influenced and inflected by the incredible multicultural population of Los Angeles. We take influences from Japan, Mexico, Korea, Thailand, El Salvador, India, Eastern Europe and other places and combine those flavors, textures, and ideas with the most stunning produce, meats, and fish available to create and exercise a cuisine that is new but familiar.

Some people might consider your food modernist. This seems to be defined by a particular presentation, as well as an abstracted flavor palate. For example on your current menu, the octopus dish with burnt butter, Sichuan peppercorn marshmallow, and panisse draws from French and Chinese cuisine, but is not either. Do you think of your cuisine, or this dish, as modernist?

I do consider my food to be modern/modernist – it is the result of classical techniques that are combined in unconventional ways and speak to where food has evolved to in the current state. If we are working with the above definition of modernist, this octopus dish fulfills the description, as abstraction in presentation and flavor palate is a keynote of modernity in general, or the arrival to something new based upon the teachings/learning of the past. I think that all of my food could, on a sliding scale, be defined in this manner.

What are your thoughts on the kitchen philosophy? Do you strive for a particular kitchen environment and workplace?

I think that the kitchen should be a calm and quiet place, not silent, but focused and fun. I strive for a strong culture of supportive competition as well as encouraging the cooks to ask for and offer help when need be. Obviously the classical tenants of cleanliness and organization remain paramount in our kitchen, and that extends to the mind as well as the workplace. A cluttered mind makes cluttered space and cluttered plates. In my mind, the days of a vicious brigade system have given way to a more earnest and human approach. I loved the 'Yes Chef' system as a line cook, and luckily our kitchen is very much disciplined in that manner. However they ask and are encouraged to ask more 'Why?' questions, which only gives them more knowledge and strength as they develop their skills and minds.

Textures you're digging:

Frozen chocolate, burnt sugar on meat, creamy beans, egg noodles, braised tendons, cartilage

Flavors/flavor profiles you're into:

Sweetness with meat, rose water with intense spice, fish sauce and unfiltered extra-virgin olive oil, aged poultry, raw turnips, strong arugula, sour citrus.

Ingredients you're excited to work with:

'Peads & Barnetts' pork, fermented mustard greens, citrus, curry leaves, dried shiitake mushrooms, aged soy sauce, seaweed, yogurt, lime leaves.

Best bite in recent memory:

Biodynamic sweet potato cooked in rose hip oil with duck fat emulsion, finger lime, Calix caviar, lemon thyme and sea lavender at Vespertine in Culver City, CA.

Where to eat in Los Angeles:

Ruen Pair, Alimento, Bestia, Bavel, Sapp Coffee House, Chengdu Taste, Rustic Canyon, Here's Looking At You, Vespertine, Destroyer.

Baby Broccoli

Recipe by Miles Thompson

Garlic Confit

Ingredients:

1 qt garlic cloves, peeled

2000 ml rice bran oil

Method:

Preheat an oven to 300 F. Place the garlic cloves in a saucepan and cover with the oil. Cover the pan with foil with the shiny side facing the contents of the pan. Place the pan in the oven for 3 hours. Remove the pan and covering, and allow the garlic confit to cool completely in the fat. Reserve the garlic in the oil in an airtight container.

Yuzu Kosho Aioli

Ingredients:

1 ea farm egg yolk

45 g yuzu kosho

80 g garlic confit, drained of oil

100 g sake

50 g rice vinegar

360 g garlic confit oil

10 g salt

Method:

Blend the egg yolk with all the other ingredients, excluding the oil, over low speed in a blender until they form a thick and creamy paste. Increase the speed and slowly stream in the oil until emulsified. Season with salt.

White Chocolate-Juniper Crackle

Ingredients:

200 g white chocolate chips

20 g coconut oil

20 g puffed buckwheat

5 g juniper berry powder

1 g salt

Method:

Melt the white chocolate together with the coconut oil over a double boiler. Once silky, remove from the heat and stir in the buckwheat, juniper, and salt. Stir well to ensure that the salt is dissolved. Transfer to a quarter sheet tray lined with parchment paper and freeze for a minimum of 1 hour before use.

Grilled Baby Broccoli

Ingredients:

baby broccoli, trimmed of woody base

unfiltered extra-virgin olive oil

kosher salt

Method:

Prepare a medium-hot grill. Toss the broccoli with the oil and season well with salt. Grill the broccoli until charred and just cooked through. Remove to a tray and cool to room temperature.

Assembly

Dress the baby broccoli with the yuzu kosho aioli and season with crushed Maldon salt. Place the broccoli on the plate and top with nine blood orange supremes. Sprinkle the dish with fresh English thyme leaves and stud the broccoli with seven shards of the white chocolate-juniper crackle. Dress the late with unfiltered extra-virgin olive oil and garnish with blue borage flowers, white borage flowers, and mustard flowers. Serve.

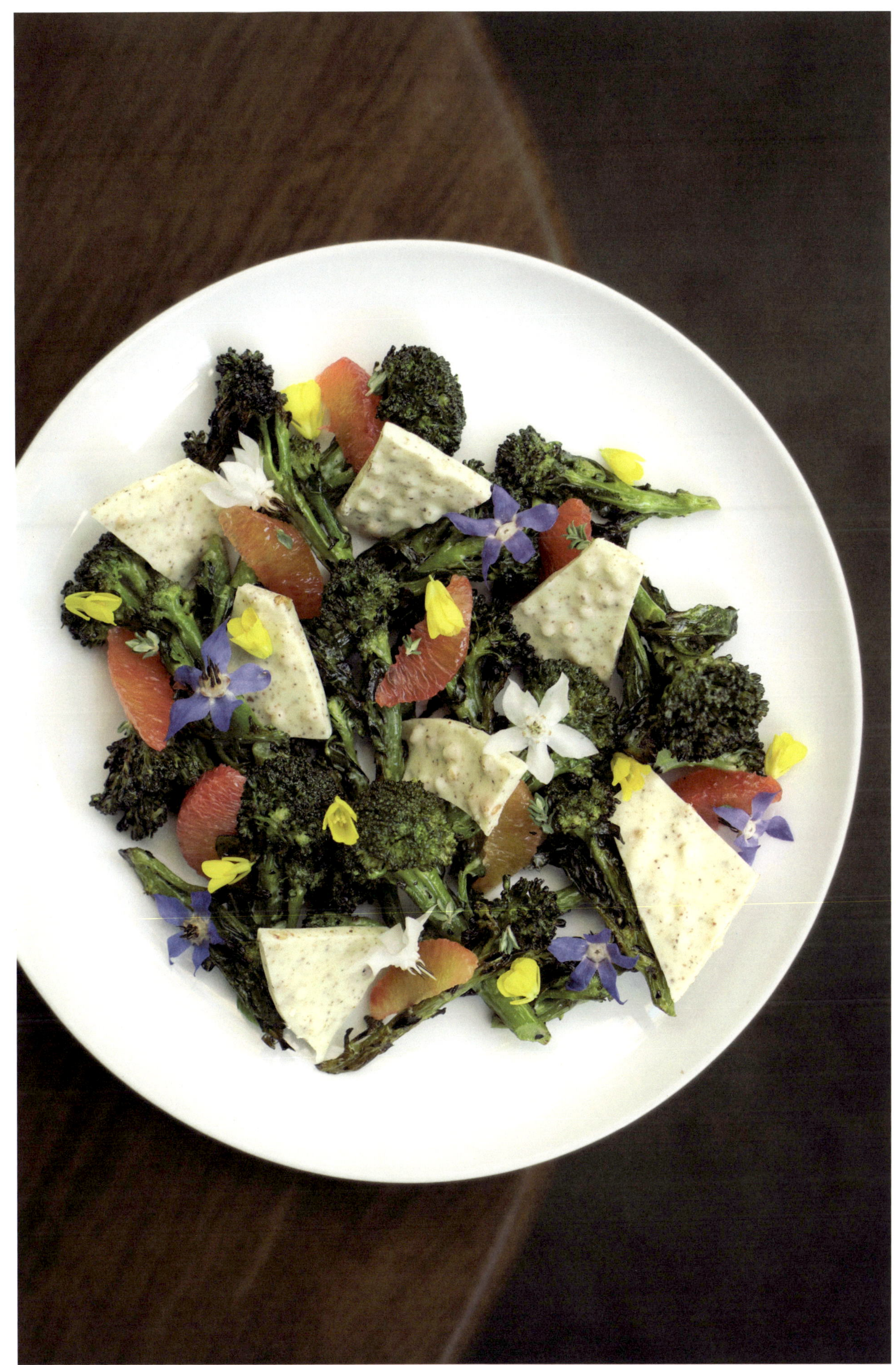

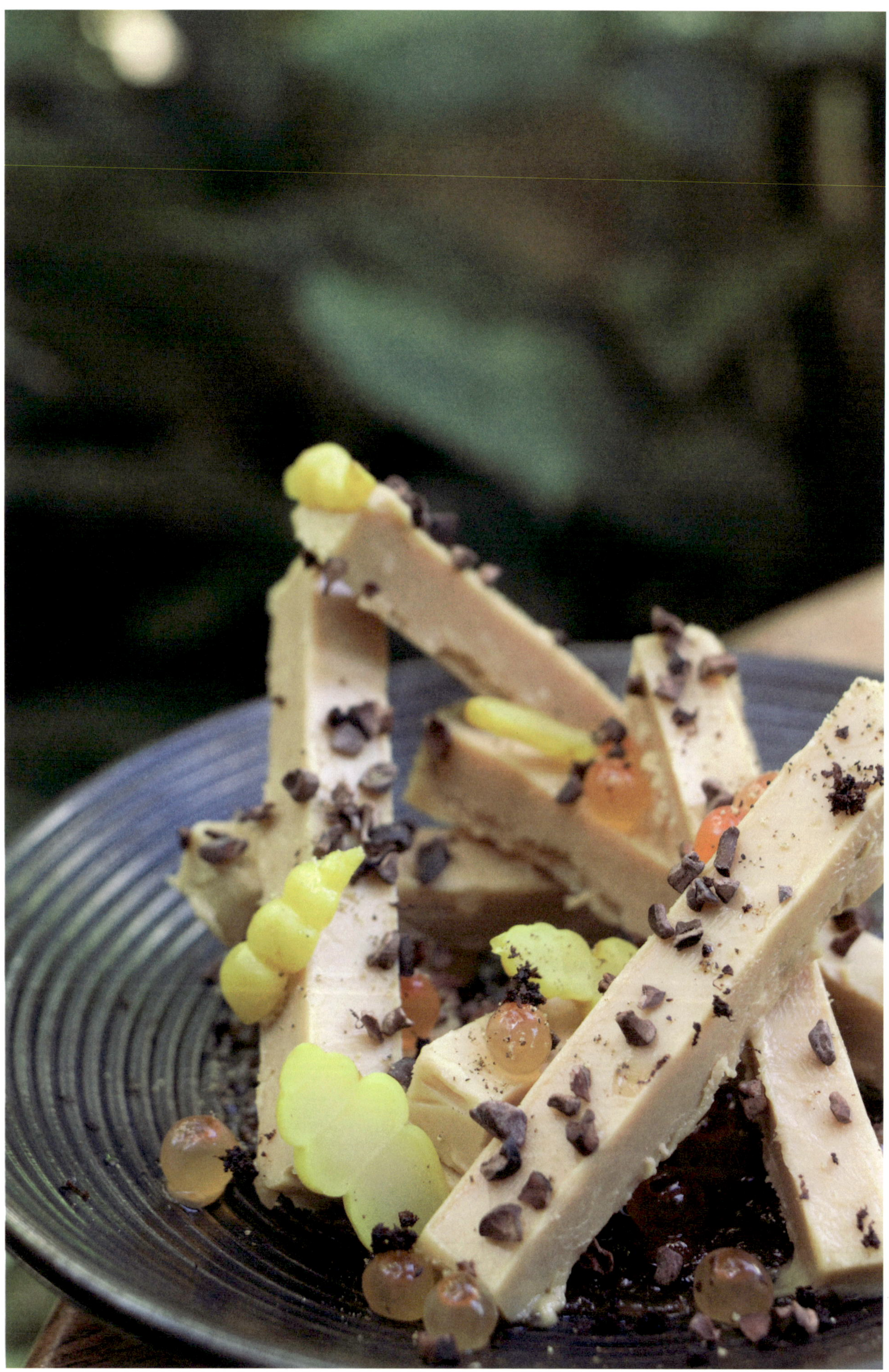

Foie Gras Terrine

Recipe by Miles Thompson

Foie Gras Terrine

Ingredients:

Foie Gras Cure:

100 g	pink salt
160 g	sea salt
70 g	granulated sugar

Cured Foie Gras:

900 g	foie gras, cleaned
12 g	foie gras cure
24 g	cognac

Method:

For the foie gras cure, combine all the ingredients with a whisk and store in an airtight container. For the cured foie gras, toss the cleaned foie gras with the cure and the cognac to coat. Place in an airtight container and allow to cure under refrigeration for 48 hours. To make the terrine, remove the foie gras from the refrigerator 2 hours prior to processing. Break the cured liver up into a hotel pan and set over the pilot light of a gas stove. Allow the foie to slowly and completely melt, whipping with a rubber spatula until it reaches 100 F. Pass the warmed foie gras through a chinois and whisk until re-emulsified. Pour into a prepared terrine mold, cover with plastic, and refrigerate overnight.

Green Tomato-Lavender Vinegar

Ingredients:

Green Tomato Water:

2000 g	green tomatoes

Green Tomato-Lavender Vinegar:

500 g	green tomato water
250 g	lavender vinegar

Method:

For the tomato water, puree the green tomatoes in a high-speed blender until liquefied. Hand the tomato puree in a cheesecloth-lined strainer over a bain marie in a cooler overnight until the tomato pulp is dry to extract a clear liquid. For the tomato-lavender vinegar, combine the two liquids, whisking well. Reserve in an airtight container in the refrigerator.

Bread and Butter Pickled Crosnes

Ingredients:

1/2 cup	salt
3 qt	water
1 lb	crosnes, scrubbed
2 cups	apple cider vinegar
2 cups	sugar
1/4 lb	onions, thinly sliced
1.5 T	yellow mustard seeds
3/4 T	celery seeds
3/4 T	turmeric
3/4 T	black pepper, coarse cracked

Method:

Dissolve the salt in water. Add the crosnes and refrigerate overnight. Drain the crosnes. Bring the vinegar, sugar, and spices to a boil, stirring to make sure that all the sugar is dissolved. Add the onions and brined crosnes. Stir and return to a gentle boil. Take off the heat and cool to room temperature.

Dehydrated Black Olives

Ingredients:

oil-cured black olives, pits removed

Method:

Preheat an oven to 180 F. Place the olives on a parchment paper lined sheet tray and place in the oven overnight or until completely dehydrated. Allow the olives to cool and reserve in an airtight container.

Pickled Ikura

Ingredients:

Dashi:

100 g	kombu
3500 ml	filtered water, cold
150 g	hon katsuo bonito

Ikura Pickling Liquid:

1000 g	dashi
100 g	green tomato water
10 g	BLiS barrel aged fish sauce
1 g	sea salt

Pickled Ikura

1 cup	ikura, cleaned
2 cups	ikura pickling liquid

Method:

For the dashi, place the kombu in the water and allow to steep for 1 hour over the pilot light. Bring the pot up to 168F. Adjust the heat to maintain that temperature for 1 hour. Remove the kombu, and strain through a chinois. Add the bonito flakes and allow to cool to room temp. Strain through a chinois, but do not press the solids. Drain until the dripping subsides. Chill in an ice bath and store in the refrigerator for up to 3 days. For the pickling liquid, combine all of the ingredients and whisk well. To pickle the ikura, cover the ikura with the pickling liquid, stirring gently to separate the ikura. Allow the roe to pickle for 2 hours under refrigeration. Discard after 36 hours.

Assembly

Smear the plate with a spoonful of membrillo. Stack the foie gras terrine in an aperture-like fashion. Drain a large spoonful of ikura and scatter over the plate. Place six pickled crosnes halves on the terrine. Microplane 1/2 of a dehydrated olive over the top. Sprinkle the dish with cocoa nibs and cracked black pepper. Serve.

Pork Collar

Recipe by Miles Thompson

Marinated Pork Collar

Ingredients:

Pork Collar Marinade:

515 g fish sauce
550 g Worcestershire sauce
165 g maple syrup
70 g lemon zest, microplaned

Marinated Pork Collar:

1 ea pork collar
pork collar marinade

Method:

For the pork collar marinade, whisk together all the ingredients. For the marinated pork collar, place the collar in a large resealable bag, cover with the marinade, and press all of the air out. Allow the collar to marinate for 48 hours in the cooler, flipping once after 24 hours. After it has marinated, pat it dry and place on a parchment lined tray. Age for a minimum of four days in the cooler before portioning into 255 g steaks.

Seasoned Extra-Virgin Olive Oil

Ingredients:

2 g chile de arbol
12 g lemon zest, by peeler
7 g garlic, crushed
100 g fish sauce
270 g unfiltered evoo

Method:

Place all of the ingredients in a resealable container and shake vigorously to emulsify. Transfer to an airtight container and store in the cooler.

Black Olive Honey

Ingredients:

Dehydrated Black Olives:

oil-cured black olives, pitted

Black Olive Honey:

500 g buckwheat honey
250 g white balsamic vinegar
500 g dehydrated black olives

Method:

For the dehydrated olives, preheat an oven to 180 F. Place the olives on a parchment paper lined sheet tray and place in the oven overnight or until completely dehydrated. Allow the olives to cool and reserve in an airtight container. For the black olive honey, place the honey and vinegar in a high-speed blender and process until smooth. While blending, slowly add the olives until a smooth paste is formed. Increase the speed to high and puree for two minutes. Cool and reserve in the cooler. Allow the sauce to come to room temperature before use.

Baby Damsom Plum Glaze

Ingredients:

Canned Baby Damsom Plums:

baby damsom plums, halved/pitted
simple syrup, hot

Baby Damsom Plum Glaze:

250 g canned damsom plums
250 g white balsamic vinegar
500 g buckwheat honey

Method:

For the canned plums, place the plums in sterilized glass jars and cover with simple syrup. Cover and process the jars for 10 minutes in boiling water. Remove and cool, inverted on towels. Reserve at room temperature. For the plum glaze, puree the plums and their syrup with the white balsamic in a high-speed blender until smooth. Pass through a chinois and combine with the honey, whisking to incorporate. Reserve in an airtight container and refrigerate. Allow the glaze to come to room temperature before use.

Pomelo Gel

Ingredients:

500 g pomelo marmalade
150 g white shoyu
150 g Frantoia Brand evoo

Method:

Blend all ingredients in a high-speed blender until smooth. Pass through a chinois before storing in an airtight container.

Assembly

Prepare a medium-hot grill. Rub the collar steak with rice bran oil and season with salt. Grill it while flipping constantly until almost medium-rare. Brush with the plum glaze and cook over the hottest part of the grill to char the glaze. Flip the steak and repeat. Remove the steak from the grill to a resting rack and allow to cool in a warm place for as long as it cooked for. Toss sprouting cauliflower, sprouting cabbage leaves, and sprouting daikon leaves and flowers in seasoned oil and salt and grill. Smear the plate with the black olive honey and place seven dots of pomelo gel on the plate. Drizzle with pomegranate molasses. Slice the pork against the grain, scatter over the sauces and cover with the grilled leaves. Garnish with sai sai radish flowers and serve.

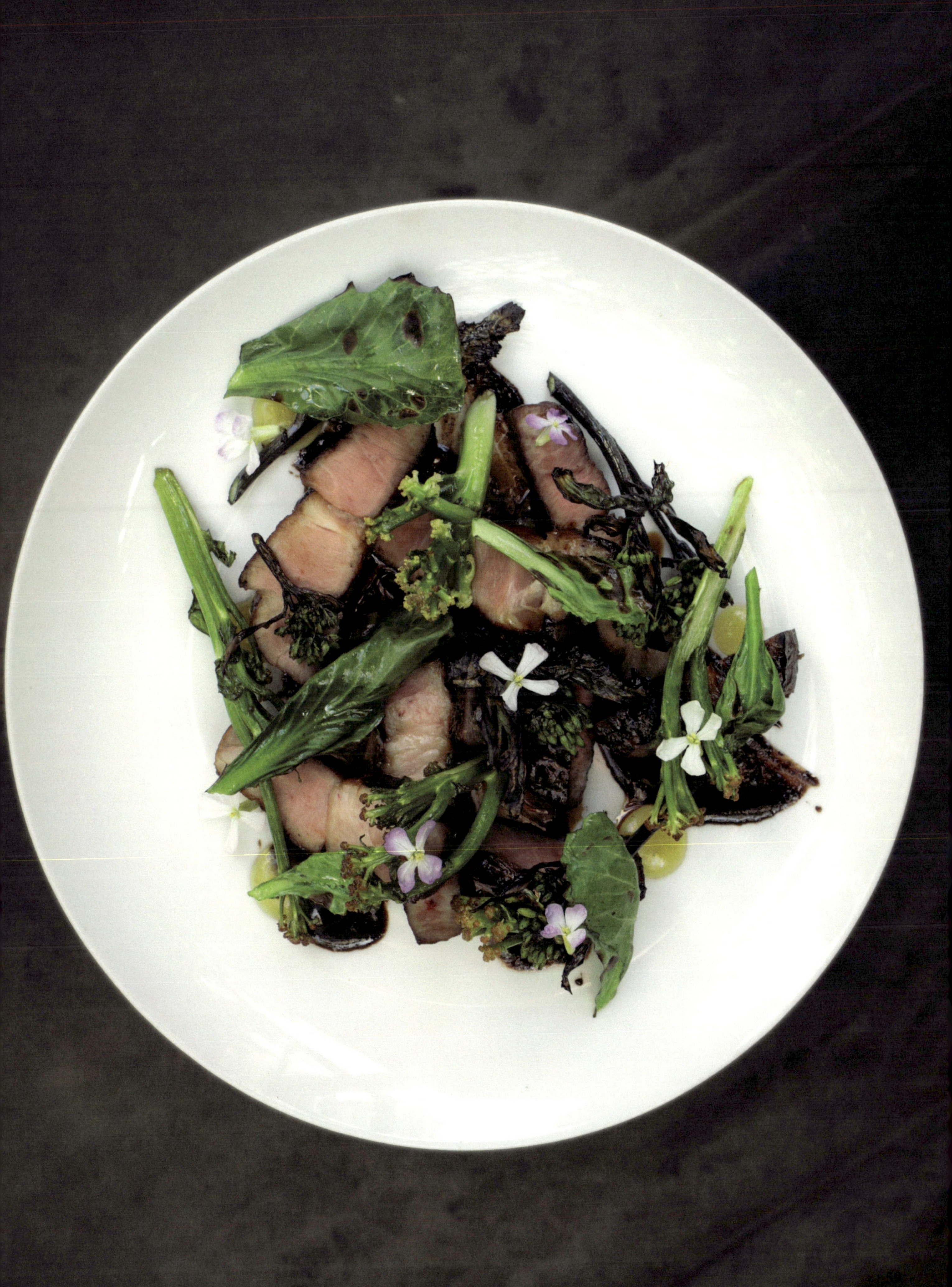

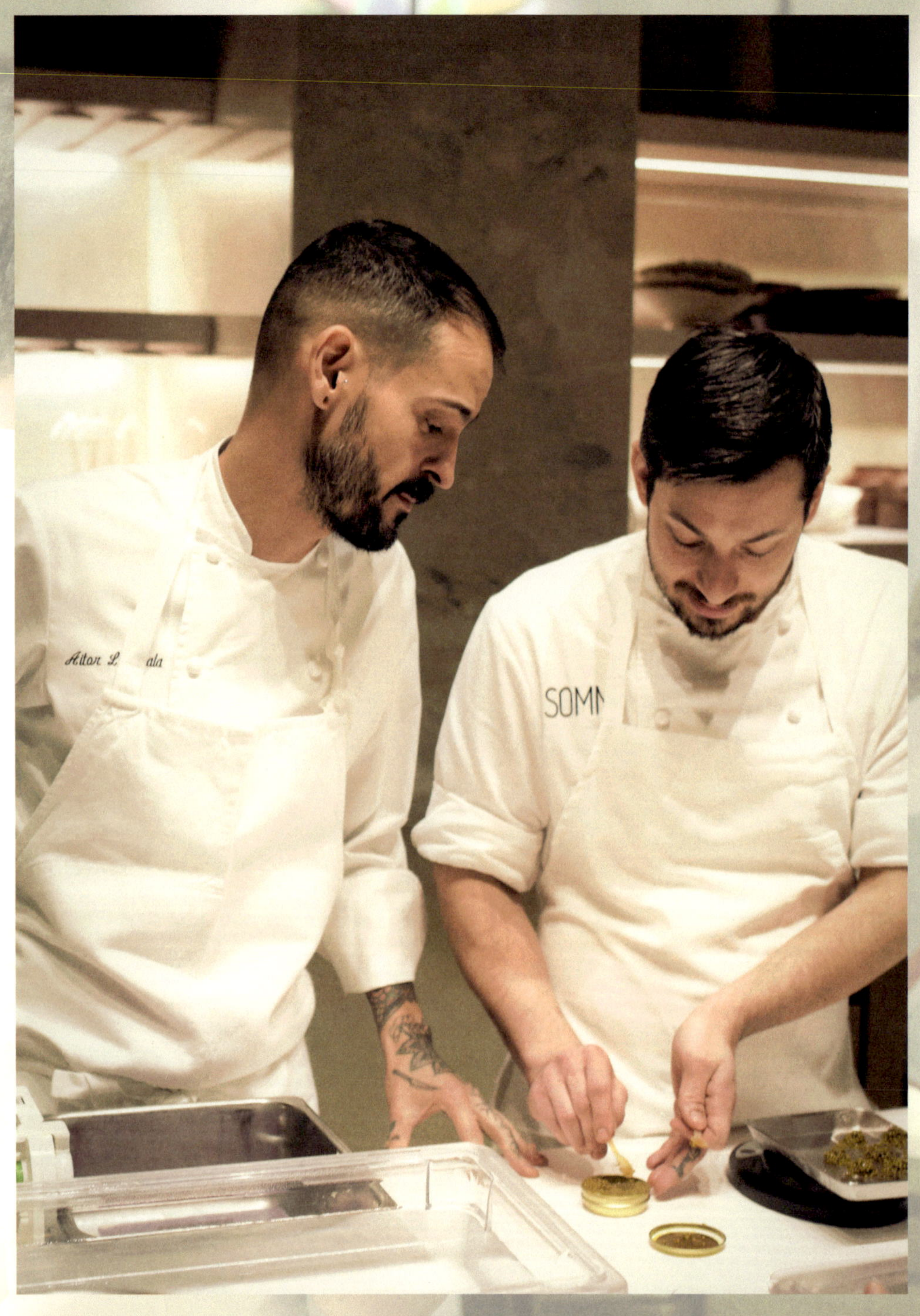

aitor zabala

somni
beverly hills, california

photos by jill paider and nick muncy

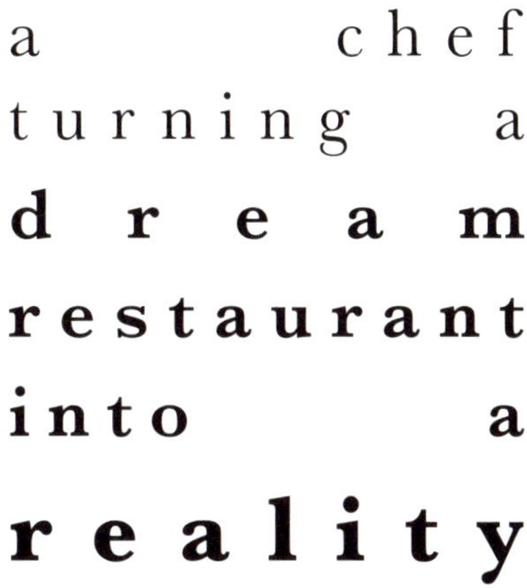

a chef turning a **dream restaurant into a reality**

Somni, which translates to "dream" in Catalan is Aitor Zabala's new space nestled inside the back of The Bazaar. The restaurant replaces Saam, which Aitor ran as one of ThinkFoodGroup's creative directors. The restaurant is a single counter that seats ten people at a time. It indeed is a dream restaurant, and its evident that a chef with a clear vision is behind the restaurant and kitchen design. The kitchen is unlike anything else. It boasts a beautiful fish tank, a temperature controlled area for dry aging meat, and a seamless kitchen workspace that blends straight into the dining area, making it unclear where the kitchen ends, and the dining room begins. The amount of planning behind this restaurant is remarkable, with custom plate ware, specialty made silicone molds and non-alcoholic drinks that mimic the flavors of quality wines like Sauvignon Blanc and Pinot Noir.

Dining at Somni is an intimate experience. Aitor invites you into his kitchen, he and his team cook for you and though the stage has been so dramatically set, no one is acting. They are just cooking their hearts out. Sitting on the other side of the counter is a true delight. Where most chefs would be uncomfortable having guests seeing and hearing everything that goes on in the kitchen, Aitor welcomes it humbly.

Aitor, who has been working with José Andrés since 2010, has an impressive resume. Before coming to the states, he worked at elBulli, as well as other great Michelin-starred restaurants in Spain such as Alkimia, ABaC, and Akelarre. His pedigree is evident in his food, with visually minimalistic dishes that hide surprising flavors and techniques.

Tell us a little bit about yourself and how you got started cooking.

I was born in Barcelona, son of Esther Zabala and Jose Luis Lozano, and the middle brother of five siblings. I started cooking when I was in the army (mandatory nine months), where we prepared meals for 3000 soldiers. After that, I decided to join the Hofmann Culinary School.

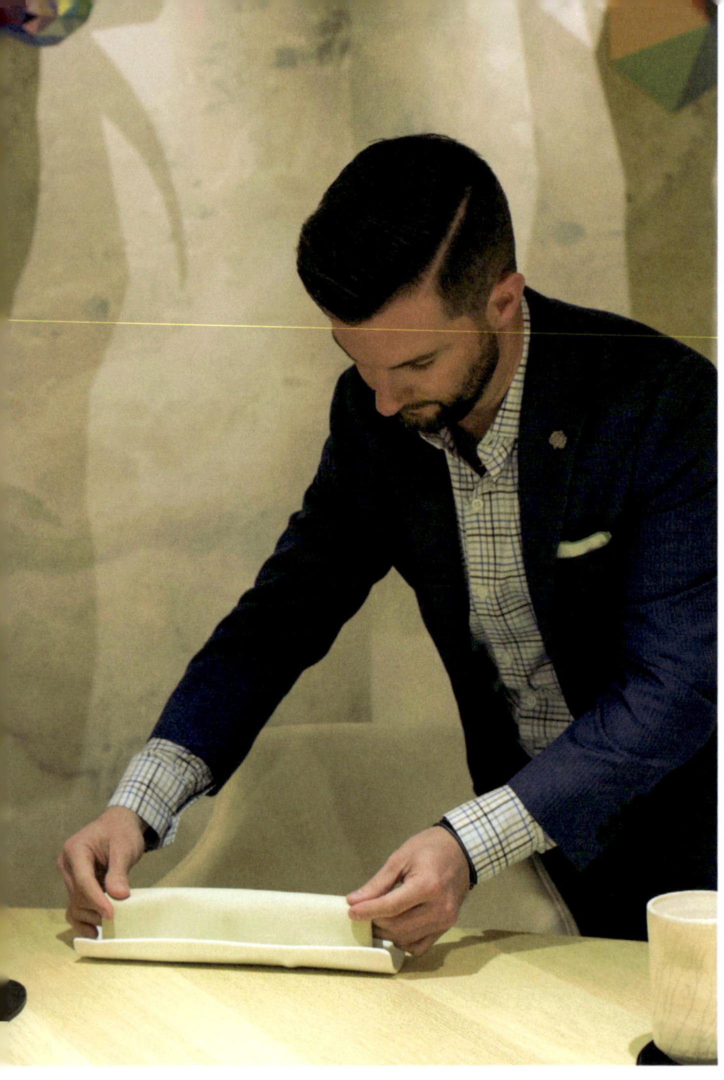

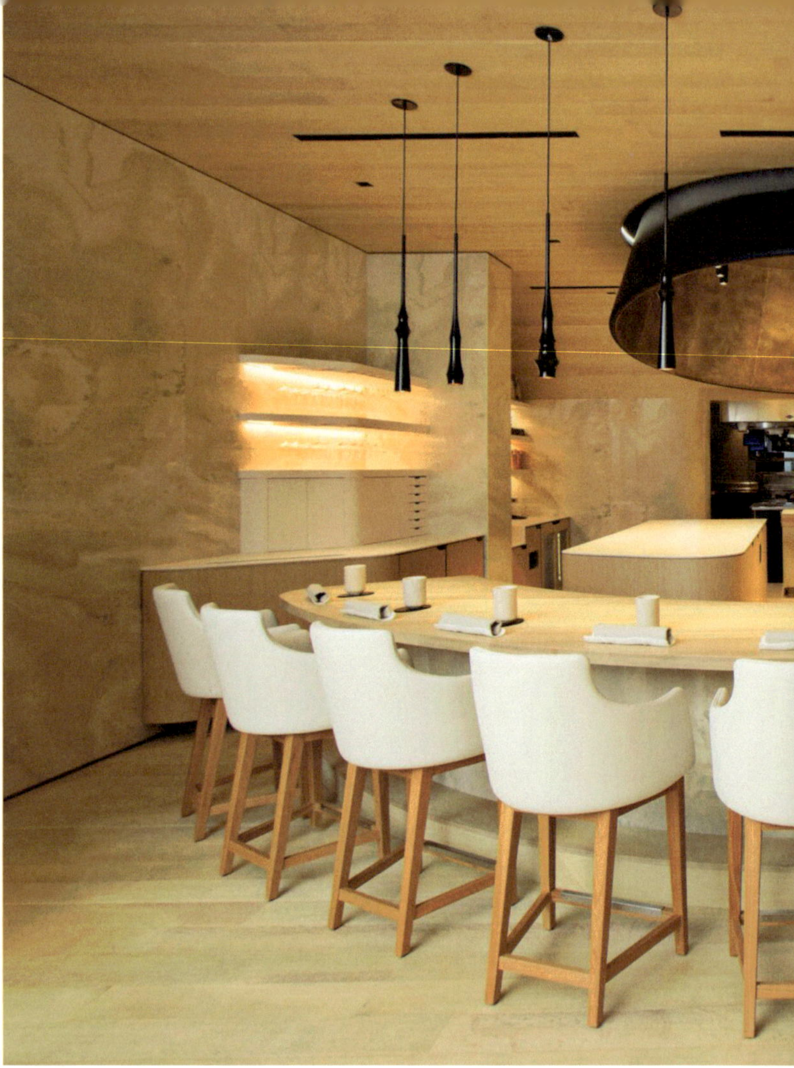

Why did you want to open Somni instead of continuing to create dishes for the other ThinkFoodGroup concepts? Why did you select LA for Somni?

That's a question I've asked myself many times (hahaha), but honestly, it has been my dream for a while, since the early days of my culinary journey. I've always wanted to have a place, where I can do "my cuisine" and emboss my style into the dishes I create. Now I have that, but it doesn't mean I've stopped creating dishes for the other ThinkFoodGroup concepts.

I didn't choose LA... It was LA that chose me. I think life takes us to places at particular times. When I came here for the first time, I felt like I was in the right place, where I wanted to be. The climate is amazing, the products here are beautiful, so everything seemed to be a perfect fit for me at that time.

How is Somni different from the other ThinkFoodGroup concepts?

Every single venue from TFG has something different from the others, and that's why we think, we are pretty successful. They have our DNA, yet they are all different from each other, with a common concept tailored to different cities (The Bazaar, Jaleo, Zaytinya, etc.). Somni is a whole different story with elements that are familiar for TGF.

How much planning has gone into the opening? How involved are you with the decisions of creating Somni?

Wow, it was a lot of planning, and in the end, we forgot about many things (hahaha). It took several months to select all the elements that create this restaurant.

I have drawings from 2013 when we tried to decide what will be the best use of space... We picked everything (art, materials, colors, silverware, glasses, tableware, kitchen, equipment, uniforms, name, logo, etc.).

I had a lot of freedom in being able to take care of all the details. One of the things that make me even more proud of this project is that I've been here from the very beginning - when SOMNI was just an idea floating in our heads, till now, when it's a real restaurant.

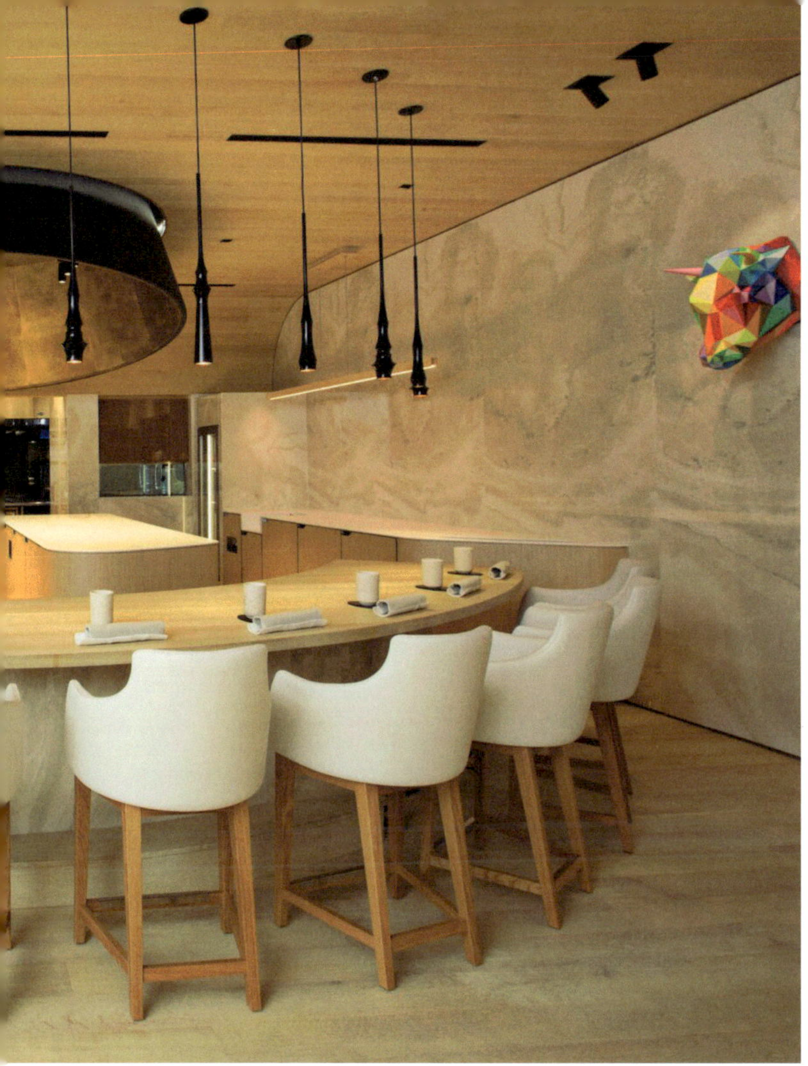

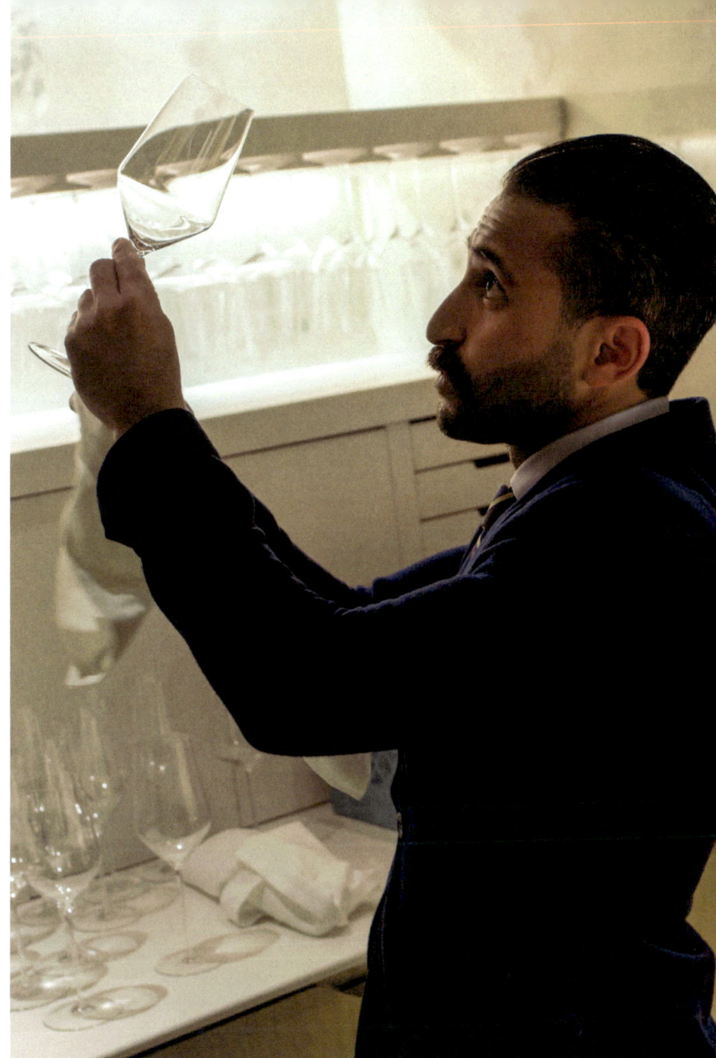

How much was José Andrés involved with the creation of Somni?

José is involved in all the big decisions (name, design, style, etc.). The information is running smoothly between us, so we are both up to date on what's happening in the restaurant. I'm glad that José made me the lead on this project. I'm always learning and have the opportunity to develop my ideas.

The cooks serve and clear most of the plates. Why did you choose this style of service vs. the traditional FOH?

I love the concept of a dialogue between the chefs and our guests. It also allows us to see their reaction. Plus who can explain a dish better than the person who made it? It's incredible to have a team of people who know how to cook and also how to serve the food they've prepared. We're developing a team with more skills and more variety.

Where does your inspiration for your dishes come? Does Somni have any theme?

This is the million dollar question.... Inspiration comes from everywhere. A trip, conversation, shapes, images, the food you already know. It can be everywhere, and that's the beauty of it. You only need to open up all your senses and then find a way to bring the inspiration to life.

What is the most important lesson you have learned from creating Somni?

Besides how to create a concept from scratch, I've learned two big lessons.

Nothing is possible without real involvement from the whole team. They need to feel responsible, knowing they are an important asset of the whole operation.

The other thing is that you might think you know it all. You've gained enough knowledge and experience over the years, but the truth is you know nothing. You've got to start learning every day over and over again, and that's the only way to move forward.

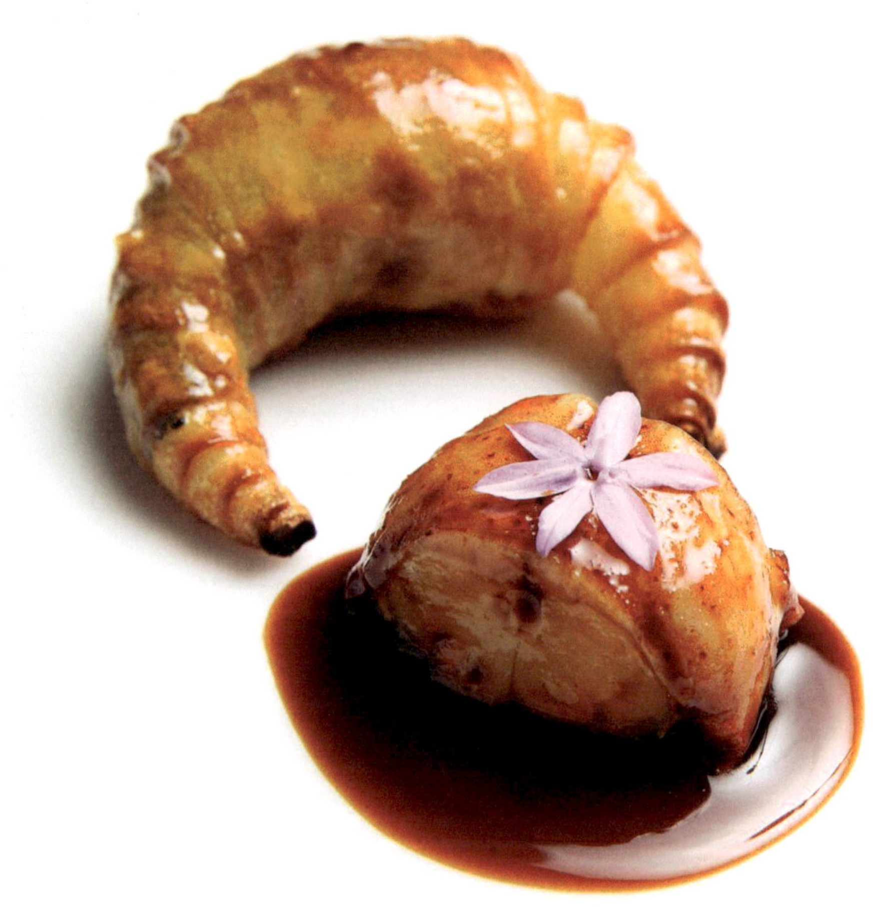

potato "croissant" and lobster

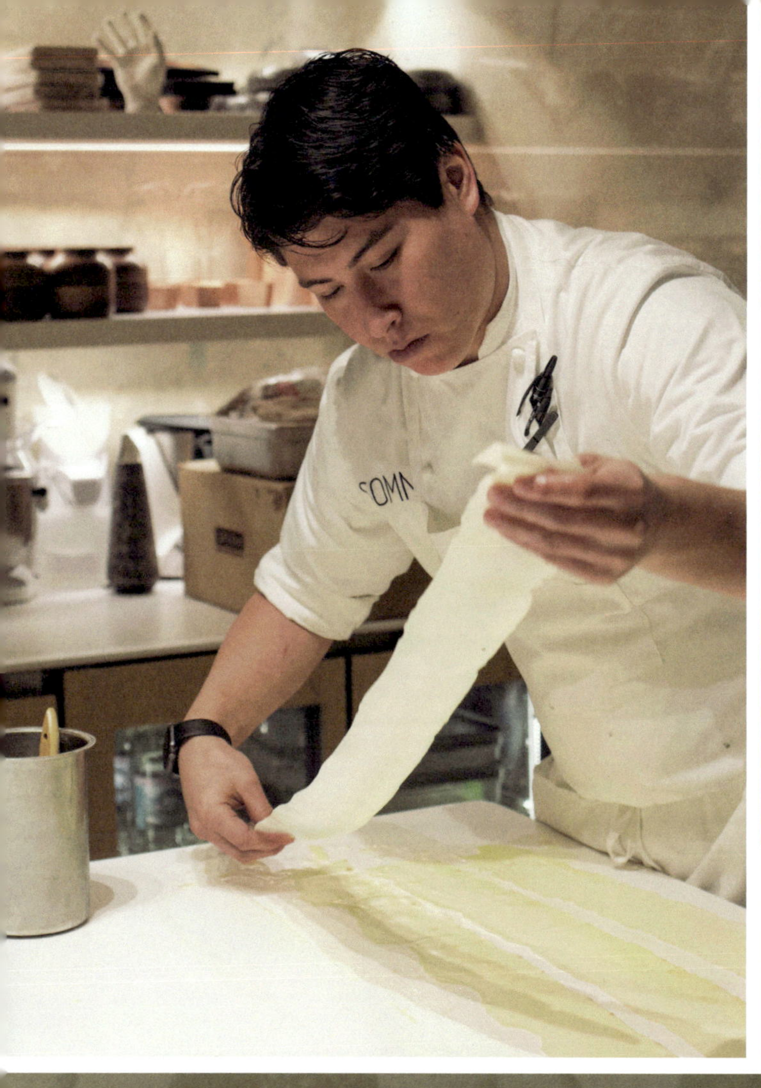

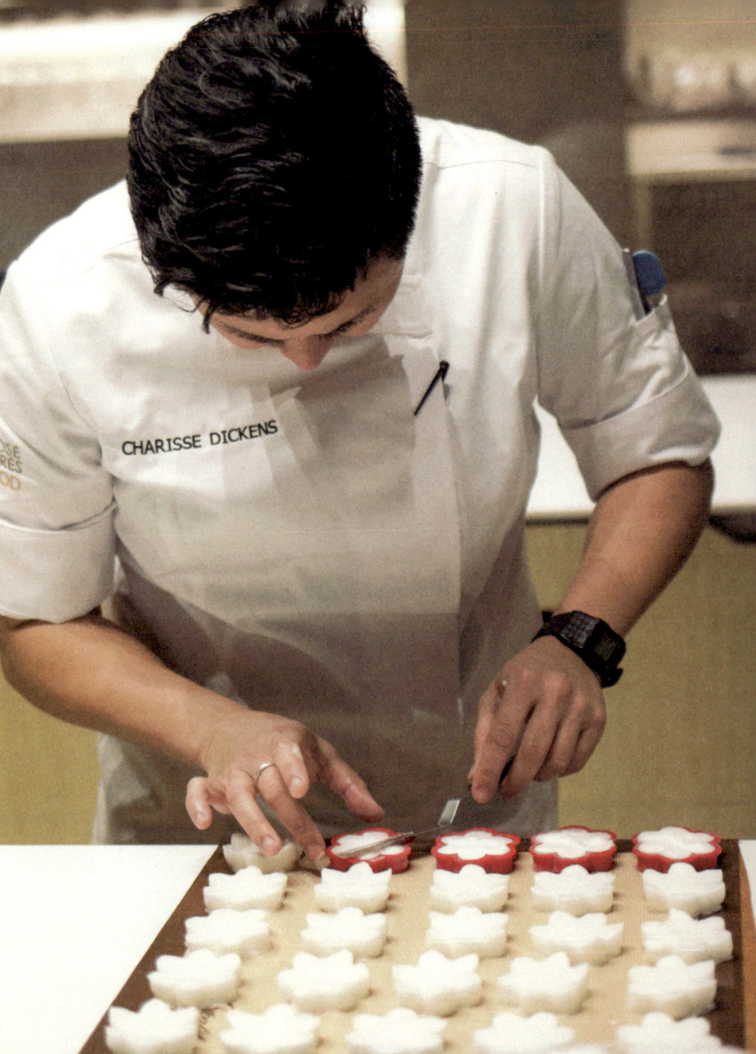
CHARISSE DICKENS

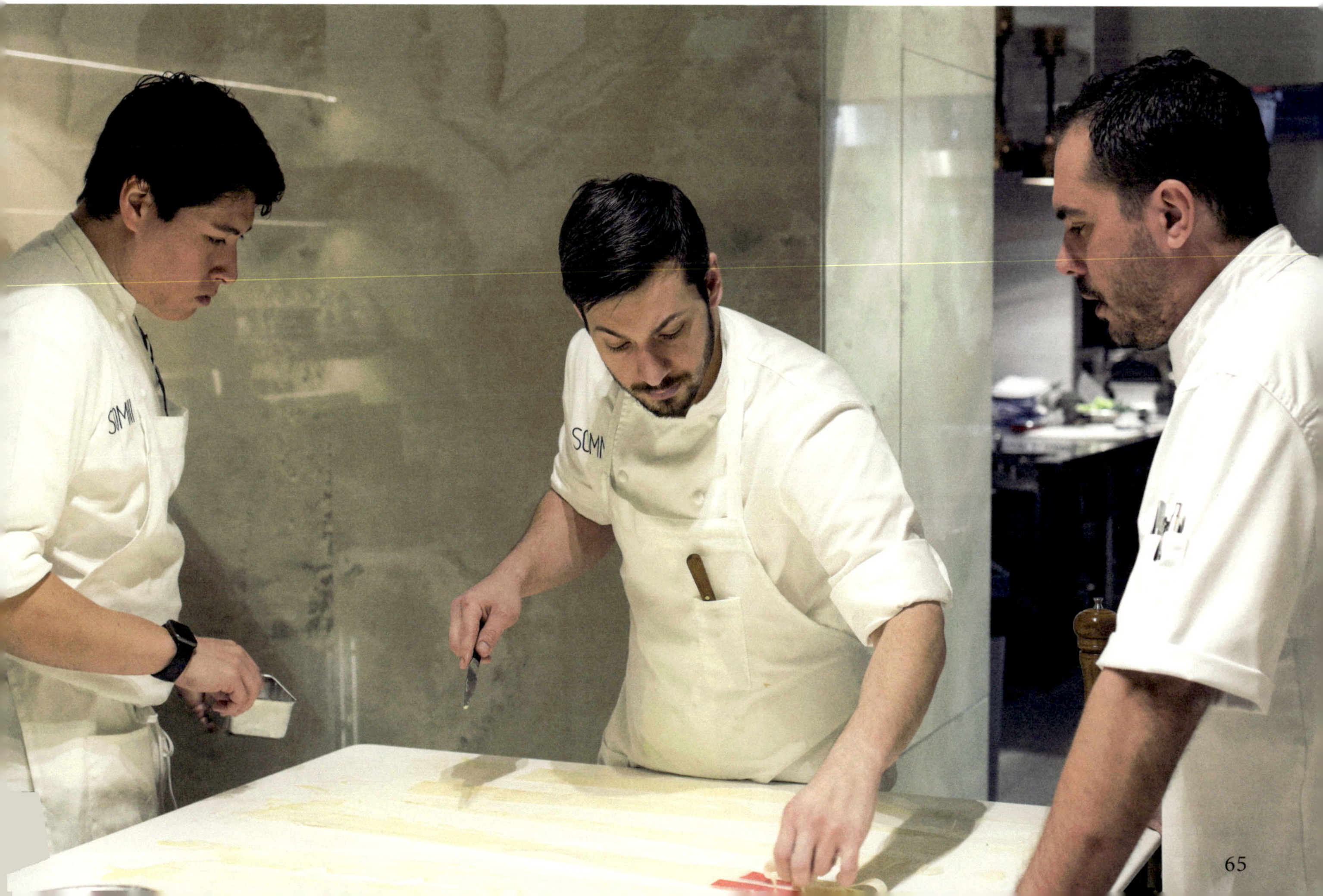

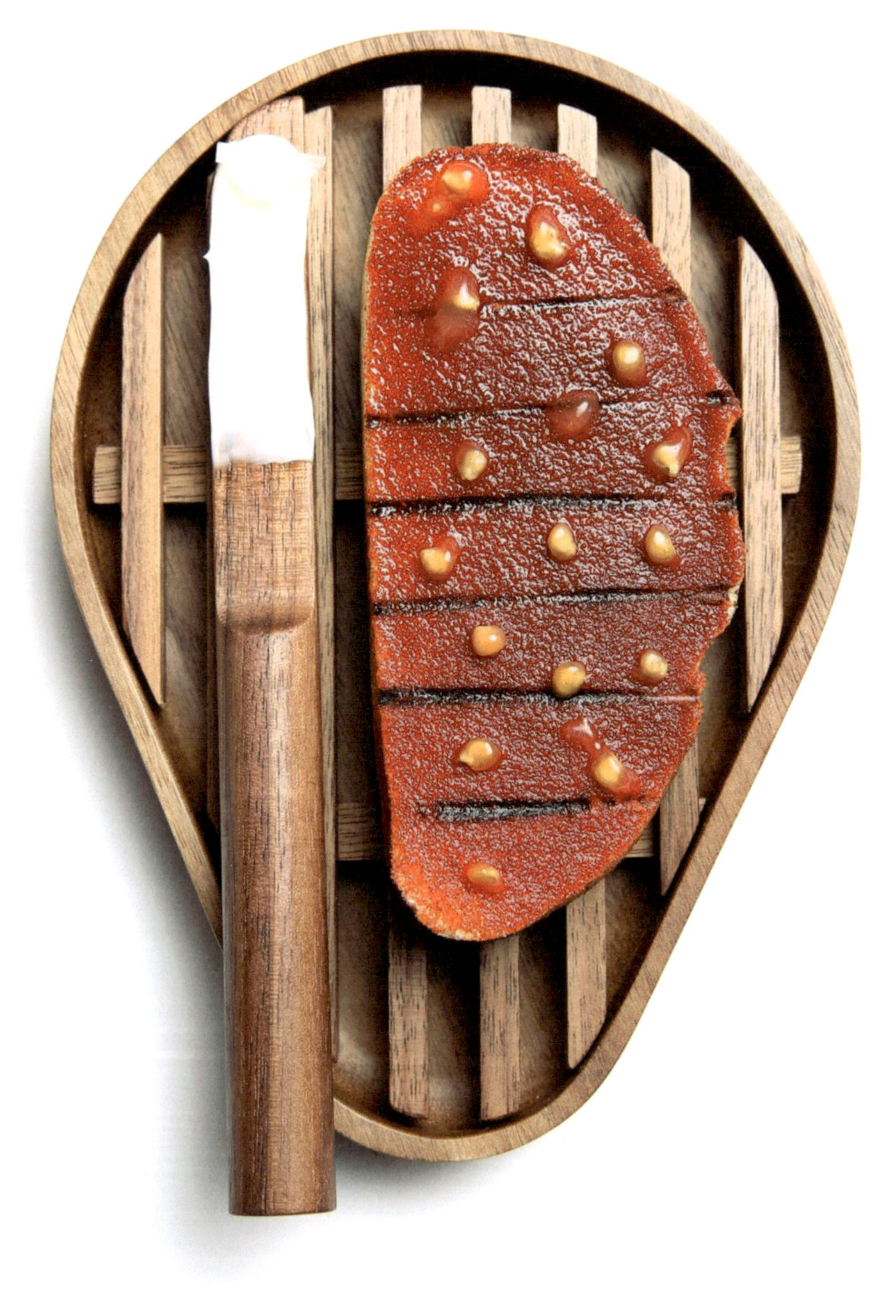

left: tomato bread

top right: vienetta

bottom right: snow ball

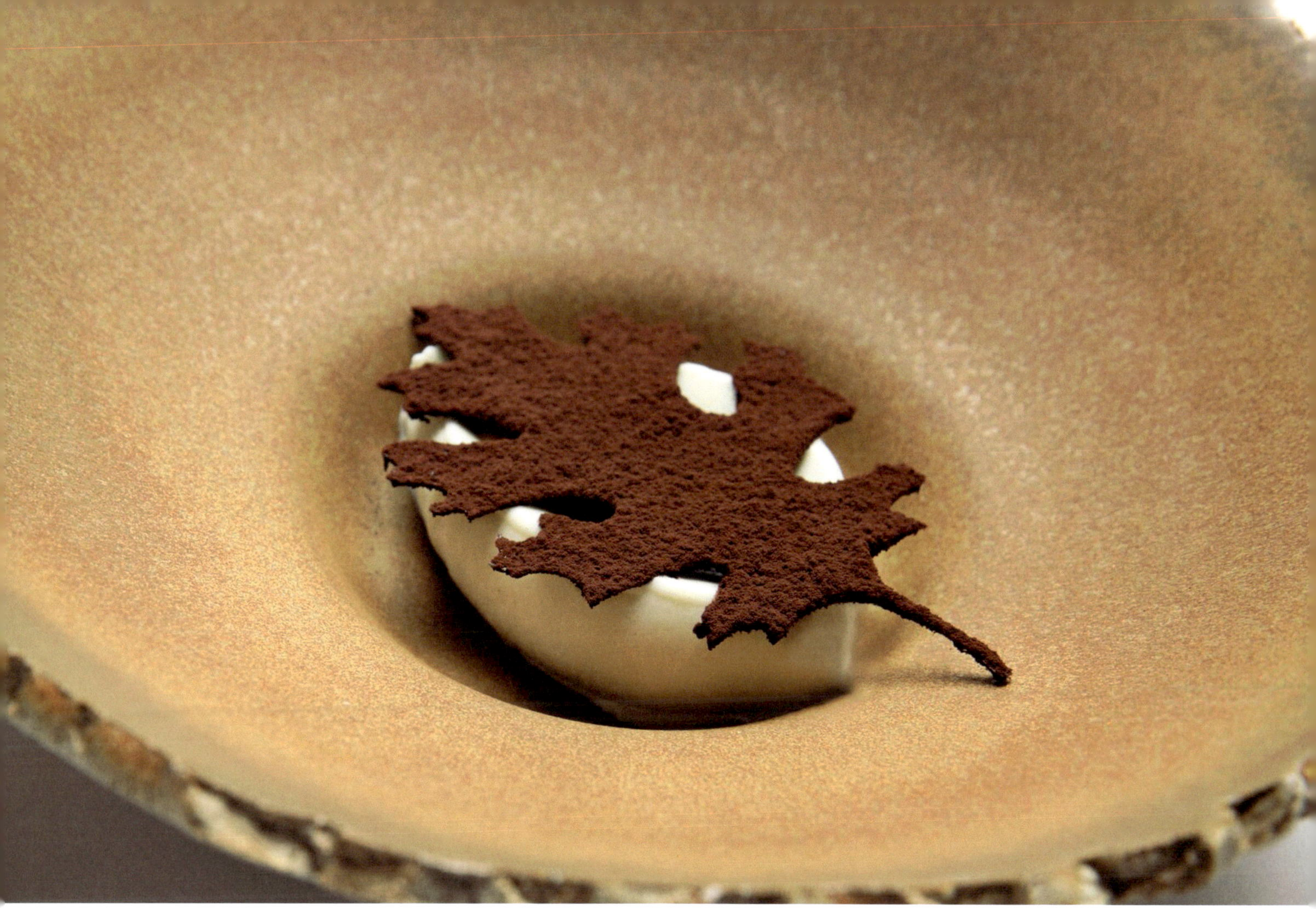

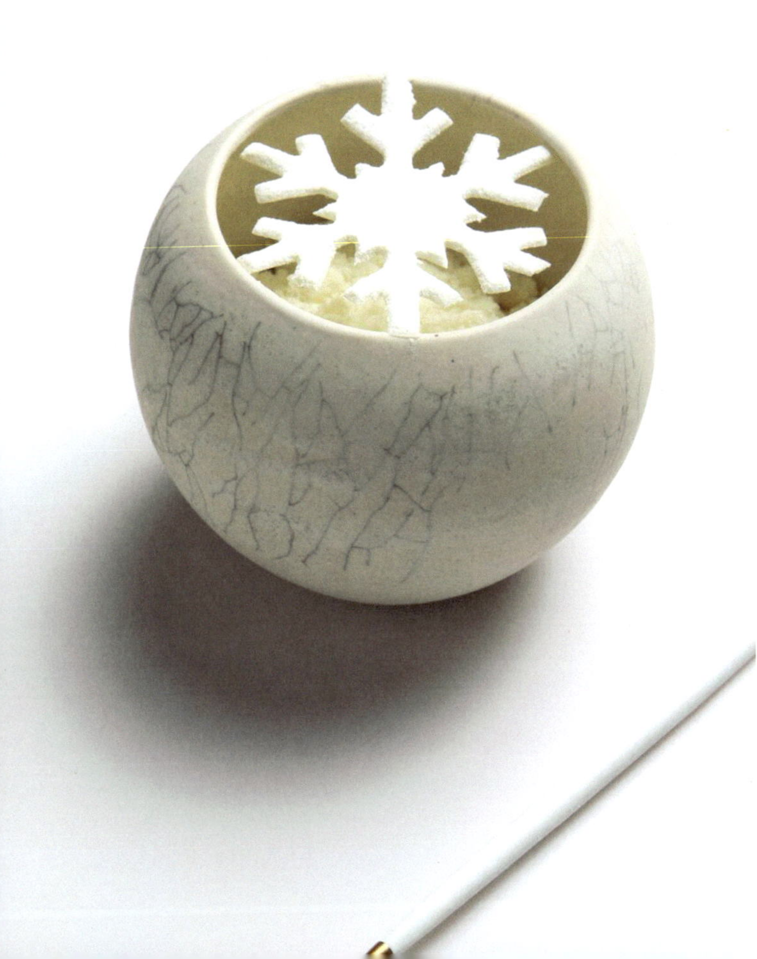

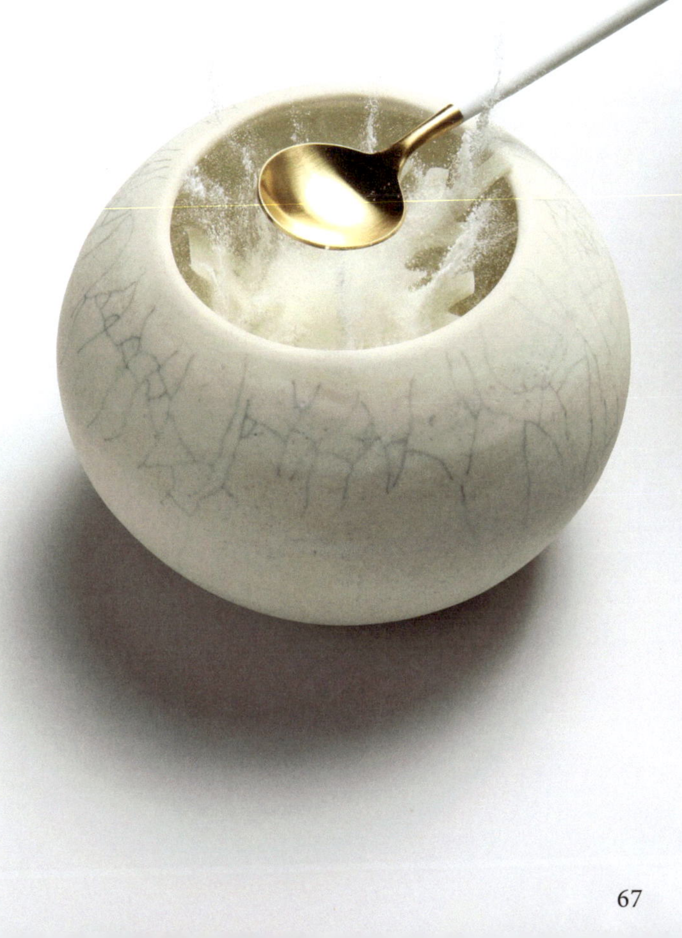

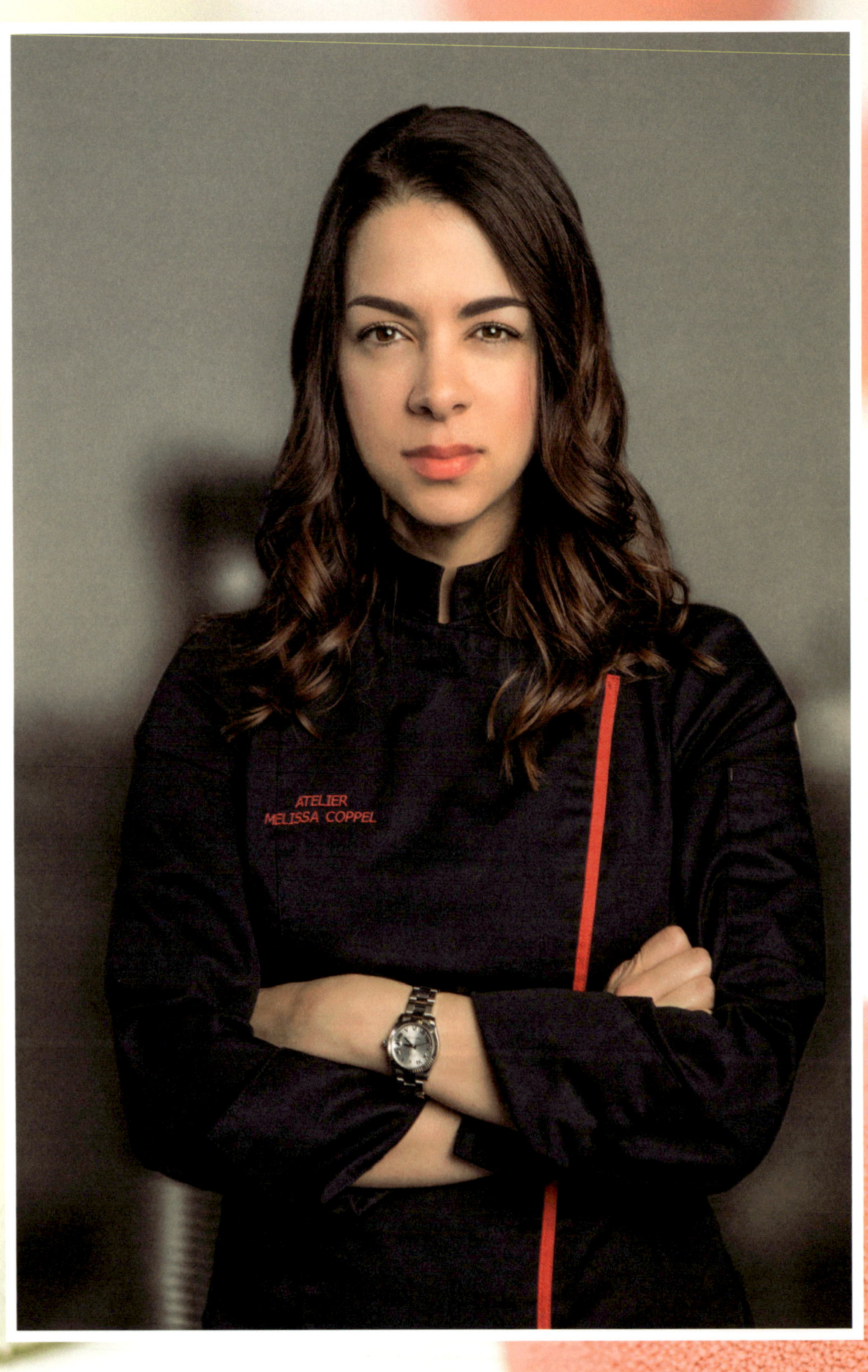
ATELIER
MELISSA COPPEL

Melissa Coppel

atelier melissa coppel

las vegas, nevada

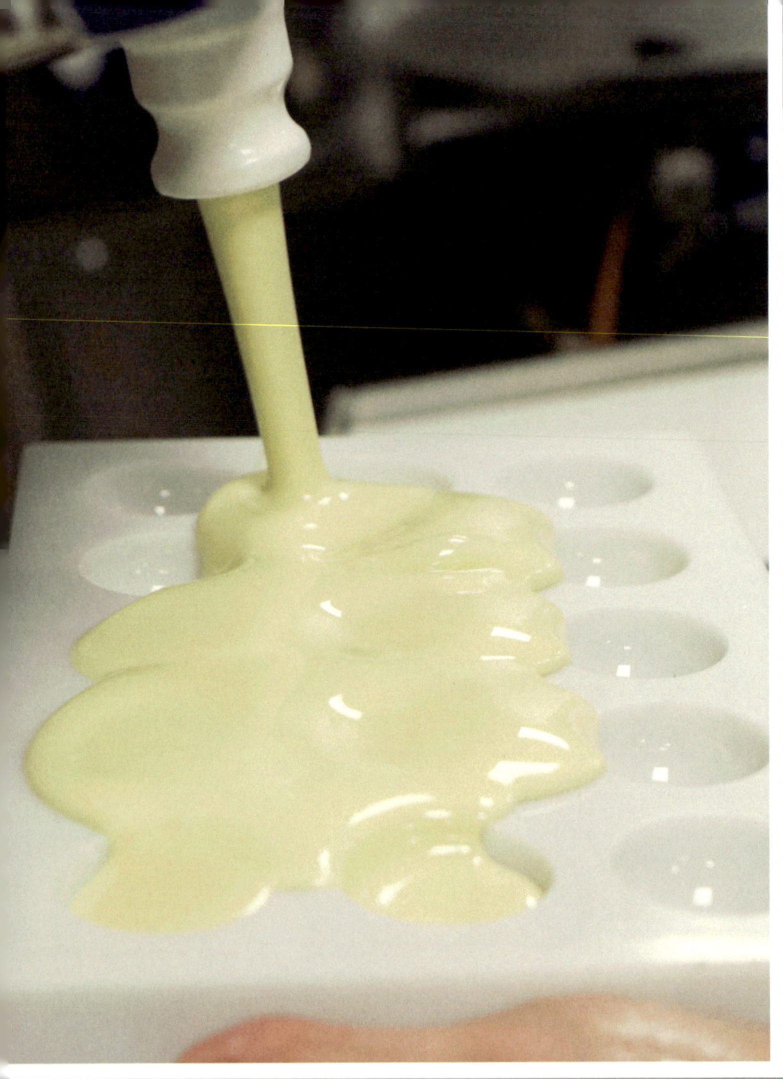

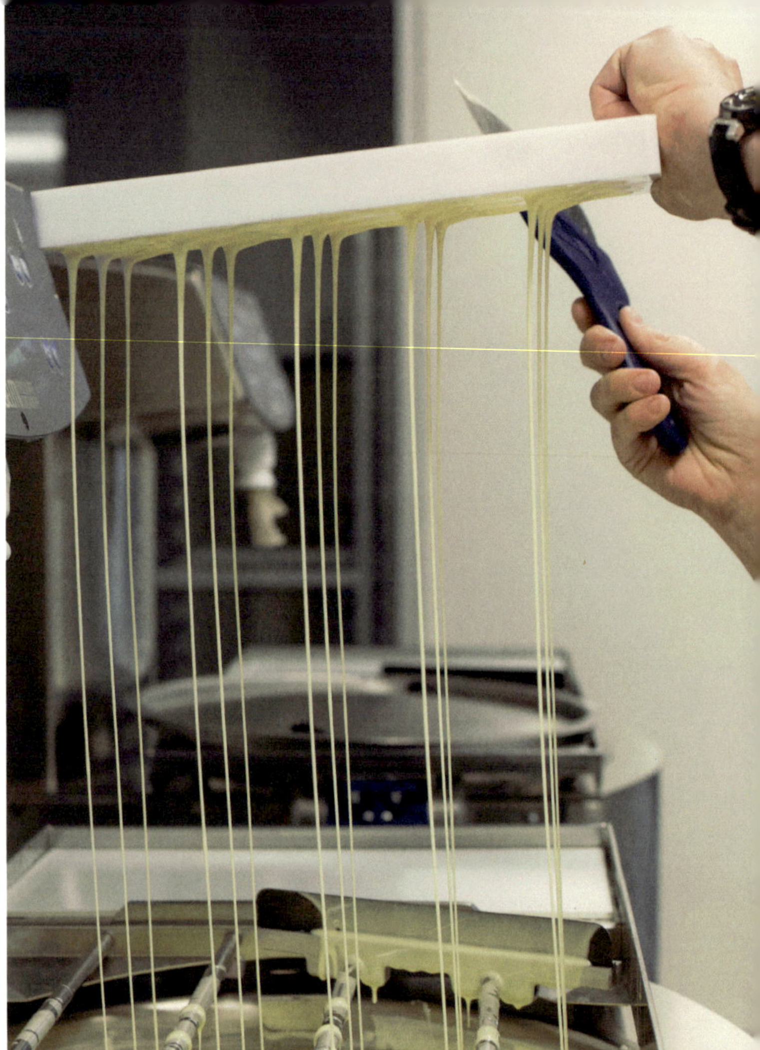

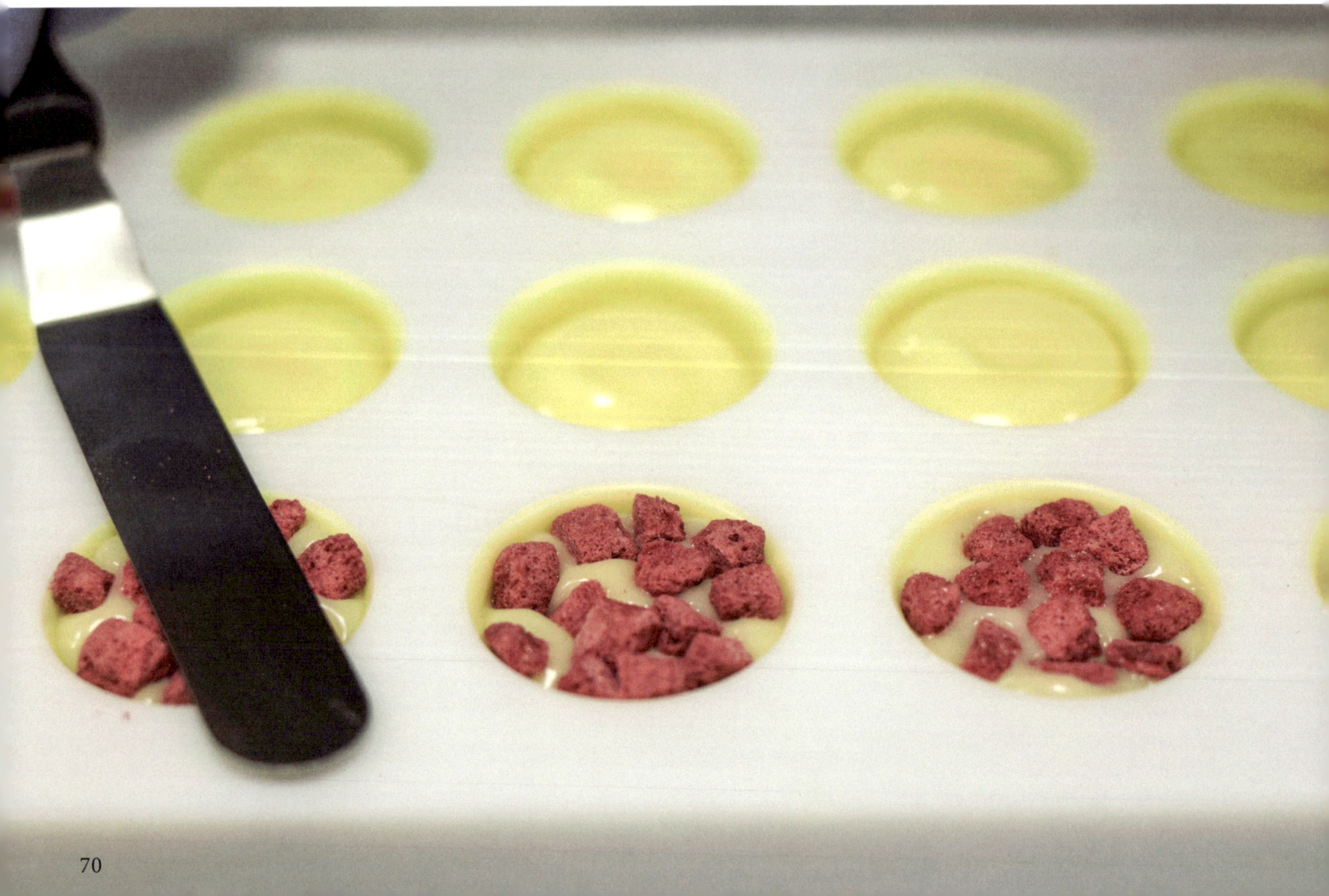

You were in our first issue of Toothache a year ago. Catch us up on what you have been up to since then.

Lots of exciting things had happened in the last year!

I've been to Japan, Australia, Belgium, Italy, Mexico, Singapore and Colombia to teach. It has been such an enriching experience for me, and I can only feel grateful.

Atelier Melissa Coppel School also moved to a much larger space, and we are offering a greater variety of workshops. I'm teaching a few different chocolate ones and also inviting lots of incredible pastry chefs from around the world to teach pastry, gelato and viennoiserie classes.

In September, I will finally be opening MELISSA COPPEL CHOCOLATIER - an online chocolate shop where I will be able to sell my products - I cannot wait!

You are getting some amazing pastry chefs to teach at your school. Do you feel you learn from them? Do they inspire you?

Of course! There is always so much to learn!

Cedric Grolet was here last month; I was very inspired by his philosophy of flavor and his beautiful "décor free" products. When Gabriele Riva taught last September, he made a statement about simplicity and the importance of finding the right balance between the components in your creations. Every time Daniel Alvarez comes I learn something new about viennoiserie...

I feel very lucky to be constantly surrounded by incredible chefs!

Do you ever get bored of chocolate? How do you keep it interesting for yourself and stay creative?

I get bored really easy actually, which is why I have to keep reinventing myself. I am always finding new ways of doing things, and I am always questioning my work. Finding time to let my creativity fly is extremely important for me... it keeps me alive!

What is the most common mistake you see pastry chefs or chocolatiers making?

It's really important at a certain point in our careers to start creating our own recipes. To start thinking for ourselves, to develop our own style. I do not see that desire often, and for me that is the biggest mistake.

Also, I do the scary "taste test" to check if a confection is still good. What are the rules you follow to keep things shelf-stable?

First, I pick the flavor I want to work on. Then I use an excel sheet to balance my recipe.

Once I have made the ganache - or any other filling - I use an AW meter to check the water activity, or amount of free water in the recipe. Free water is the water that is not tied, and it's available for microorganisms to live and reproduce.

Having that measurement helps me decide what I need to adjust in my next test, based on the AW, flavor and texture I currently have. To resume, there are three very important rules to make a shelf-stable product:

1. Work extremely clean.

2. Use a well-balanced recipe with a good AW.

3. Keep your products stored at the right conditions: either frozen or in a non-fluctuating room temperature of 17 C with 60% humidity.

A lot of chocolatiers, especially when they are just starting their careers, are obsessed with how shiny and pretty they can make the outside. What are your thoughts?

YES! There is a real obsession with the aesthetics. This is the impact social media is having in our lives, and it's hurting our profession a lot. Forget about the flavor that doesn't get us likes, right? It's crazy!

How do you balance the focus between beauty on the inside versus outside?

I work backwards. I start with a simple shell without any spray or decoration and test my flavor. Once I am satisfied with the flavor, I move on to the decoration stage. But flavor will always be my priority.

Why do you think most chocolatiers limit themselves to a singular ganache center?

Maybe they want to keep their products more traditional? Maybe they want to limit their labor cost by simplifying their production? Maybe they are afraid of trying new things? Maybe they prefer it that way.

I really enjoy playing around with my fillings, so I would say only 10% of my bonbons are one single layer.

Some of your chocolates have 3 different components. At what point do they stop being a chocolate and start becoming a bite sized dessert?

Around 6 years ago, I came up with a concept that allowed me to bring my pastry background into the world of chocolate, and "Dessert Bars" were born. These are inspired by traditional desserts like apple tart, apricot cobbler, strawberry cheesecake, lime pie, and crème brûlee.

So you are totally right. I take it very seriously when it comes to recreating those flavors inside a chocolate. Those tend to have a shorter shelf life, because I allow myself to think like a pastry chef... For once.

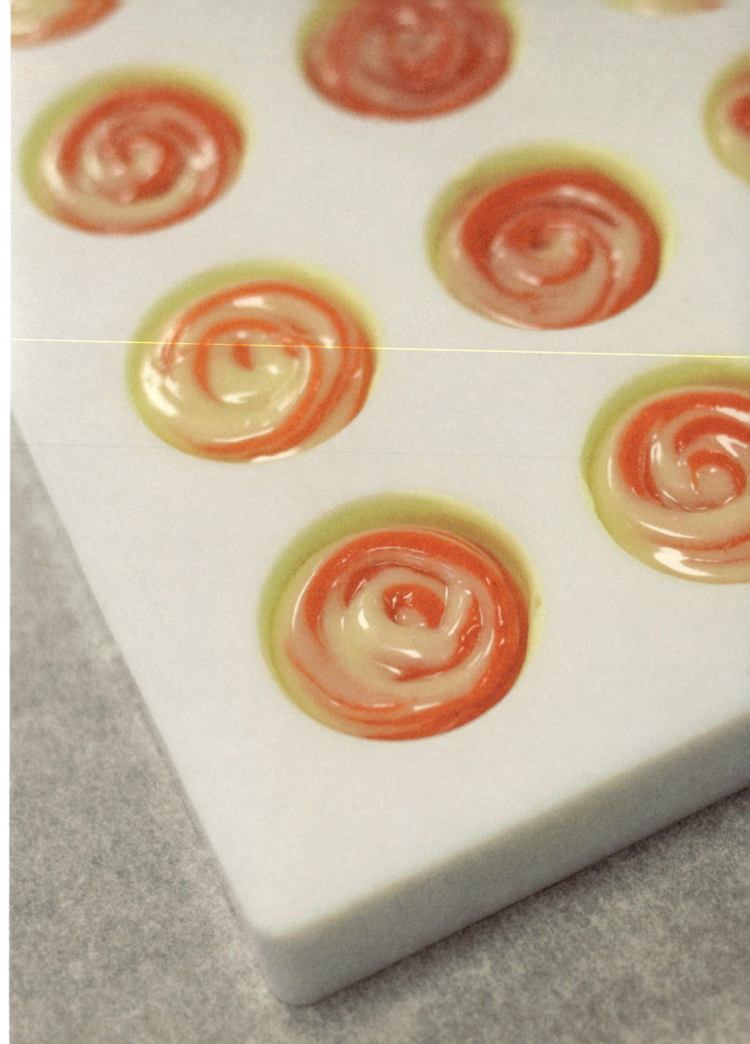

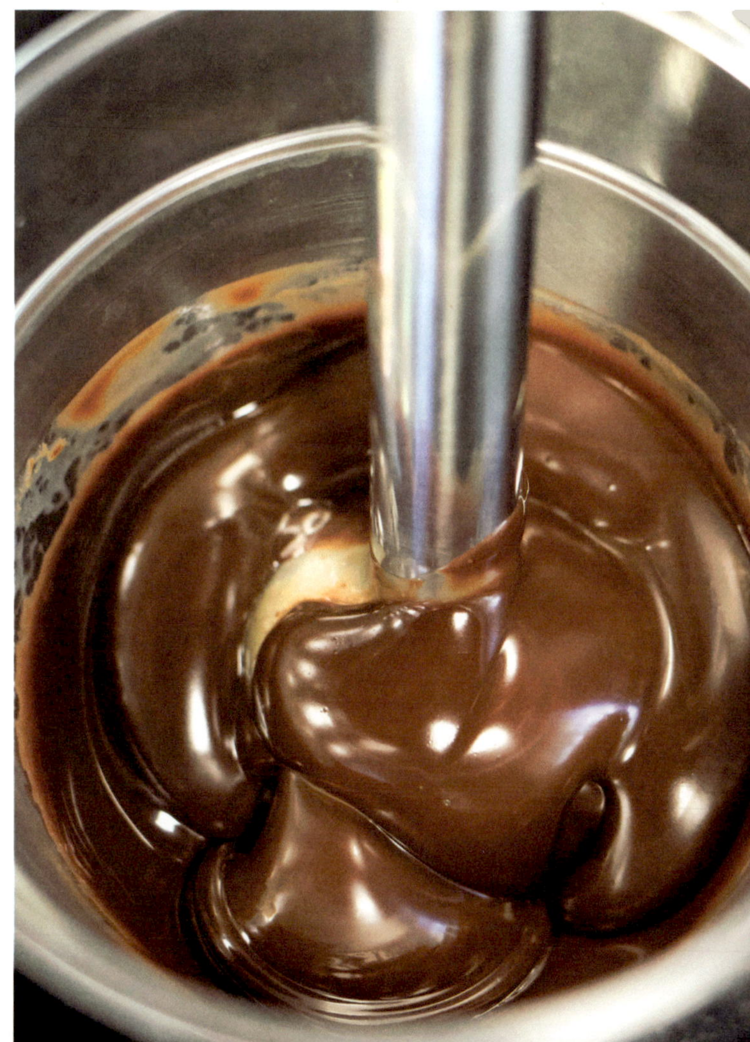

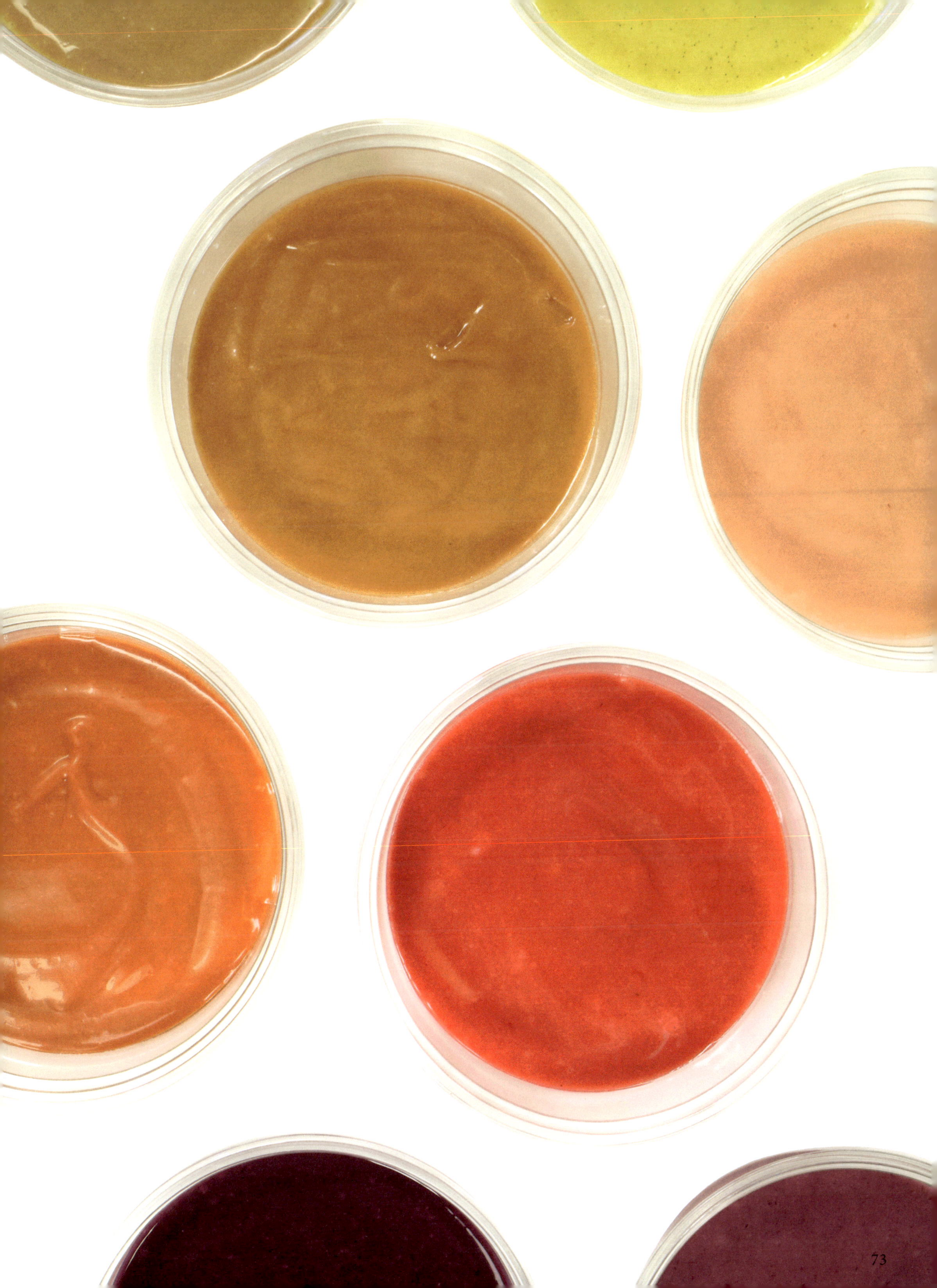

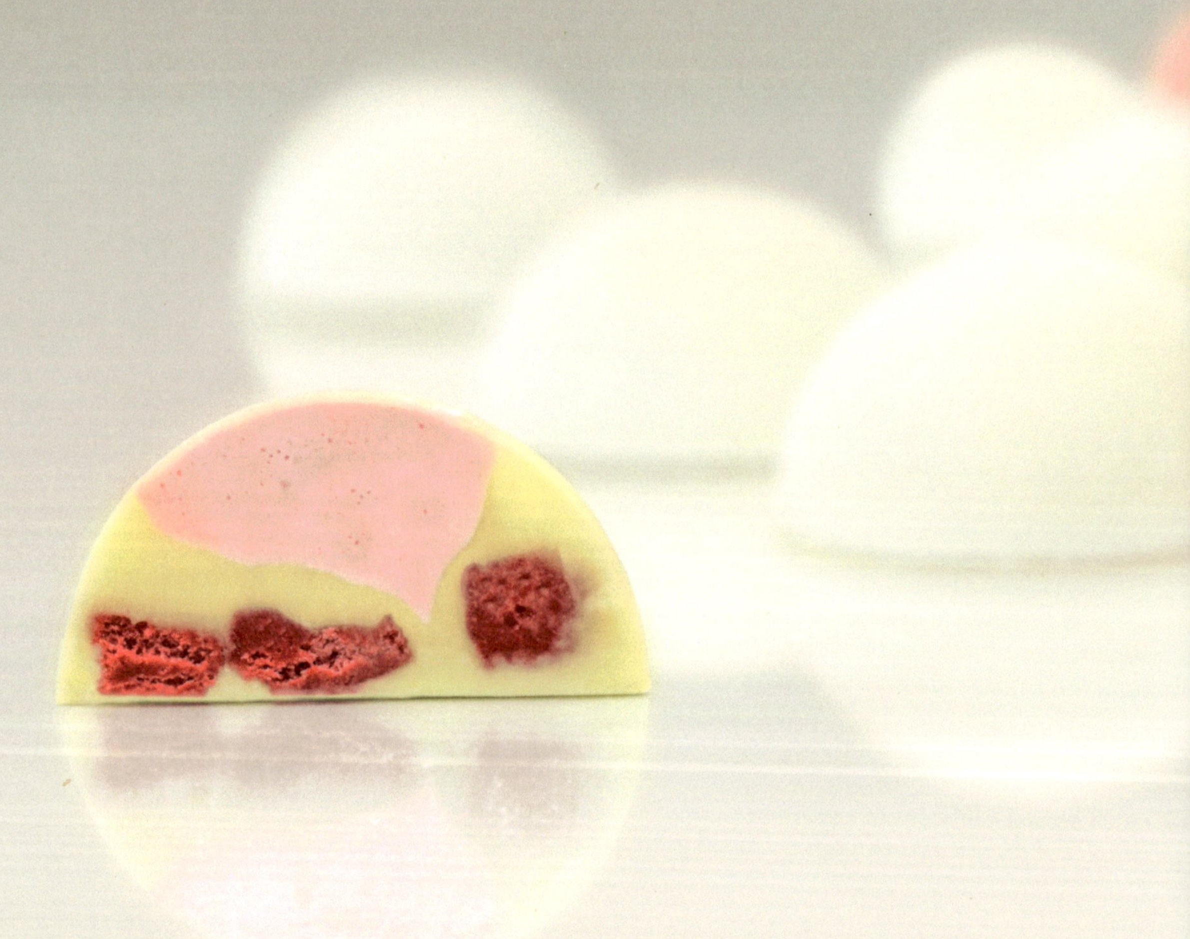

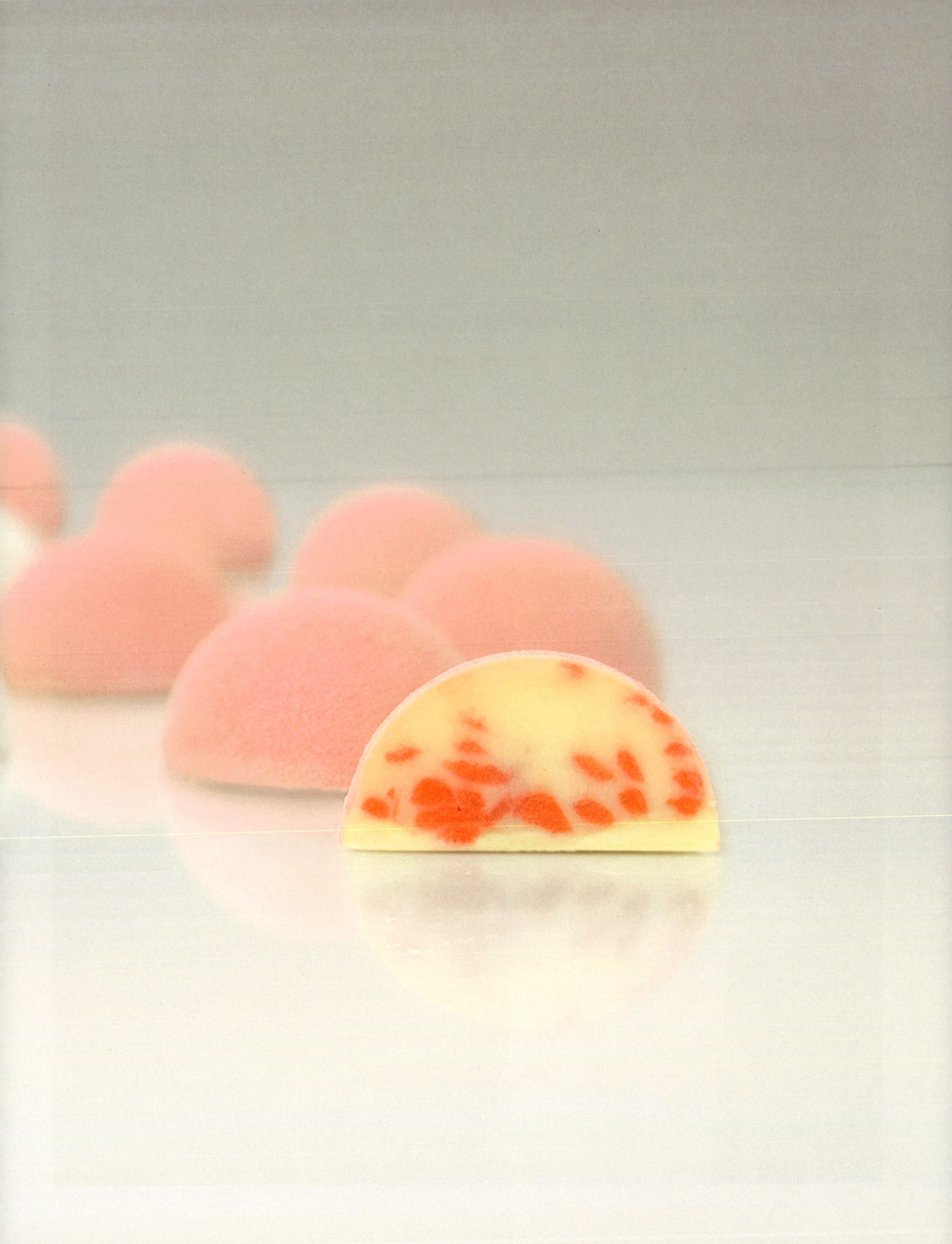

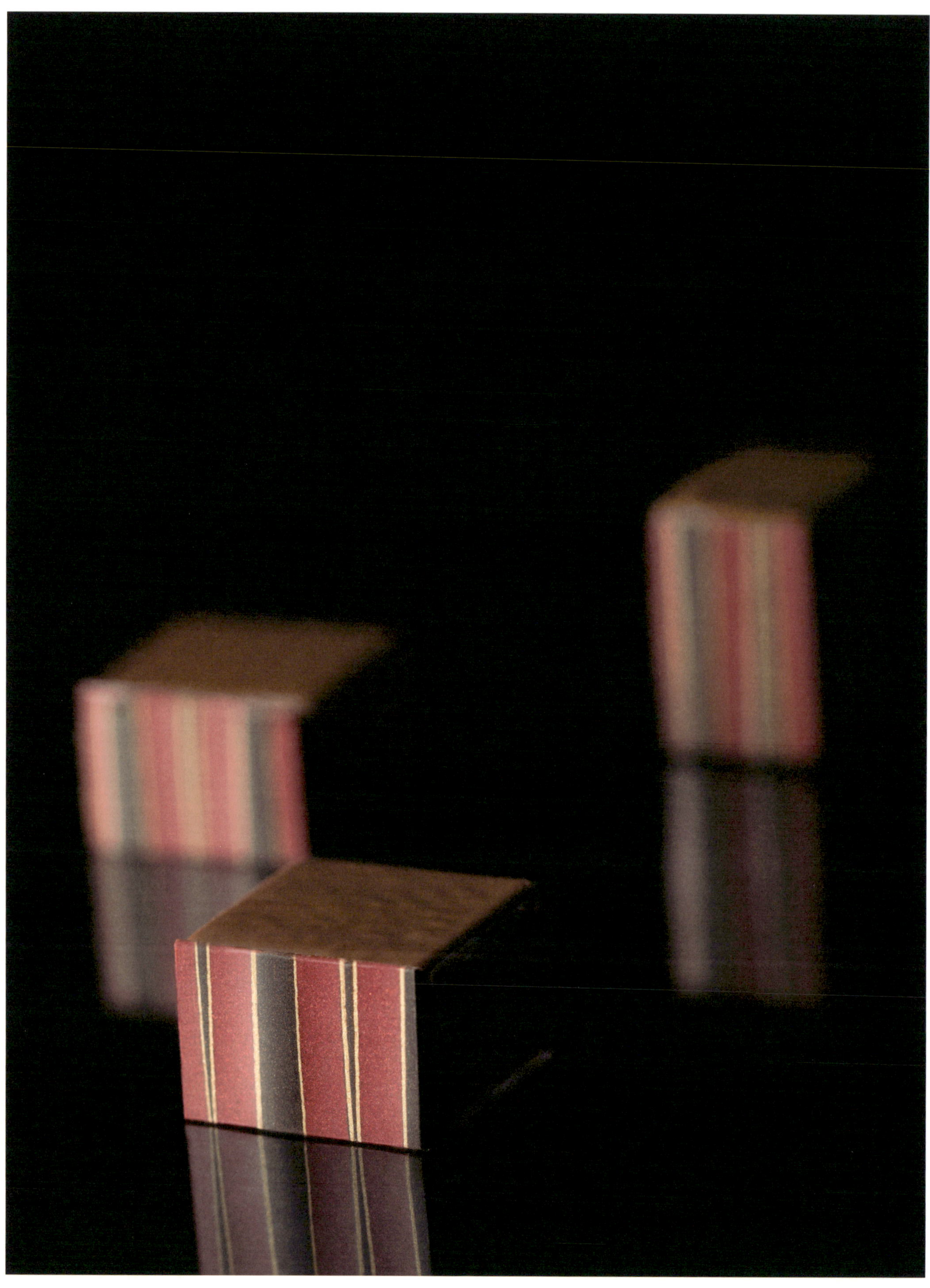

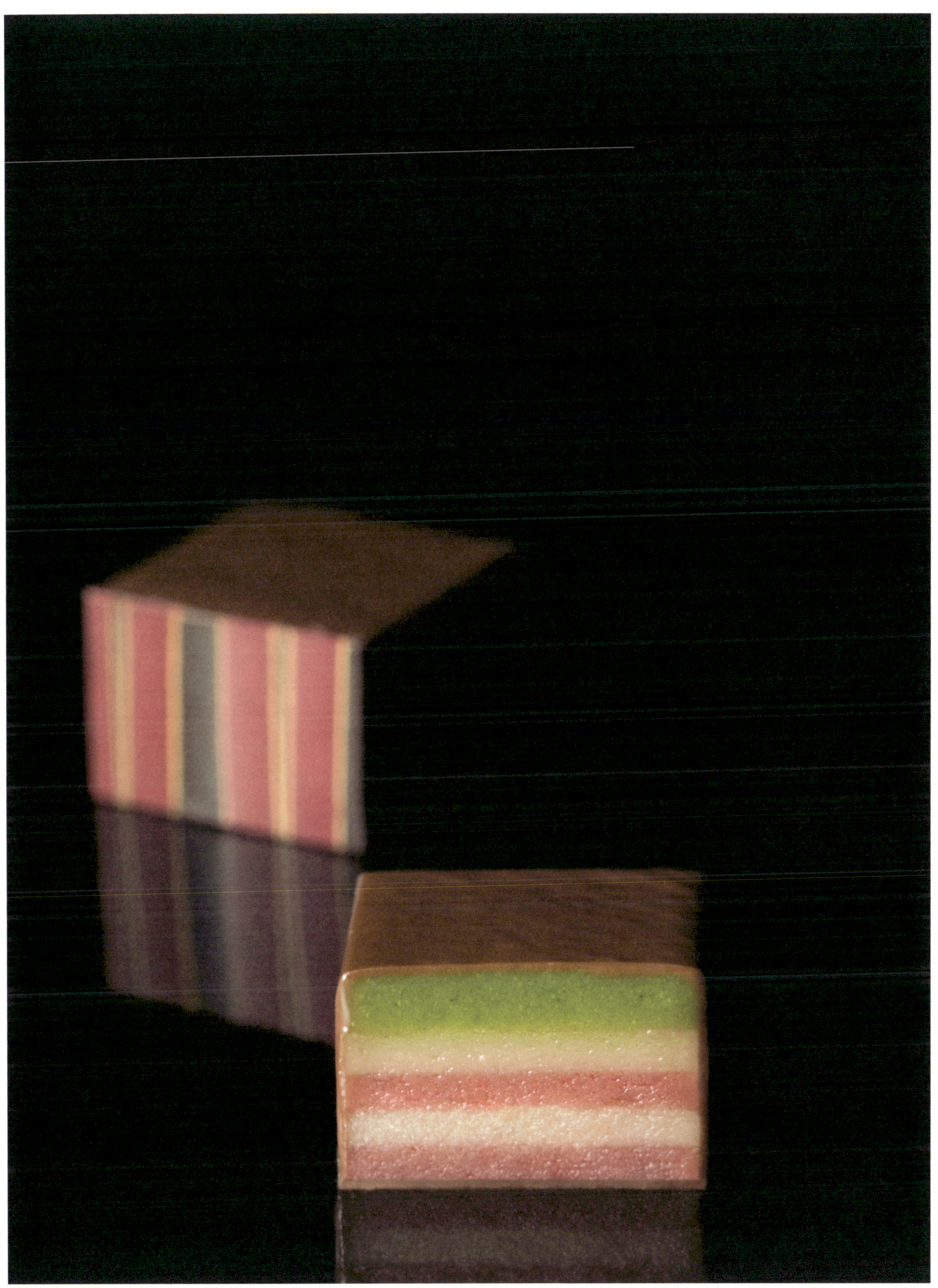

Strawberry Fields

Recipe by Melissa Coppel

AW: 0.82 - 3 to 6 weeks shelf life if stored at 16 C

Featured on page 75

Yogurt Ganache

Ingredients:

120 g cream
32 g sorbitol powder
25 g glucose syrup
3 g invert sugar
36 g unsweetened sheep's milk yogurt
35 drops SOSA yogurt extract
2 g Chef Rubber citric acid
210 g Cacao Barry Zephyr 34% white chocolate

Method:

In a pot, warm the cream and sugars to 40 C. Add the extract, fresh yogurt, and make an emulsion with the melted chocolate. Pipe at 27 C.

Strawberry Yuzu Compote

Ingredients:

160 g strawberry puree
40 g yuzu juice
35 g sucrose #1
6 g pectin NH
30 g sorbitol powder
70 g dextrose
60 g sucrose #2
15 drops SOSA strawberry extract
1.5 g citric acid powder

Method:

Mix pectin with sucrose # 1. In a pot bring purees and the rest of the sugars to 40 C. Add the pectin mix. Boil for 2 minutes. Add the citric acid and pour on a silpat to cool down completely. Hand blend before using.

Assembly:

Pour the yogurt ganache in a piping bag. Pour the compote in another piping bag. Place both piping bags inside a third one and pipe inside the white chocolate shells. Let crystallize at 17 C overnight. Next day close with tempered white chocolate.

Decor:

Place the half spheres in the freezer for 15 minutes. Spray pink cacao butter at 36 C.

Tokyo

Recipe by Melissa Coppel

AW: 0.82 - 3 to 6 weeks shelf life if stored at 16 C

Featured on page 76-77

Green Tea Ganache

Ingredients:

98 g	cream
7 g	matcha green tea
25 g	sorbitol powder
31 g	glucose powder
3.5 g	invert sugar
21 g	butter, 82% fat
.5 g	citric acid powder
189 g	Cacao Barry Zephyr 34 % white chocolate

Method:

Warm the cream, tea, sugars and butter to 40 C. Add the citric acid and make an emulsion with the melted chocolate. When the ganache is at 28 C, pour over the marzipan. Place in the fridge for 15 minutes. Then keep overnight at 17 C. Next day, cut with the guitar.

Raspberry Marzipan

Ingredients:

280 g	almond marzipan. 50 %
20 g	syrup, 50 %
10 g	raspberry powder
30 drops	SOSA raspberry extract
50 g	Cacao Barry cacao butter
2 g	citric acid solution

Method:

Knead the marzipan with all of the ingredients. Cover and let it rest in the fridge for 1 hour.

Lemon Marzipan

Ingredients:

280 g	almond marzipan, 50 %
20 g	syrup, 50 %
3 ea	lemon zest
50 g	Cacao Barry cacao butter
2 g	citric acid solution

Method:

Knead the marzipan with all of the ingredients. Cover and let it rest in the fridge for 1 hour.

Assembly:

Roll out the raspberry marzipan inside a frame. Place a second frame and roll out the lemon marzipan with a rolling pin. Place in the fridge for 30 minutes, then cut in half and place inside a frame. Stick another frame on top and pour the ganache at 27 C. Let crystallize overnight covered at 17 C. Next day make a chablon op top with off-temper chocolate and cut squares with a guitar.

Decor:

Enrobe in tempered milk chocolate. To make the plaquette, using tape make the desired design on a guitar sheet. Spray with tempered cacao butter at 29C, then remove the tape and spray again with a different color of tempered cacao butter. Spread tempered milk chocolate on top to make the plaquettes. Cut and tick on the side of the bonbons.

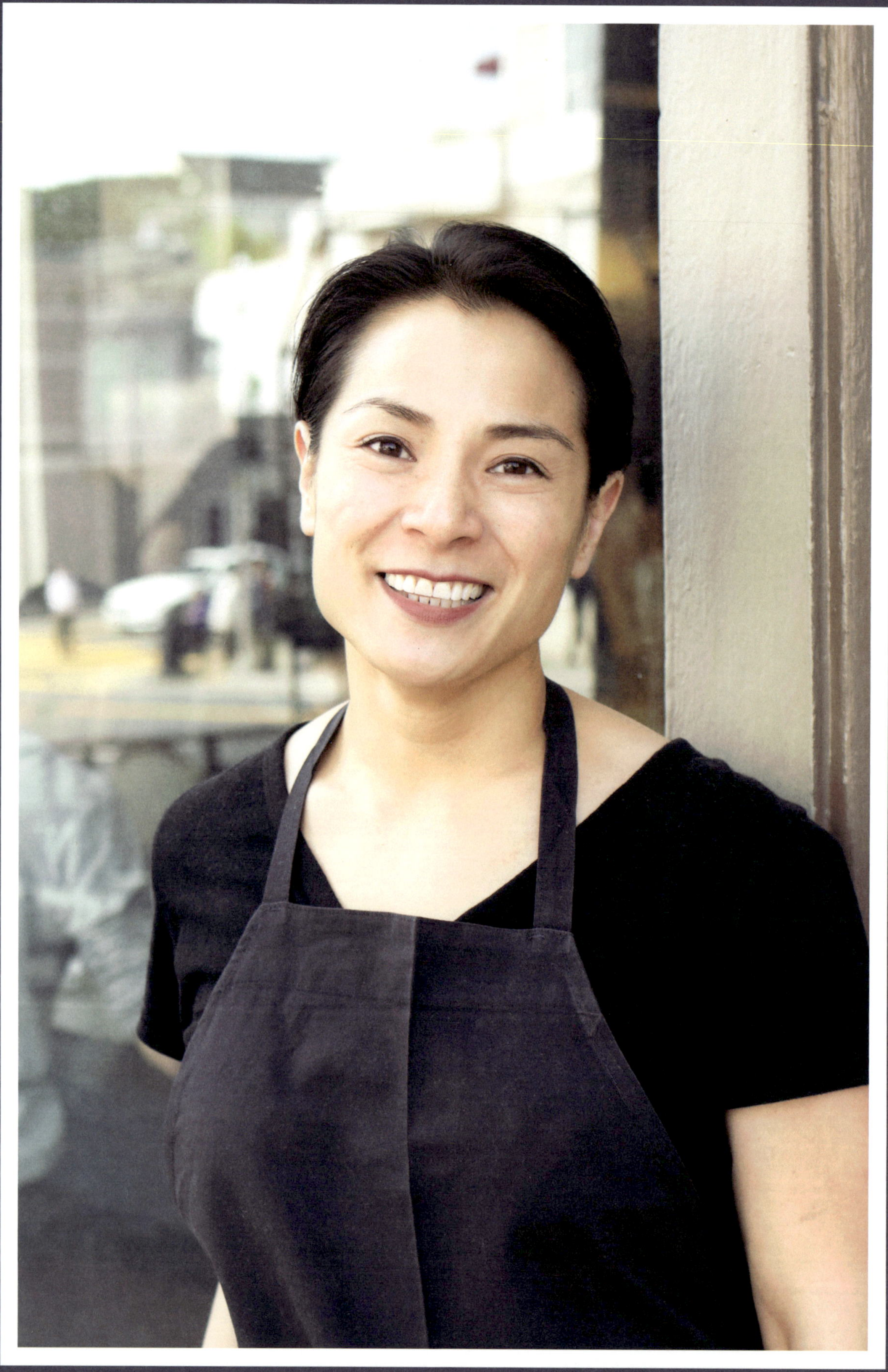

Belinda

re-imagining the flavors of her plated desserts into patisserie creations

Leong

B. Patisserie, San Francisco

How did you get started cooking?

I started working at Aqua in 1997 on the garde manger and pastry stations, and I was more focused on being a savory cook. After Aqua, I attended the City College of SF Hospitality Program and did my internship at Restaurant Gary Danko in 1999, also on the garde manger and pastry stations. Chef Danko had difficulties finding a pastry chef in the beginning, so I would often fill in. It was at that time that I decided I wanted to pursue pastry. After a year, Chef Danko gave me the executive pastry chef position. I stayed for eight-and-a-half years. After I left the restaurant, I staged for almost two years around Europe.

What was your interest in transitioning from restaurants to a bakery?

I've always had a dream of opening something for myself. I wanted to have a place of my own where the focus of the product is mainly pastry. I knew working in a restaurant, I would always have to follow the direction and style of a chef.

For you, what's the difference between a pastry chef and a baker?

A pastry chef has a lot more elements to work with than a baker, and their creativity with flavors, textures, and seasonality can be greater. There are many more techniques, along with developing your own style. The challenge for a pastry chef is balancing flavors with texture and presentation, creating a dessert that uses all the elements without being too sweet.

A baker's ingredients are only water, flour, yeast, salt, and fermentation. With these few, they must have the skill of controlling the dough's activity from the time of mixing, shaping, proofing, and baking. The flavor changes with different flours and mainly through the fermentation process the baker chooses. The final consistency of the bread really depends on the skill of the baker knowing the dough and being able to feel the dough.

How does the experience of presenting a dessert in a restaurant compare to the space/experience of a bakery?

There are different pressures for the pastry chef in each space. The presentation of a plated dessert is the closure of a full dining experience. The style of the dessert must follow the style of the chef. If the guests are having a wonderful experience, the dessert must follow through to continue that. If the guests are having a terrible experience with the food, the dessert is the last opportunity to change the guests' mind.

At a bakery, a guest's experience is the beginning, the middle and the end. People go to a bakery to treat themselves. It's a casual and more relaxed atmosphere where people can gather.

Tell us about changing a plated dessert into a bakery item. How do you transform the components into a dessert that can sit in the pastry case?

It is definitely more challenging to create a dessert that will sit in a pastry case, as opposed to making a dessert a la minute. Plated desserts have separate components that are assembled as ordered, so you don't need to worry as much about the stability of the structure.

Desserts that are in a display case need to be stable for a length of time without compromising presentation. All the components are in one structure, while still having to maintain texture throughout the day and during transportation.

Do you interpret traditional French pastry, or do you try to replicate it exactly? For example, the Kouign-amann in Brittany is large and incredibly buttery. How does yours differ?

Our style of viennoiserie are influenced by traditional French pastry, particularly French technique, but we incorporate our own flavors and textures. Our kouign amann is very different from that of Brittany. I believe the 'original' kouign amann is very heavy and sweet, which would not please many of today's consumers. The texture of our kouign amann is light, flaky and moist in the center, which makes someone consume the whole thing without realizing it.

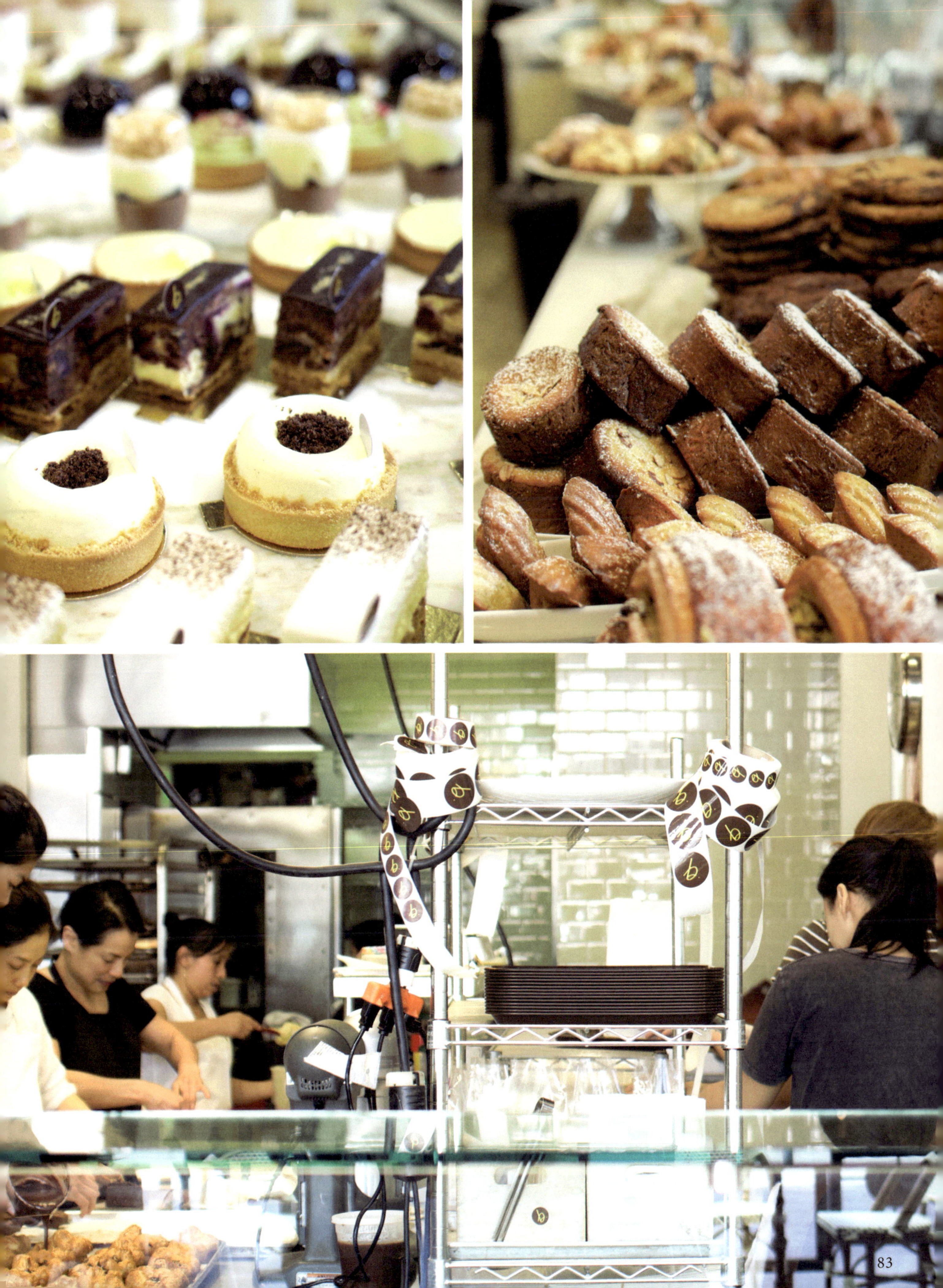

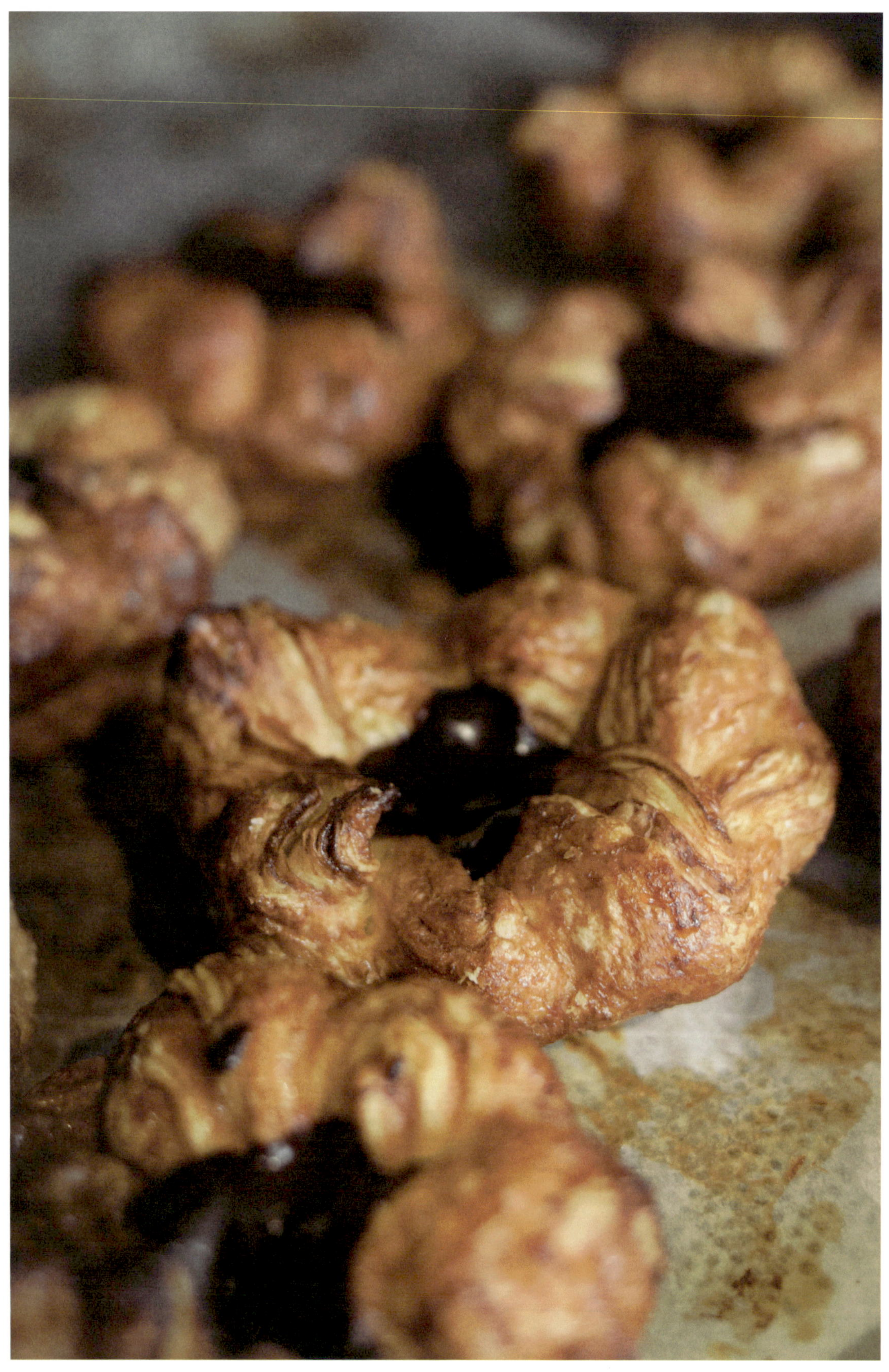

In your experience, do you feel there are prominent differences between the American and French palette?

I'm not sure if I can say there are differences in palette, but I believe there are prominent differences in the food culture. The French are more classic and conservative, and they believe in quality before quantity. The Americans used to be quantity before quality, but now there is a drastic change where people are more knowledgeable and exposed to food. It is starting to be a part of the culture to meet and entertain around food. There is greater accessibility to product, along with a melting pot of cultures in America. They are more open to having classics tweaked with unique flavors and presentations, compared to the French.

San Francisco is known for several incredible bakeries. What are your thoughts on the city's bakery culture?

San Francisco has a good amount of retail bakeries that are diverse and producing high-quality product with a neighborhood feel. As a bakery owner here, it is definitely not as competitive, and each bakery has their own individual style. SF and NYC are the two cities that started high-quality breads in the 80's. And in the last ten years, the movement of high-quality pastry shops started to grow.

Why did you decide to open a B. Patisserie in Hawaii and Korea? Did you have to change any recipes or techniques to accommodate your different bakery locations?

We opened in Hawaii and Korea because it was a great opportunity for our employees to travel and share their knowledge. Hawaii and Korea were also ready for our style and bakery concept. The partners we associated with in both locations had the same vision and philosophy for running a business.

In Hawaii, the only factor we needed to deal with was humidity. We adjusted that by working a different baking schedule through the day. In Korea, we had to adjust some of the recipes due to the availability of ingredients. We adjusted mixing, emulsion, and fermentation times according to some recipes, to achieve the same texture and flavor.

Do you miss working in restaurants and creating plated desserts?

I sometimes miss working in restaurants because of the service rush. But I don't miss the long, late hours. I do miss plating desserts, but I do sometimes get the opportunity when there are collaborative events with other chefs. To replace the plated desserts in our bakery, I create desserts in verrines, which allows me not to be so limited with textures and components.

Why pastry?

I love pastry because it's fun, playful, whimsical, and colorful. It gives happiness and a soulful feeling to people.

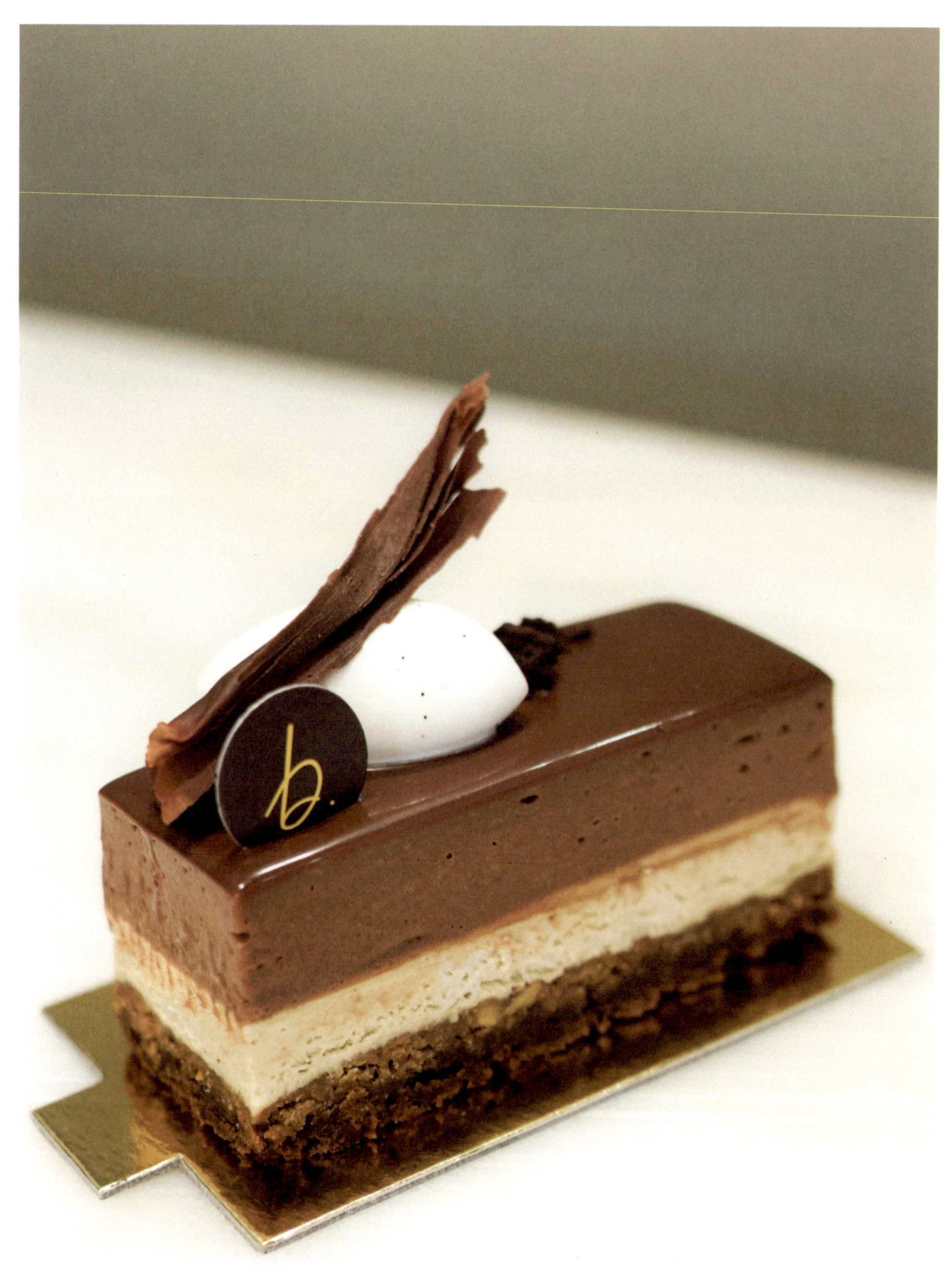

CHOCOLATE, COFFEE AND HAZELNUT

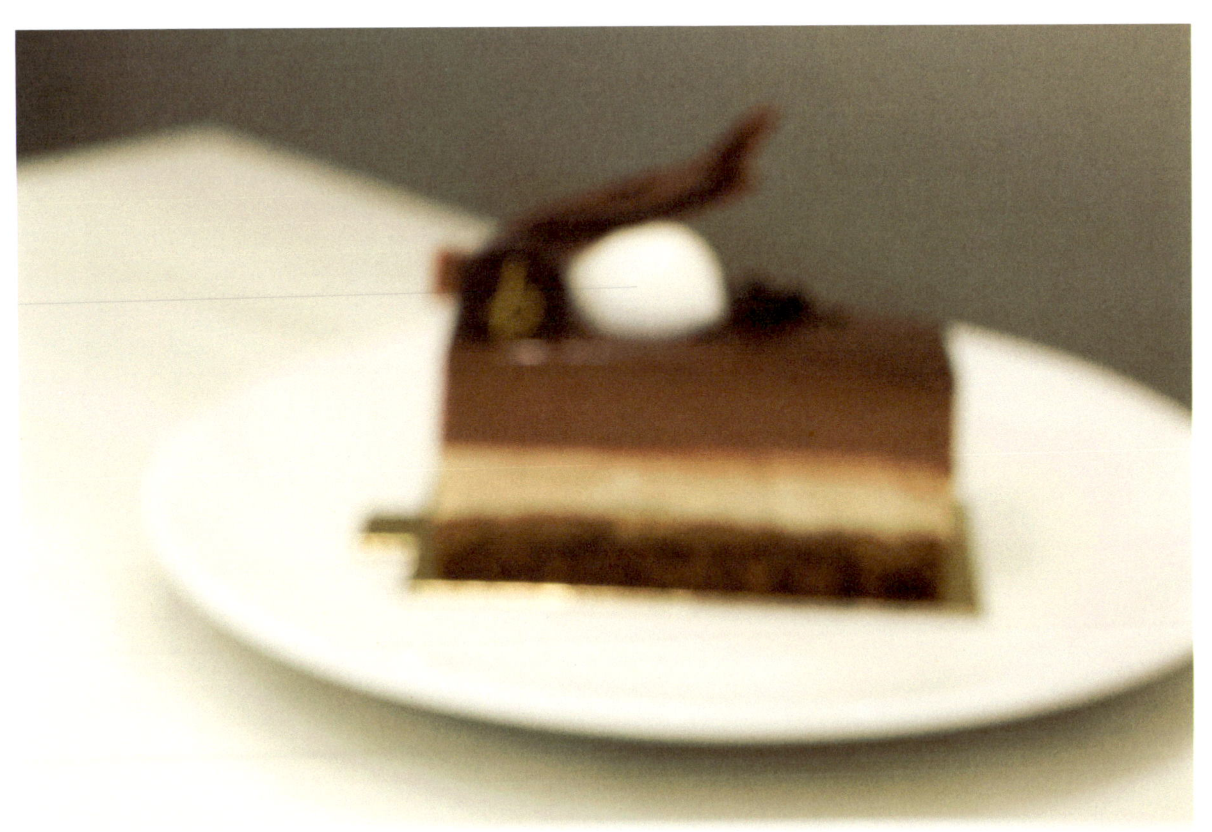

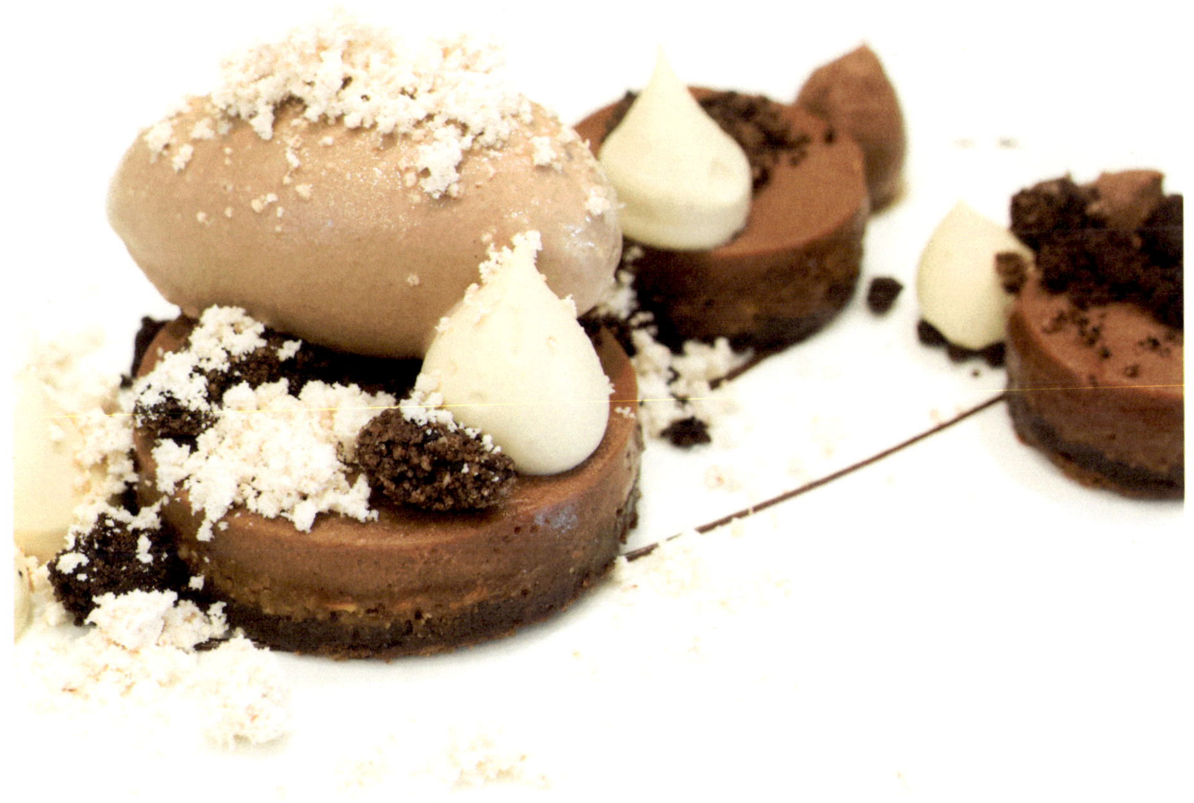

CHOCOLATE, COFFEE AND HAZELNUT

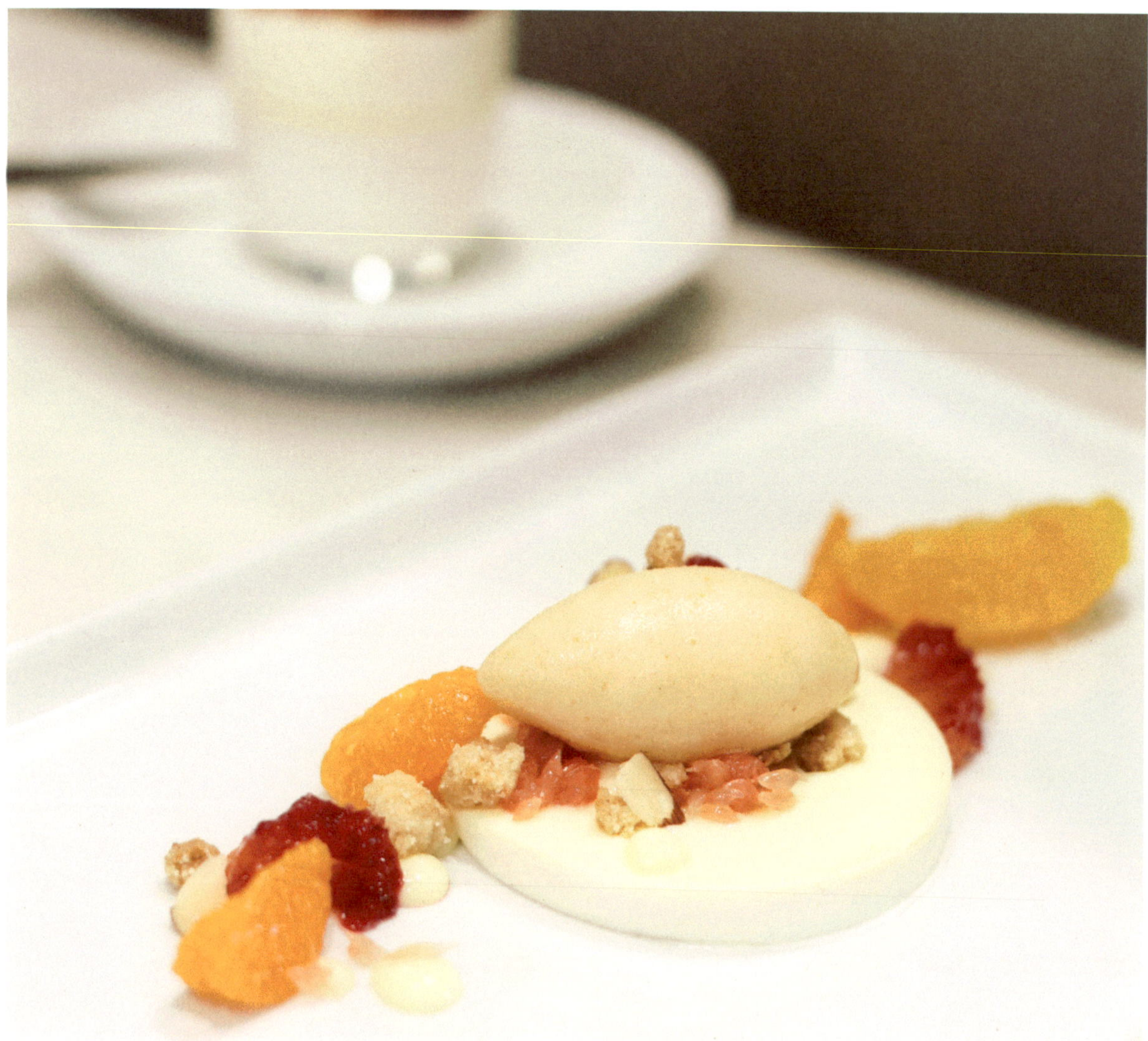

Yogurt, Citrus and Almond

Yogurt Panna Cotta

Ingredients:

223 g granulated sugar
563 g heavy cream
5.5 g gelatin
1 ea vanilla bean, scraped
1 kg Greek yogurt
1/2 tsp kosher salt

Method:

Bloom the gelatin in ice water and set aside. In a sauce-pot, heat the sugar, vanilla bean and cream to scald. Strain the gelatin from the water and dissolve it into the warm cream mixture. Once dissolved, pass through a strainer over the yogurt and add the salt. Portion into cups or ring molds.

Yogurt Mousse

Ingredients:

60 g granulated sugar
30 g water
60 g glucose
100 g egg yolks
14 g gelatin
80 g trimoline
600 g Greek yogurt
550 g heavy cream, whipped

Method:

Bloom the gelatin in ice cold water and set aside. Whip the heavy cream in a bowl and set aside in the refrigerator. Make a pate a bombe with the sugar, water, glucose, and eggs. Drain the gelatin and place into a small container. Melt the gelatin and trimoline together and pour it into the pate a bombe when it's almost ¾ way ready. When the pate a bombe is cooled, add in the Greek yogurt then fold in the whipped cream.

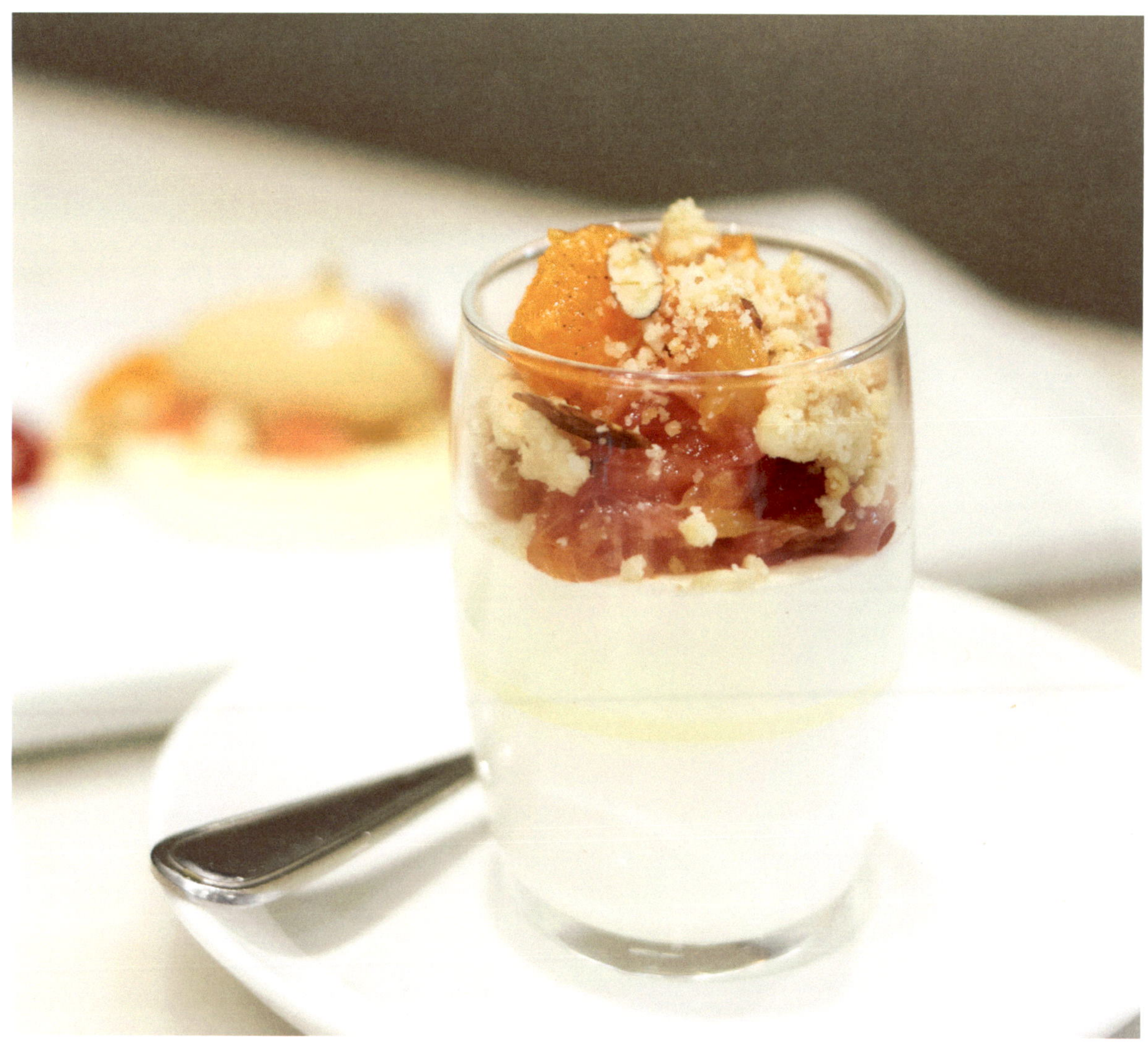

Citrus Cream

Ingredients:

660 g granulated sugar
9 ea zest of lemons
600 g whole eggs
280 g fresh lemon juice
200 g passion fruit puree
900 g butter

Method:

In a large mixing bowl, rub the zest and sugar together, then add the eggs and whisk together. Add the lemon juice and passion fruit puree. Pour into a heavy-duty sauce-pot and cook over medium heat, until thickened. Strain the citrus mixture and cool to 40'c and add the butter with a buerre mixer.

Almond Streusel

Ingredients:

250 g powdered sugar
1 g kosher salt
175 g almond flour
325 g AP flour
15 g baking powder
310 g butter
25 g whole eggs

Method:

In a large mixing bowl, mix the powdered sugar, salt, almond flour, all-purpose flour and baking powder. In a mixing bowl with a paddle, cream the butter, then add the dry ingredients. Halfway through mixing, add the eggs and mix to incorporate. Place the dough onto a parchment lined sheet pan in large pieces. Bake until golden brown and mix the dough during the baking process. Cool and use as garnish on top of fresh citrus.

AMERICAN CLASSICS

with recipes that will give grandmas meltdowns

As I worked on this issue, I set aside a few pages titled "My Content." I knew that I wanted to carry on the theme of including a section like the "Custards" section featured in issue one, and "Siphons" in issue two. But as the magazine progressed, these pages stayed blank. It needed to be something that would force me to create and learn some new recipes, something out of my comfort zone. Four weeks before the magazine's deadline I saw it. A simple piece of cake.

I'm a pastry chef, but like others, I started out as a savory cook. I don't have a classic pastry background. I trained in fine-dining restaurants and spent my years making plated desserts for tasting menus. I've never worked in a bakery or pastry shop, and I don't have very many American classic dessert recipes. Like many restaurant pastry chefs, I like playing with the flavors of traditional desserts and re-imagining them on a plate. But I imagine I'm not the only pastry chef out there that has little experience making these classic desserts.

I began to think about my favorite childhood desserts. They were always overly sweet recipes found on the back of the cake mix box. Add three eggs, a half cup of oil, and bake. No skill needed and it always tastes the same as you remembered it growing up.

So I did the opposite. I wanted to create versions of these desserts using more advanced techniques and ingredients to see if its possible to make them better than the box. My primary goal was to amplify the flavors. If it's coconut, I wanted coconut flavor to kick you in the face. For the carrot cake, I tried to pump as much carrot in as I could.

These are the recipes that came out of this process. They are not the type of recipe passed down by your grandma. In fact, she would hate these recipes.

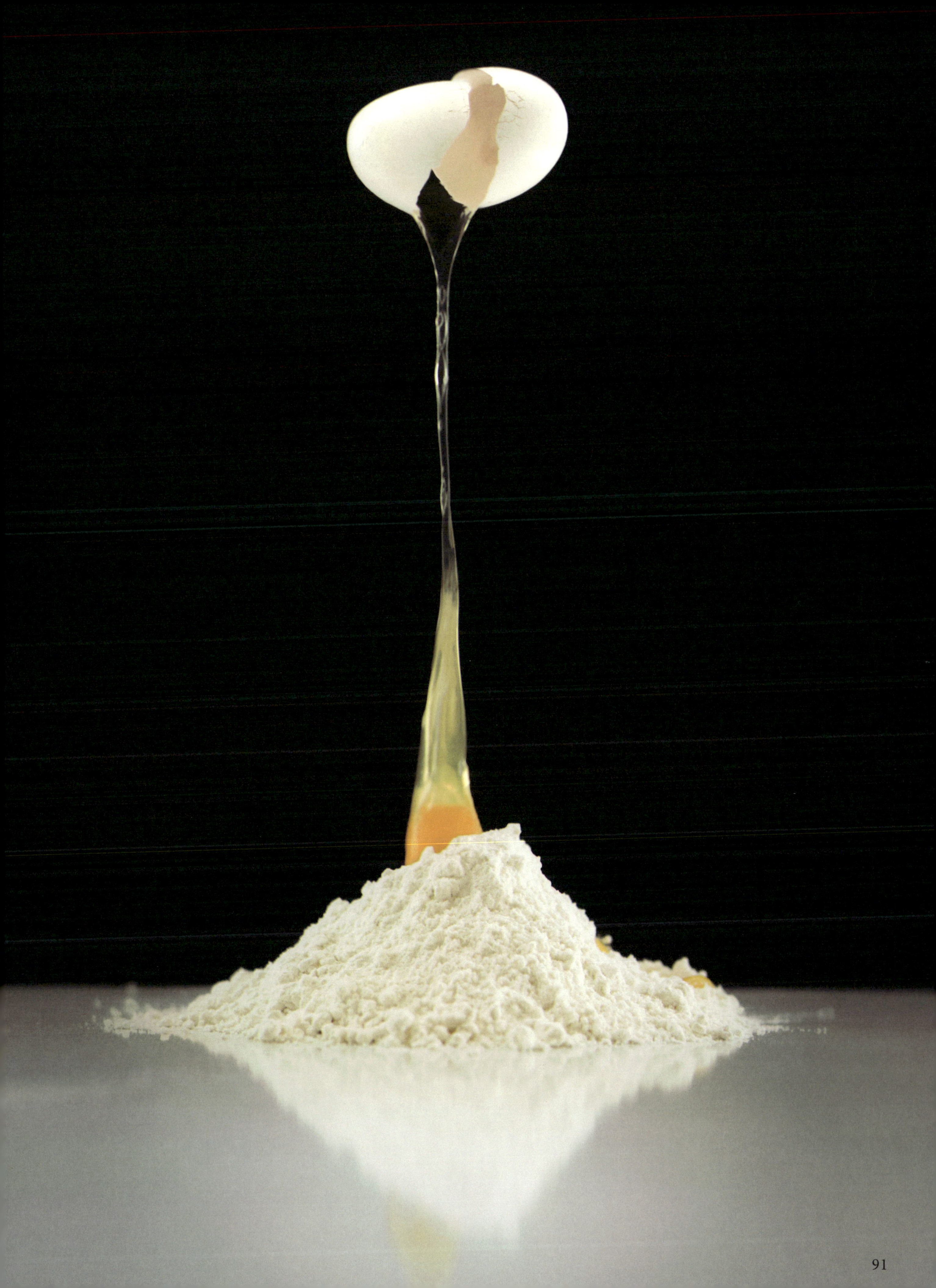

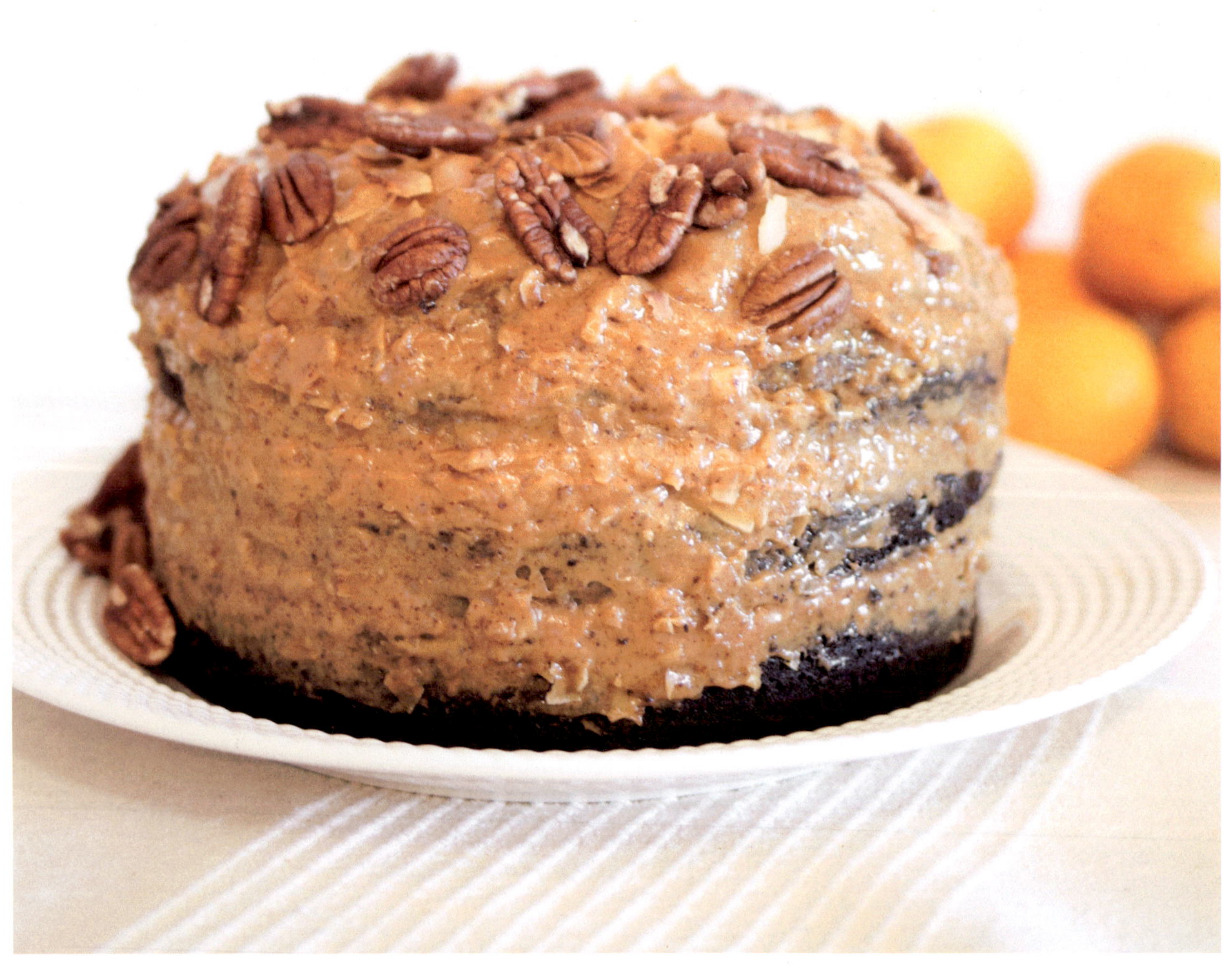

German Chocolate Cake

Recipe by Nick Muncy

Devil's Food Cake

Ingredients:

330 g	egg whites
150 g	sugar
300 g	cake flour
90 g	cocoa powder, dark
24 g	baking powder
9 g	salt
360 g	sugar
255 g	coconut oil, melted
354 g	coconut milk
2 g	vanilla paste

Method:

Whip the egg whites and first amount of sugar in a standing mixer until stiff peaks. Reserve in a bowl. In the standing mixer with the paddle attachment, mix the cake flour, cocoa powder, baking powder, salt, sugar, and coconut oil until a thick paste forms and all the ingredients are dispersed. Add the coconut milk and vanilla paste and mix until smooth. Gently fold in the whipped egg whites. Separate the batter into three greased and lined 8-inch cake pans and wrap the tops of each in foil. Bake at 350F for 30 minutes, then remove the foil cover and finish baking uncovered for 15-20 more minutes. Let cool to room temperature before inverting the cakes onto a tray. Reserve for assembly.

Notes: This recipe happens to be dairy free. It wasn't something that I was aiming to do. Often when I'm making a coconut flavored dessert, I try to replace all the milk with coconut milk to get as much coconut flavor in as I can. The coconut oil also worked as a great substitute for butter in these recipes.

Coconut-Pecan Frosting

Ingredients:

100 g	pecans, toasted
120 g	coconut flake, toasted
150 g	sugar
50 g	glucose
250 g	coconut milk
55 g	coconut oil
60 g	egg yolks
5 g	vanilla bean paste
2 g	sea salt
90 g	egg whites
150 g	sugar

Method:

Grind the pecans in a robot-coup or grind them through a meat grinder. Combine with the toasted coconut. In a medium pot, combine the sugar and glucose and make a very dark caramel. Once caramelized, slowly add the coconut oil and coconut milk. Bring the mixture up to a boil and then temper in the egg yolks. Whisk the mixture over medium heat until the eggs thicken the caramel to a pudding consistency. Remove from the heat and add the vanilla bean paste, sea salt, pecans, and coconut flakes. Chill over an ice bath. In a standing mixer, make a French meringue out of the egg whites and sugar and whip to stiff peaks. Fold into the chilled caramel mixture and let chill in the refrigerator.

Assembly

Layer the devil's food cake with the coconut-pecan frosting. Garnish the top with toasted pecans and toasted coconut flakes.

Angel Food Cake

Recipe by Nick Muncy

Angel Food Cake

Ingredients:

100 g	sugar
125 g	cake flour
20 g	almond meal
430 g	egg whites, room temp
200 g	sugar
15 g	lemon juice
2 g	almond extract
1 g	salt

Method:

Blend granulated white sugar in a blender until super fine and powdery. Measure the sugar amounts with the blended sugar. In a bowl, sift together the 100g of sugar, cake flour, and almond meal and set aside. In a standing mixer, start whipping the egg whites. When they have started to become frothy, add the lemon juice, almond extract, and salt. Whip to soft peaks before slowly adding the sugar in small amounts. Once the meringue is whipped to stiff peaks, vigorously mix 1/3 of the meringue into the dry ingredients until it is a thick, smooth paste. Gently fold in another 1/3 until barely incorporated, followed by the last 1/3. Once all of the meringue is mixed in, gently pour into an un-greased two piece tube pan. Bake at 350 F for approximately 40 minutes. The cake should be golden on top. Invert the pan on a wine bottle with the neck of the bottle going into the tube pan hole. Let the cake cool completely while hanging upside down. To remove the cake, run an offset spatula around the outside to release it.

Rhubarb Glazed Fruit Topping

Ingredients:

Rhubarb Juice:

300 g	rhubarb, chopped with skin
150 g	strawberries
120 g	sugar
50 g	water

Rhubarb Glaze:

225 g	rhubarb liquid (from above)
25 g	lemon juice
10 g	kudzu starch

Cooked Rhubarb:

2 ea	rhubarb stocks, peeled and cut
1 pt	strawberries, halved

Method:

For the rhubarb juice, combine the rhubarb, strawberries, sugar, and water in a medium sauce-pot and cook over low heat until the fruit breaks down. Strain through a chinois and cool over an ice bath. Once cooled, make the rhubarb glaze by dissolving the kudzu starch into the rhubarb liquid with your fingers, and then bring the mixture to a boil. The juice should turn clear and thick. Once cooked, pour the boiling rhubarb glaze over the peeled rhubarb pieces and let it sit at room temperature until cooled. The heat from the sauce should poach the rhubarb enough to where it is cooked but has a little bite left to it. Add the lemon juice and strawberries to finish the fruit topping.

Assembly

Whip some sweetened cream with lemon zest to stiff peaks. Serve a slice of the cake with a couple of spoons of fruit topping and a dollop of the whipped cream.

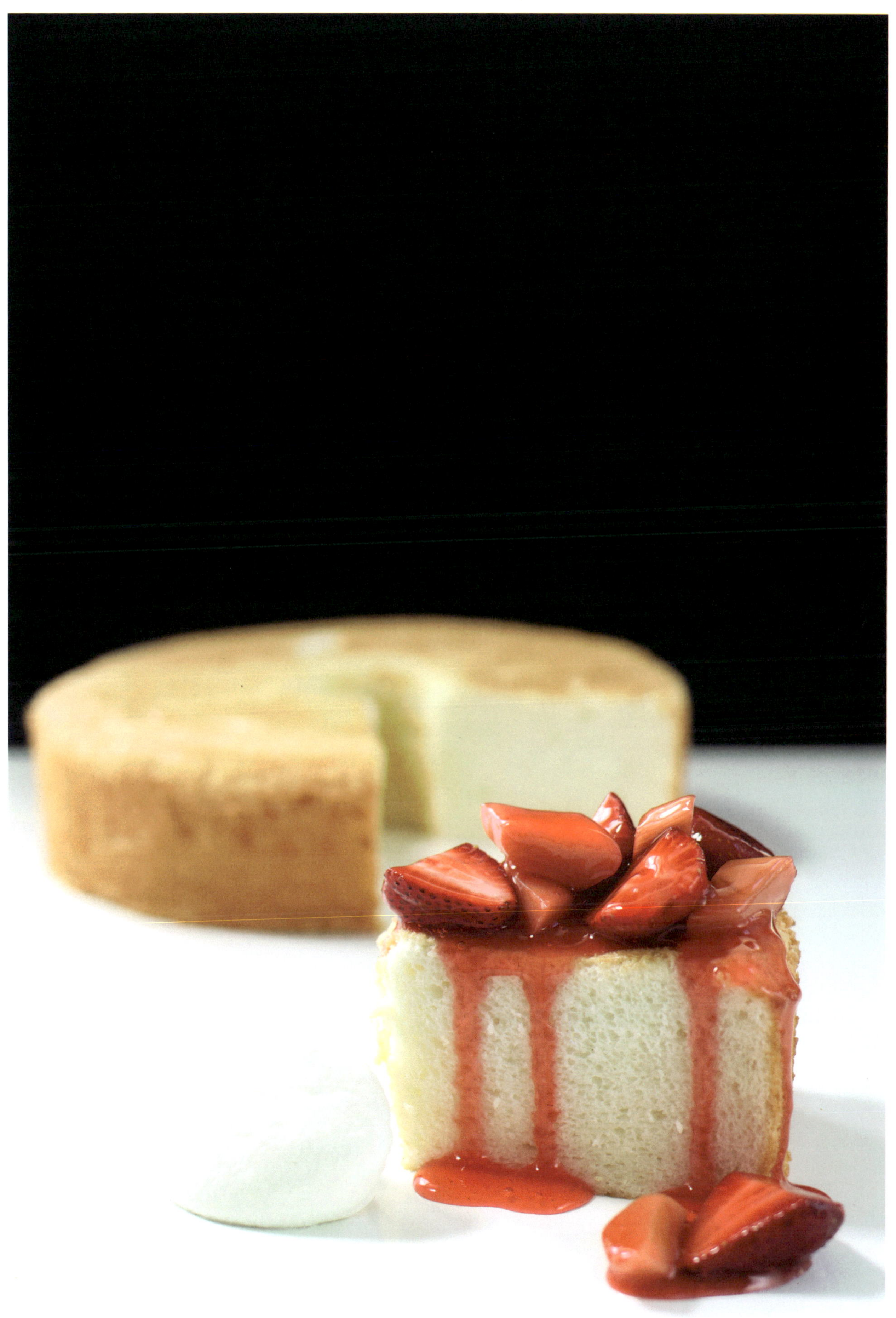

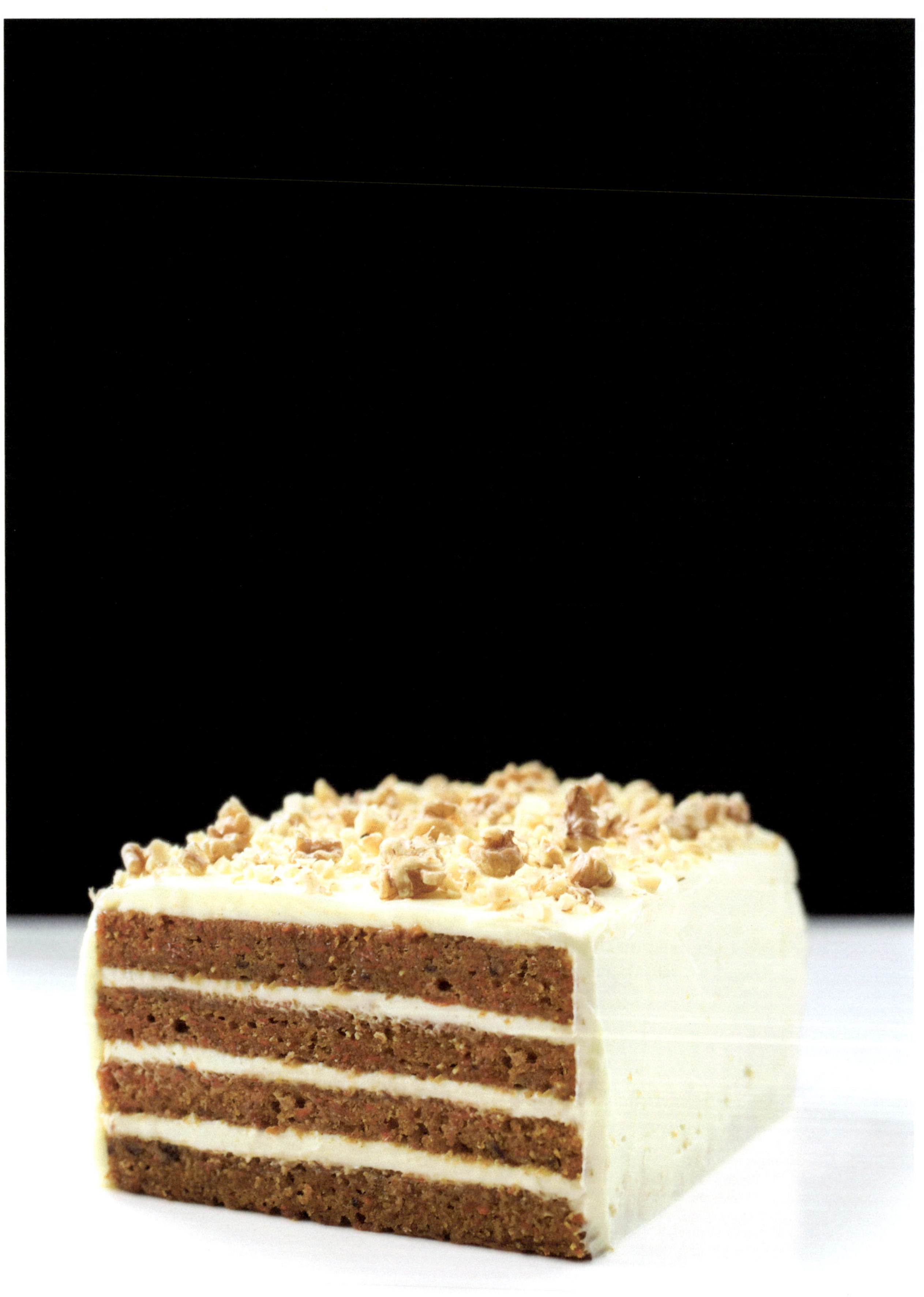

Carrot Cake with Cream Cheese Frosting

Recipe by Nick Muncy

Carrot Cake

Ingredients:

50 g	carrot, shredded and dehydrated
400 g	carrot juice
100 g	carrot, freshly grated
40 g	prunes, pureed
100 g	walnuts, toasted and ground
2 g	salt
20 g	ginger, fresh and grated
300 g	vegetable oil
7 g	cinnamon
230 g	eggs
400 g	sugar
50 g	honey
285 g	AP flour
5 g	baking powder

Method:

In a medium sauce-pot, combine the dehydrated carrots and the carrot juice. Bring to a simmer and reduce until the dried carrots absorb all of the carrot juice. Combine with the fresh carrot in a bowl and mix in the prune paste and ground walnuts. In a separate bowl, combine the salt, ginger, vegetable oil, cinnamon, eggs, sugar, and honey. Whisk together until completely dispersed. Combine the flour and baking powder before whisking it into the wet ingredients. Mix in the carrot and walnut mixture and pour into a lined half sheet pan. Bake at 350F for 40 minutes, or until completely baked and slightly browned. Let cool and reserve.

Cream Cheese Frosting

Ingredients:

450 g	cream cheese, room temperature
480 g	powdered sugar
250 g	unsalted butter, softened
4 g	salt
60 g	orange juice
2 ea	orange zest

Method:

In the standing mixture, combine the butter, salt, and powdered sugar and mix with a paddle until completely dispersed. Add the orange zest, orange juice, and cream cheese and paddle for 5 minutes. The frosting should be slightly fluffy and completely mixed. Reserve for assembly.

Assembly

Cut the carrot cake into four pieces and layer cream cheese frosting in between each. Decorate the outside of the cake with more frosting and then top with chopped toasted walnuts.

Notes: I used the dehydrated carrots and carrot juice in an attempt to amplify the carrot flavor in the cake. I also used prunes instead of raisins because I forgot to buy some. I also used Philadelphia Cream Cheese instead of something fancy because it has to have that exact flavor to taste correct.

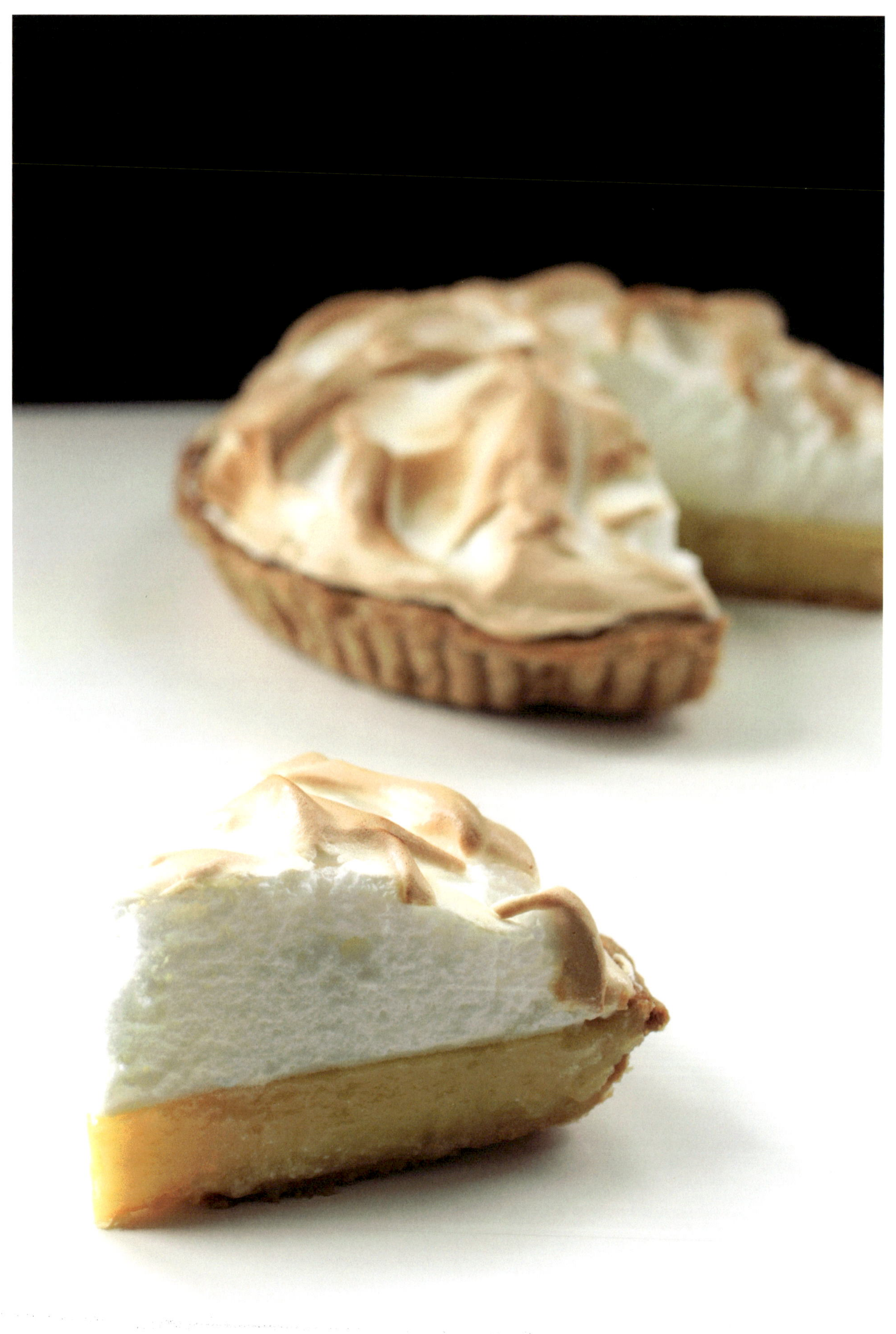

Meyer Lemon Meringue Pie

Recipe by Nick Muncy

Pie Crust

Ingredients:

175 g	AP flour
10 g	sugar
2 g	salt
130 g	butter, small diced
78 g	water, ice cold

Method:

In a bowl, combine and mix the flour, sugar, and salt. Add the butter and mix with your hands, pressing the mixture between your hands to smash the butter cubes. You want there to be a good mix of different sized butter chunks. Add the ice water and gently mix to bring the dough together. Wrap the dough in plastic wrap and press into a thick disk for easier rolling later on. Refrigerate the dough for 30 minutes, then pull out and roll to fit a 9-inch pie pan or tart mold. Fit the dough to the pan and place in the freezer to firm up the dough. Once frozen, place a piece of parchment paper in the middle and fill with beans for blind baking. Bake the crust in a 350 F oven until browned.

Candied Preserved Meyer Lemons

Ingredients:

100 g	preserved lemon peels
200 g	sugar
100 g	water

Method:

Rinse the preserved lemon peels off to remove the excess salt and sugar. Bring a small pot of water to a boil, and blanch the preserved lemons for 30 seconds in the water to help further remove the excess saltiness. Place the blanched preserved lemons in a bowl. Combine the sugar and water in a small pot and bring to a boil, and then pour over the preserved lemons. Let cool at room temperature. Cut to the desired size. The flavor of these should be a nice a mix of sweet and salty.

Meyer Lemon Curd Filling

Ingredients:

300 g	water
300 g	sugar
100 g	egg yolk
40 g	cornstarch
150 g	meyer lemon juice
45 g	butter
1 g	salt
1 ea	gelatin sheet, hydrated
2 ea	meyer lemon zest
30 g	candied preserved lemons, chopped

Method:

In a pot, combine the water and sugar and bring to a boil. In a bowl whisk together the egg yolks and cornstarch. Once the water and sugar have come to a boil, temper it into the egg yolk mixture. Combine together and return to the heat. Bring to a full boil. It should become very thick. Once cooked, whisk in the lemon juice, butter, salt, gelatin sheet, and lemon zest. Pour into the baked pie crust and let set up in the refrigerator. Sprinkle the chopped pieces of candied preserved lemon over the top of the curd.

Meringue

Ingredients:

120 g	egg whites
1 g	cream of tartar
1 g	salt
100 g	sugar

Method:

Preheat an oven to 350 F. In a standing mixer, whip the egg whites, cream of tartar and salt to soft peaks. Then slowly add the sugar and whip to firm peaks. Top the cooled lemon curd filled pie with the meringue and bake for 15-20 minutes, until golden brown on top. Let cool in the refrigerator before serving.

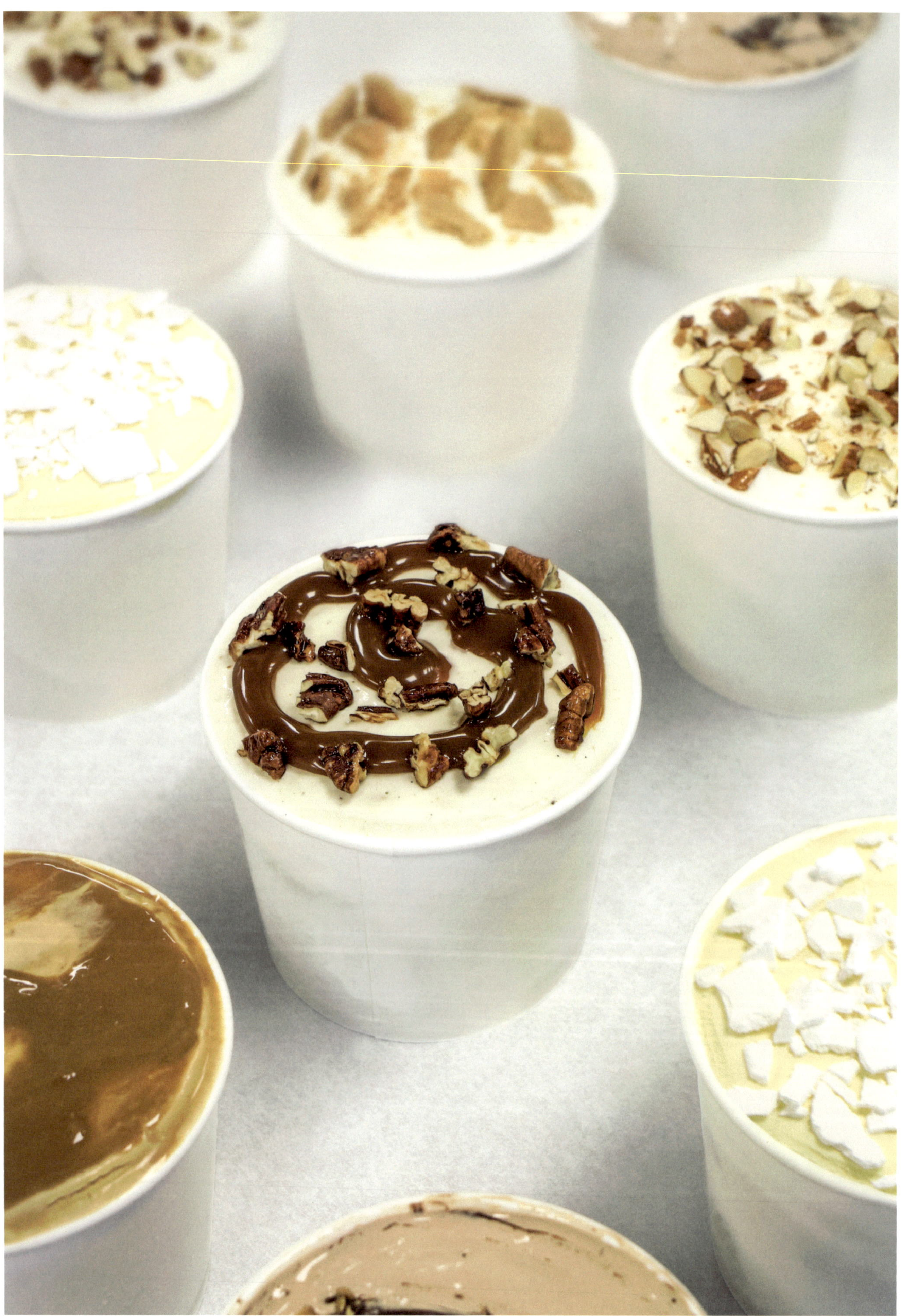

Gabriele Riva

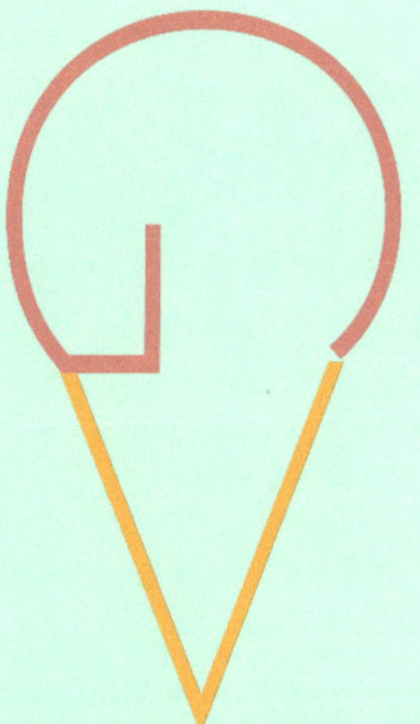

VERO GELATO

las vegas, nevada

One of the best parts about creating Toothache is meeting new chefs and making new friends. I first started talking with Gabriele Riva when working on issue one, and we have since been able to get to know each other better. For the third issue, I spent a couple of days in Las Vegas hanging out with Gabriele and Melissa Coppel at Atelier Melissa Coppel to see them both in action.

While taking photos in the kitchen with Gabriele, I watched him make gelato for his new company, Vera Gelato. He makes some traditional flavors like chocolate and vanilla, but also has unique twists on flavors like coconut, passion fruit, and dulce de leche that taste anything but conventional.

Gabriele currently makes his gelato in Melissa Coppel's pastry school, Atelier Melissa Coppel, and has some pretty amazing equipment to use. Though he has a large ice cream machine and a blast freezer, he's still not entirely set up for production. Half of his day was spent filling containers of gelato by hand and cleaning up the meticulous kitchen.

He currently sells his gelato locally on UberEats, as well as a few restaurant wholesale accounts. Gabriele is also a Cacao Barry Ambassador, so while he works on his new gelato concept, he is always thinking about chocolates. As an Ambassador, Chef Riva conducts demonstrations of his chocolate ideations, judges pastry competitions, and continues to develop recipes and ideas.

Gabriele's resume includes working with Silvano Lullini at Pasticceria Piave in Milan, being the pastry chef at Nobu in London and New York, and Executive Head Chef at the Gramercy Park Hotel. He is often known for incorporating Japanese ingredients and Asian flavors into his beautiful creations. In Toothache issue one, he spoke about incorporating probiotics like koji rice and dashi into his chocolates.

After a few days in the kitchen, we sat down for some beers, and I recorded a candid conversation, pastry chef to pastry chef.

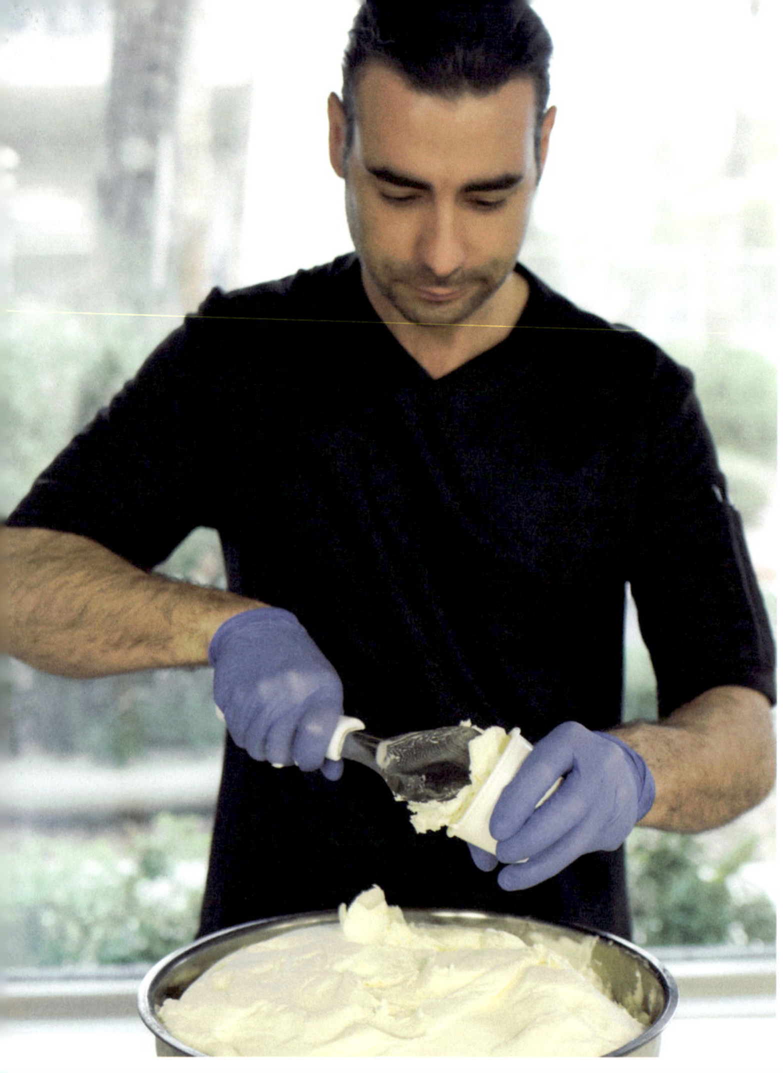

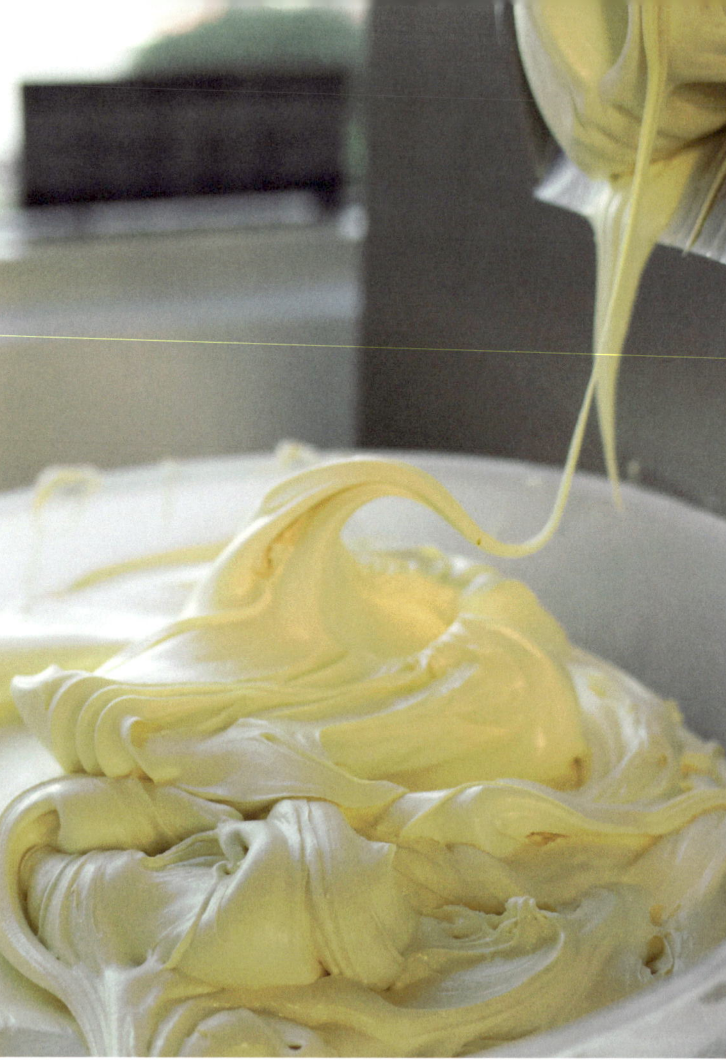

Gabriele: What are your thoughts after spending a few days in the kitchen and seeing what I do?

Nick: I feel like because there isn't a storefront, it'd be hard to stay motivated. You don't have to personally turn away customers when you run out of a flavor, and if you're feeling like crap, you can turn off the app for the day. I mean, I have that issue now working for myself at home. If I wanted to take a day off, it'd be pretty easy to get away with.

Yeah, it's tough.

But on the flip side, you're also working in a dream kitchen with every tool and piece of equipment you could ever want to play with. It's probably pretty fun to test new desserts and work on ideas in that space, but also must be hard to make the same gelato again and again when you have a chocolate idea on your mind.

That's exactly right. In a way having a store is great because people walk in, and it's easier to sell the product in person. But I feel like not having a store pushes me more. Especially selling ice cream by the pint, because it needs to be very stable. Otherwise, after a couple of weeks in people's freezers, it's not good anymore.

I'm sure a lot of people buy your gelato, eat a third of it, and then it sits in their shitty home freezer for a couple of days. Or maybe it sits out for a while, and then goes back into the freezer...

That's why the formula is important. For example, I know how to balance my recipe to be able to quenelle it straight out of a - 18-degree freezer in a restaurant setting. But if I do that recipe in a pint container for customers, then somebody is going to buy it, and by the time they're home, it's going to be melted soup.

Why did you decide to start making and selling gelato? What is different about your gelato?

The gelato that I'm doing is with the perspective of a pastry chef and chocolatier, which is very different from a gelato maker.

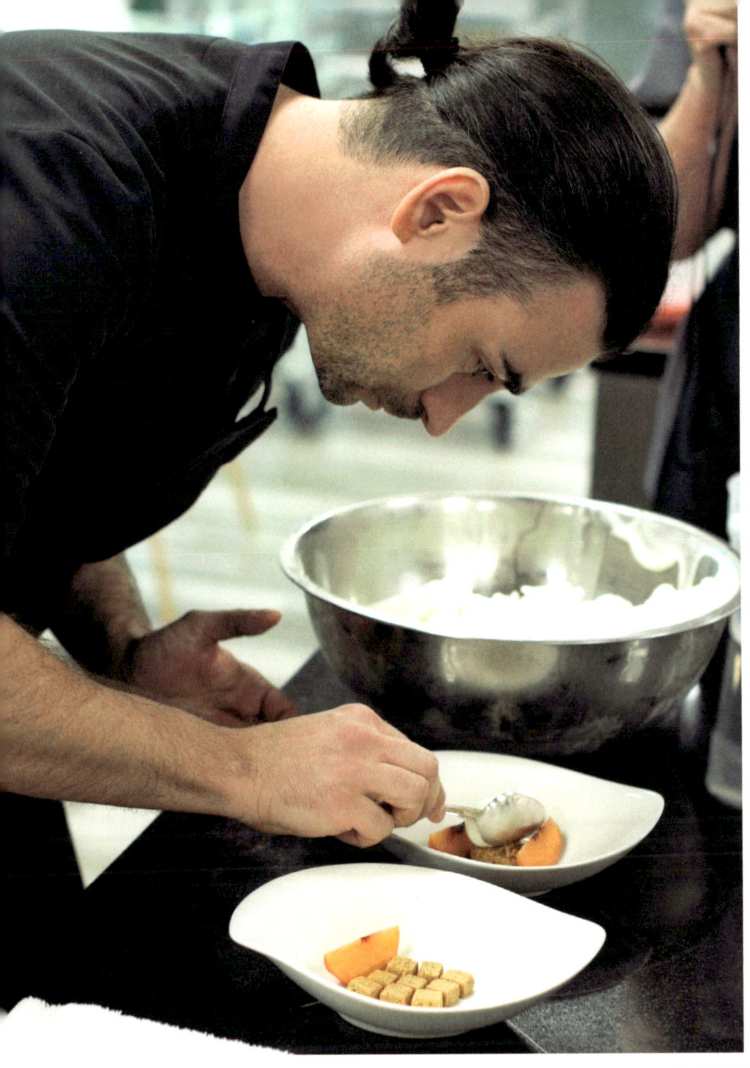

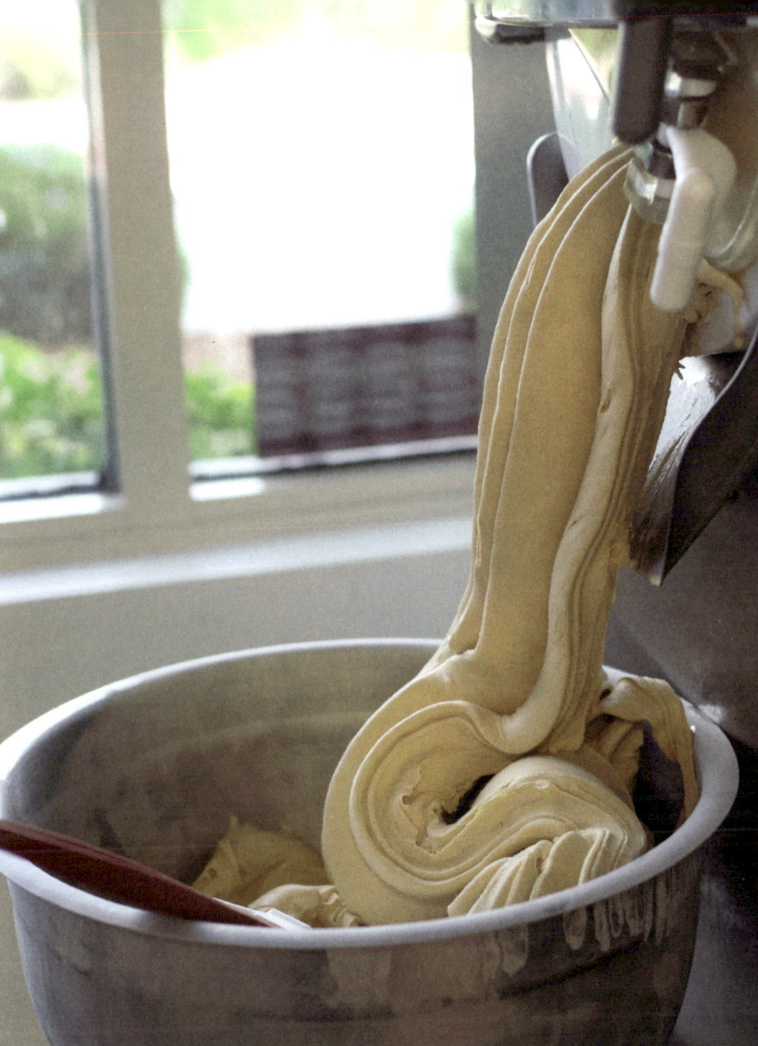

There are some gelato makers or ice cream makers that are much better than me. There are a few Italian gelato makers that are seventy or eighty years old, and that's all they've done their whole life. As a pastry chef with a lot of restaurant experience, creating ice cream is not just about calculating a formula. It's about showing the sensitivity and subtlety of a flavor. So I do unconventional flavor combinations, infusions, textures, cookies, and sponges in my gelato.

Gelato is something that I like, and there isn't any good gelato here in Las Vegas.

Even though you do unique flavors, I'm sure there are the people that only want vanilla or chocolate or strawberry.

Sometimes it's difficult for business to do non-traditional flavors. Because, if you do a peculiar flavor, you need the demand. That's the only thing. But I do things like changing the name of the Gianduja gelato to "Nutella", because the average American only knows that flavor as Nutella.

I feel like restaurant pastry chefs want to do everything, because they've gotten a taste of all aspects of pastry. It's hard for a restaurant pastry chef to entirely focus on one thing like ice cream and forget about all the rest.

Especially for me, growing up with a pastry chef father. He had a pastry shop in Milan for 30 years, and after opened a separate gelato shop that he ran for 15 years. So I grew up learning how to create traditional pastries and classic Italian desserts, including everything from chocolate, pastry, and gelato.

I think a lot of specialized chefs like ice cream makers and bakers are very good at making those foods, but they're almost confined by traditions and what they have been taught. They aren't interested in innovation and only do what they've been shown regarding specific flavors and methods. Do you want to be known for gelato?

As a professional, I don't want to be defined as a gelato maker. It's one thing that I do, and I want to make it as good as I can, but I'm a pastry chef as well.

I love the gelato business, but I want to keep doing things as a pastry chef and as a chocolatier. The ultimate goal is to incorporate it into a mochi concept. With the gelato as a filling. Of course, not just gelato. Although I think ice cream fillings are the most refreshing, I also want to incorporate centers, crunch components, mousses, and creams.

Cooking mochi, rolling it out, and wrapping it around ice cream adds a lot of labor to a one-man gelato business.

It's expensive to get where I want to be with the mochi business. I need three expensive machines. It's one thing to make it by hand for a picture or a magazine, but for production, I'm not going to cook mochi in the microwave. In New York, I consulted for two years full time on a mochi ice cream company, Mochidoki, and they are doing very well. I created the product from A-Z. When I started to develop the product, I tried using rice flour from Korea, China, Japan, and rice flour from Japan but made in the USA. I tried everything. I was also working with a scientist, so for me, it was a fantastic experience.

I once tried to do it by hand for an event at the MGM. I did three or four hundred by hand, and it took me all day. Since I don't have a walk-in freezer, I had to blast chill the ice cream and wrap two at a time. I'm glad that I did it, but if I count my labor, I lost money. It was good to see, because if you want to do business, you need to know its limits. It's like creating a chocolate company and tempering chocolate by hand. Are you kidding me? It's stupid. Don't do it.

Once you start the mochi part of the business, do you want to get a storefront?

Melissa Coppel and I are thinking about doing a shared storefront. It all depends on the location, but we could sell gelato, mochi, bonbons, and pastries. It'd be good.

Is doing the gelato on its own fulfilling for you? Do you feel your creative outlet is being satisfied? Or are you just waiting for the right time to start the mochi?

While I'm doing the gelato right now, I think a lot about the mochi concept. Also, I'm still working with chocolate every day, doing research and development with Melissa. So we're still working on new recipes together and pushing with chocolate.

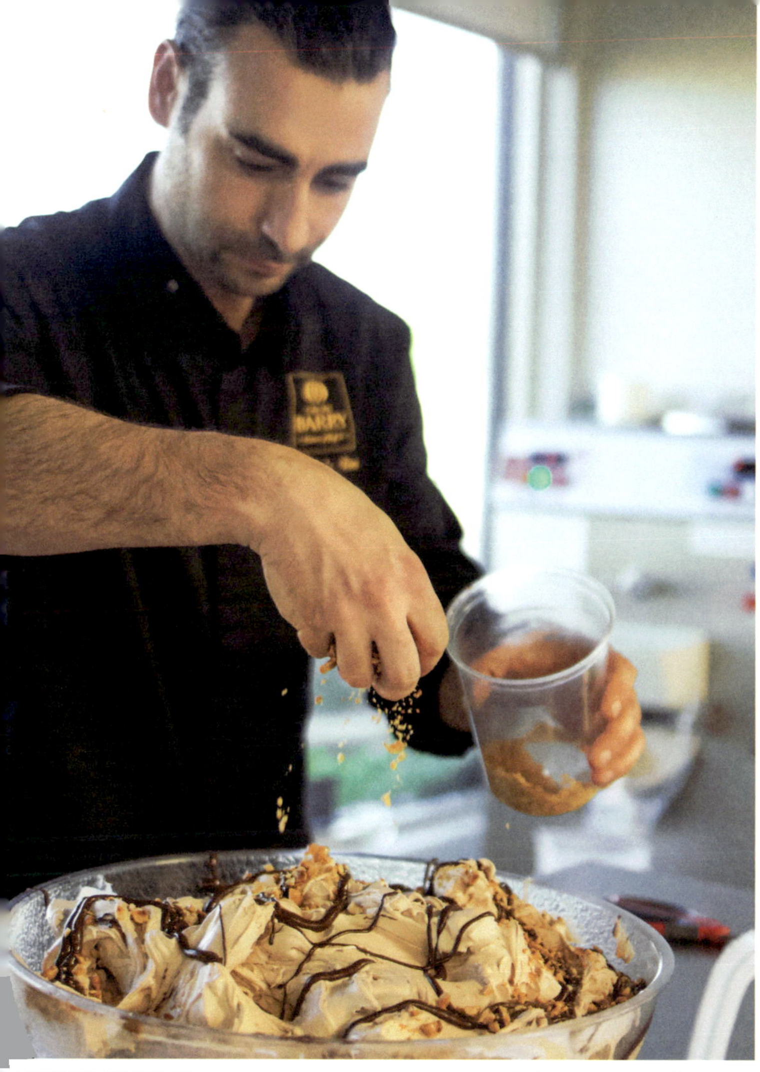

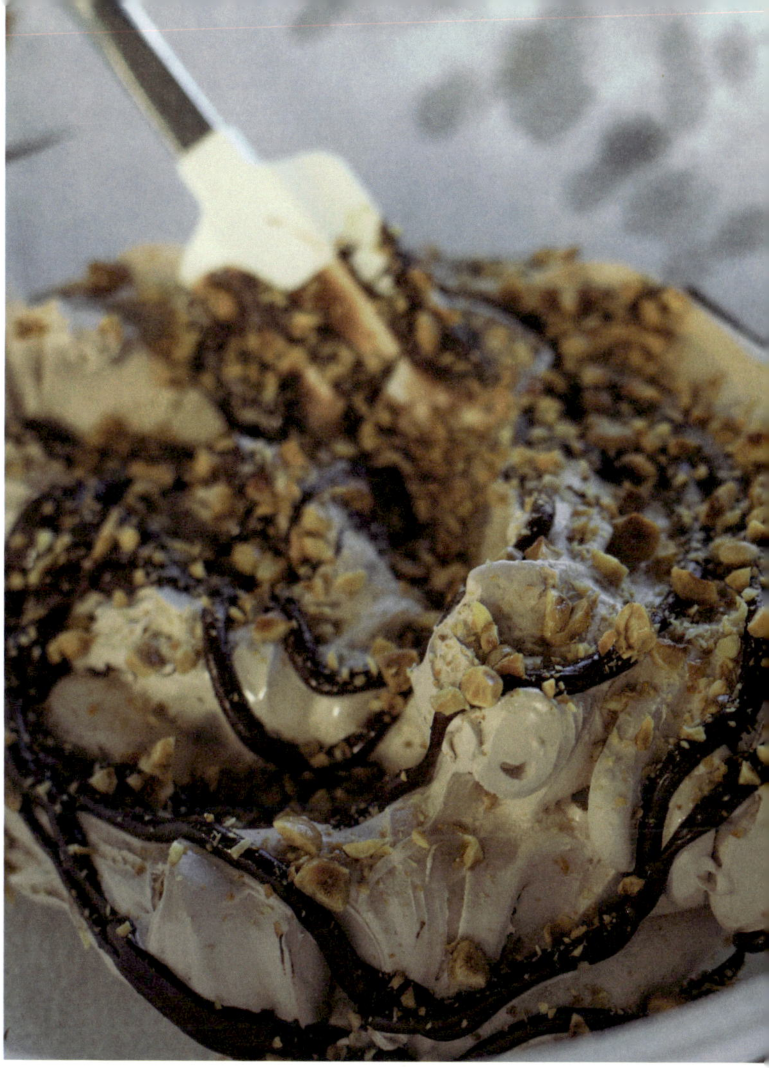

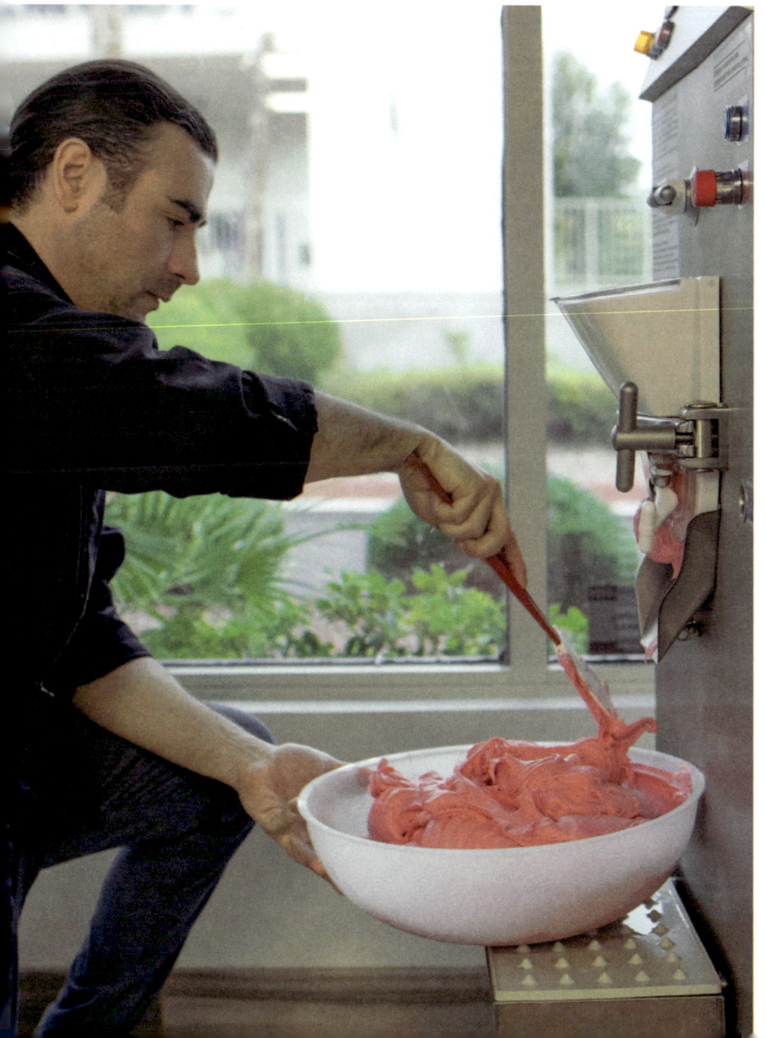

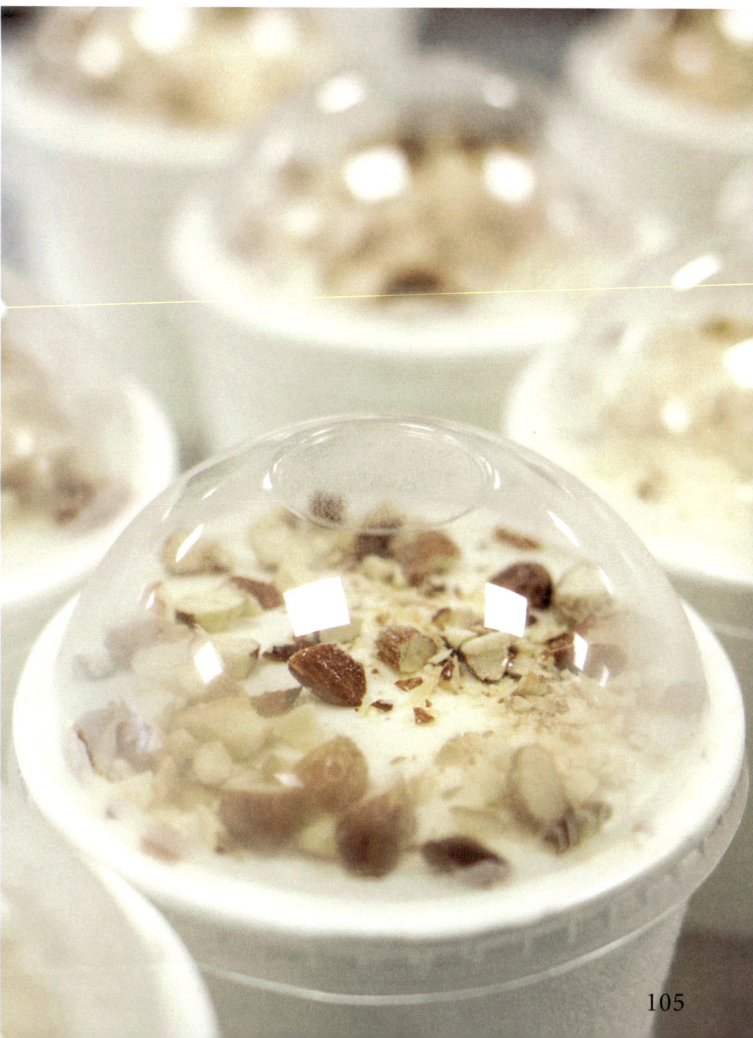

Raspberry Sorbet

Recipe by Gabriele Riva

Raspberry Sorbet

Ingredients:

1125 g	filtered water
1600 g	Boiron raspberry puree
375 g	sucrose
130 g	dextrose
200 g	glucose powder
35 g	lemon juice
35 g	sorbet stabilizer

Method:

In a pot, heat the water to 30 C. Add the dextrose and glucose powder. Dry mix the sucrose and sorbet stabilizer and then incorporate it completely into the water. While continuously whisking, cook to 82 C. Strain the sorbet base over an ice bath and let cool completely. Thaw the Boiron raspberry puree and add to base along with the fresh lemon juice. Immersion blend to fully combine.

To churn the sorbet: Strain the base. Churn to -9 in designated containers and freeze immediately. Keep in the freezer till needed.

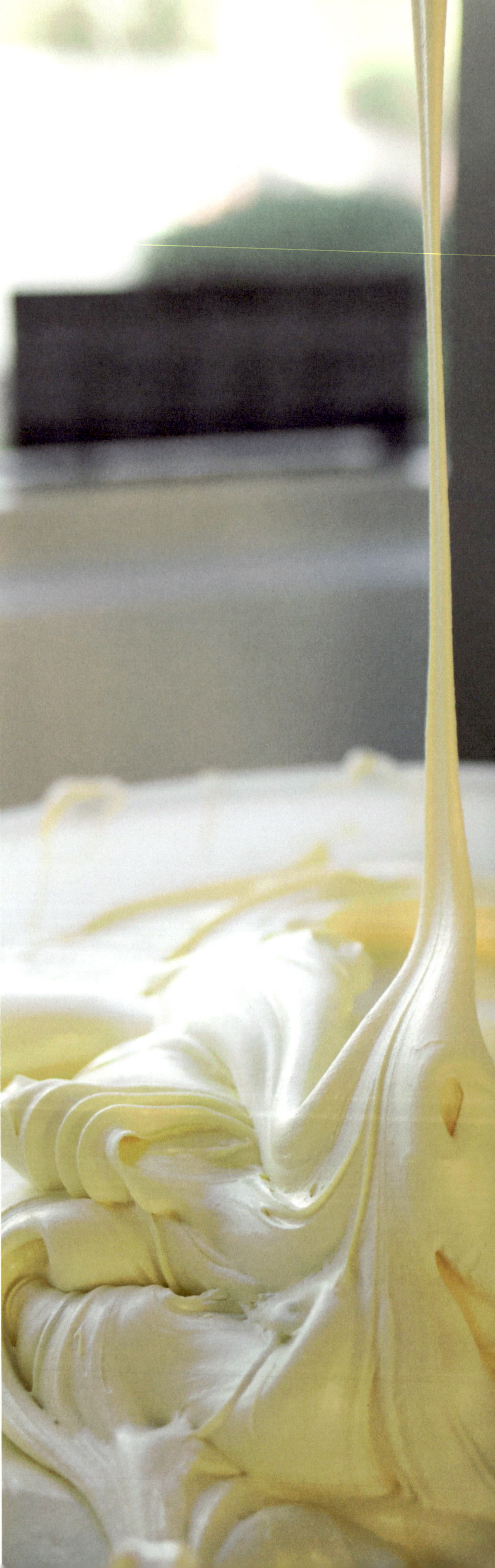

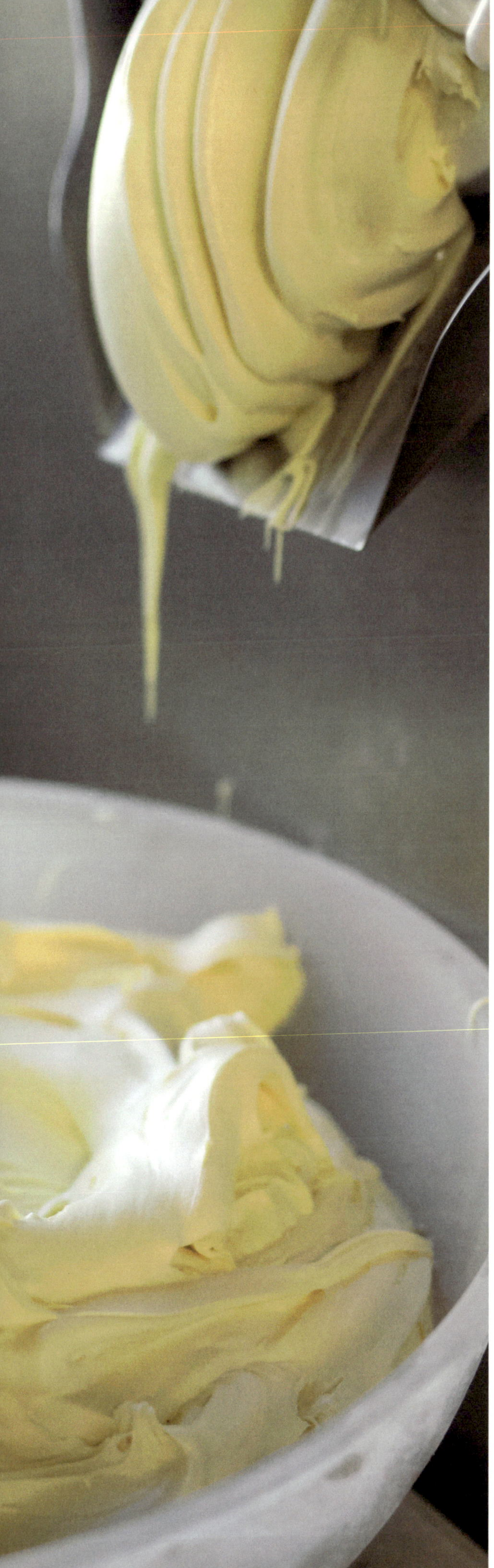

Zephyr White Chocolate-Coffee-Lime Gelato

Recipe by Gabriele Riva

Zephyr White Chocolate-Coffee-Lime Gelato

Ingredients:

435 g	milk
40 g	heavy cream
45 g	sucrose
14 g	inverted sugar
37 g	dextrose
23 g	glucose powder
7 g	Pregel gelato stabilizer
2 g	sea salt
100 g	Cacao Barry Zephyr 34%
20 g	coffee beans
10 g	lime zest

Method:

In a medium pot warm the milk and heavy cream over an induction unit. Once it reaches 30 C, add the milk powder and dissolve. Then add the dextrose. Dry mix the sucrose and IC stabilizer, glucose powder, inverted sugar and salt. Add to the gelato base while constantly whisking. Add coffee beans and lime zests. When the base reaches 85 C, strain the base on top of Zephyr white chocolate and mix to combine. Pour into a metal bowl over ice bath and Immersion mix very well. Churn the gelato base in the Bravo gelato machine the following day.

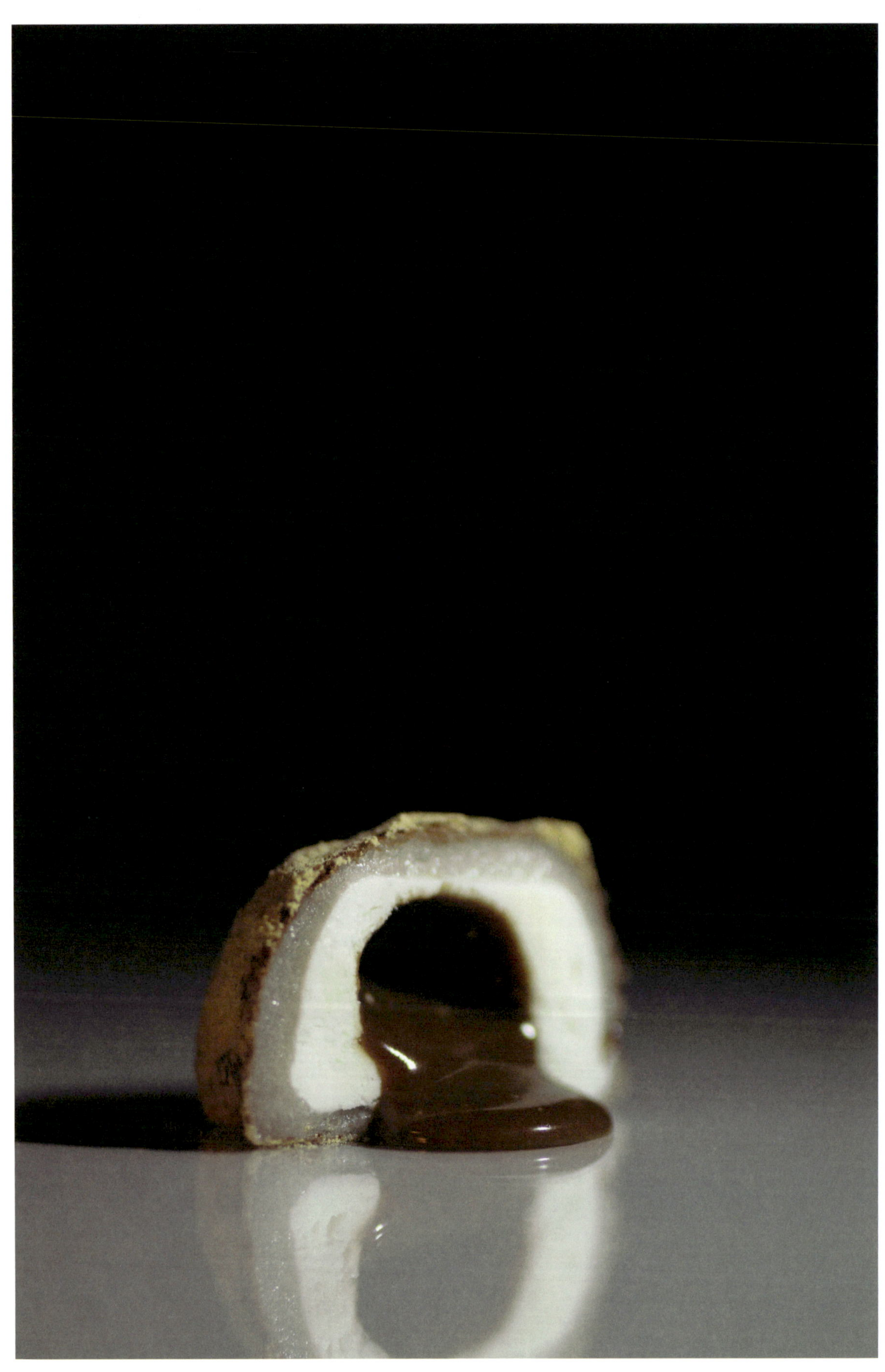

LIQUID TOFFEE MOCHI WITH KINAKO AND VANILLA

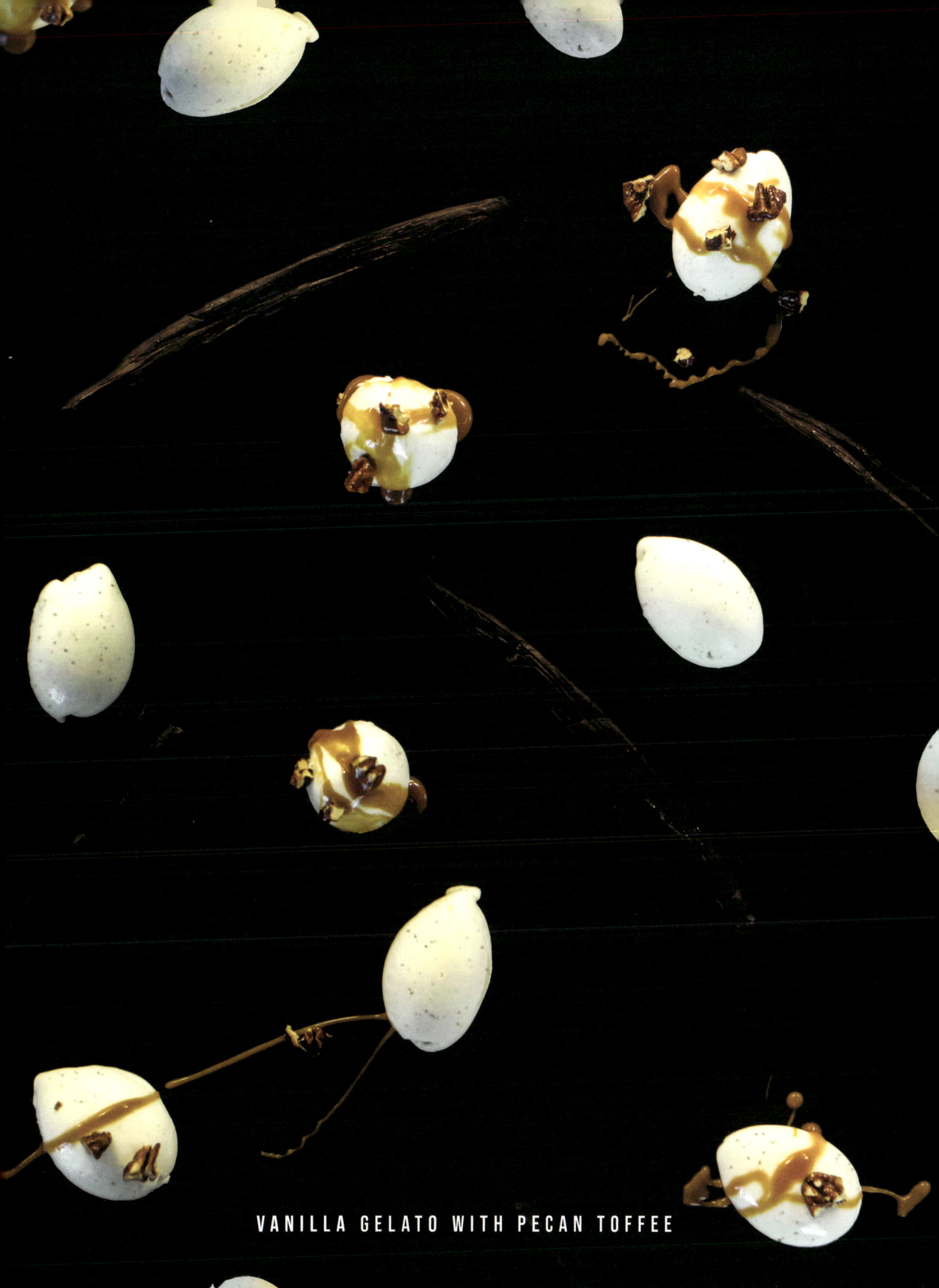

VANILLA GELATO WITH PECAN TOFFEE

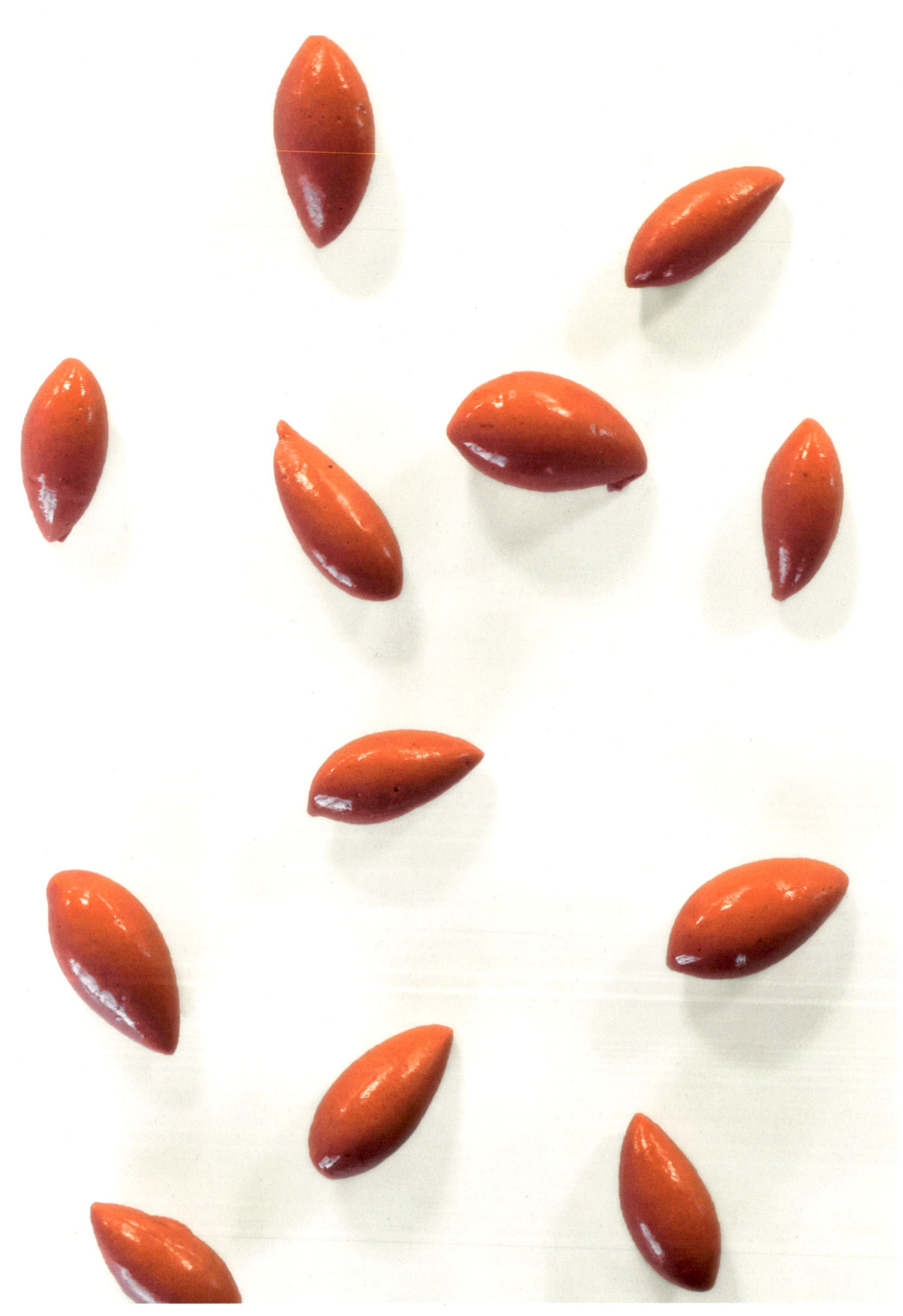

RASPBERRY SORBET

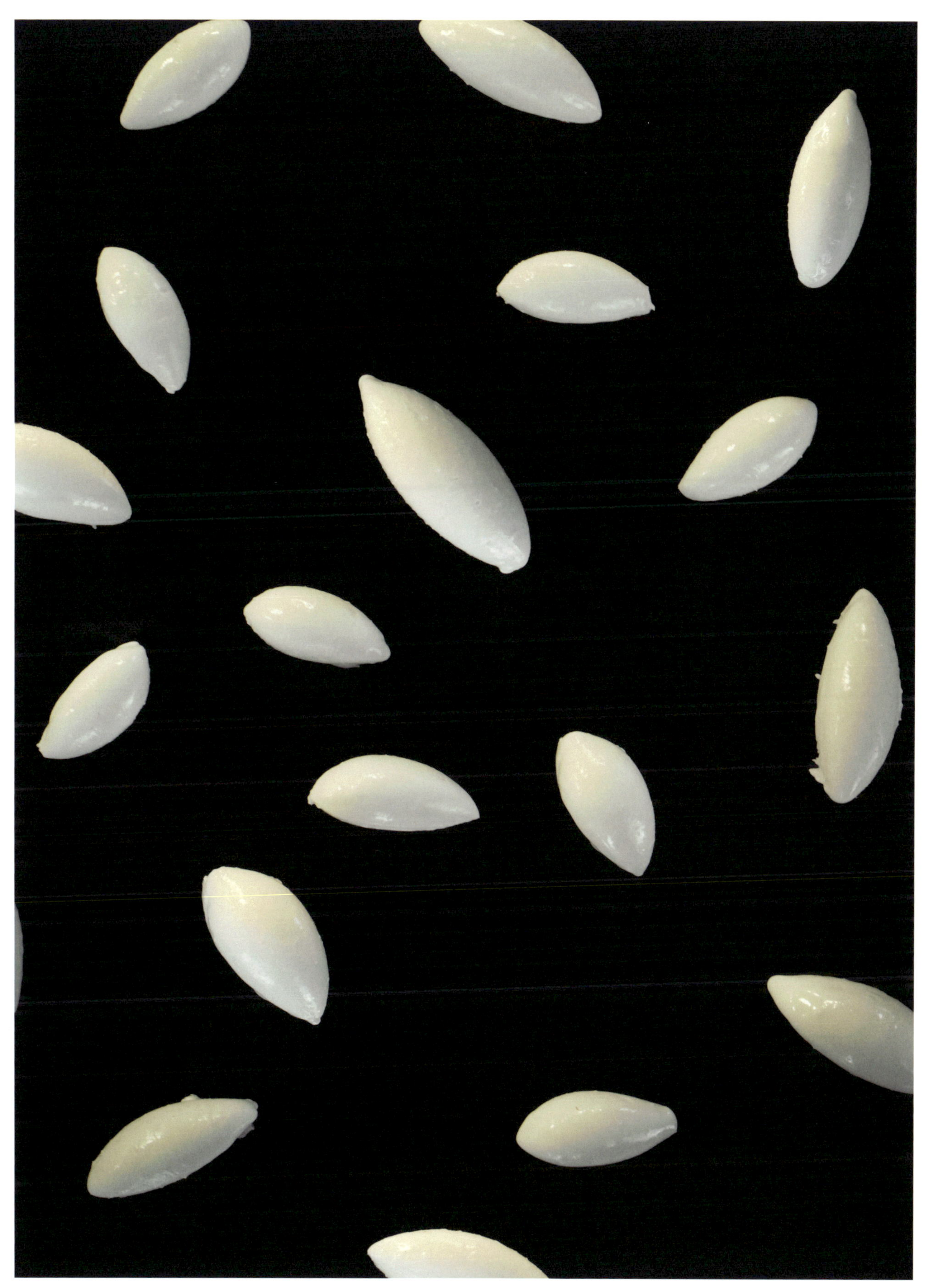

COCONUT GELATO

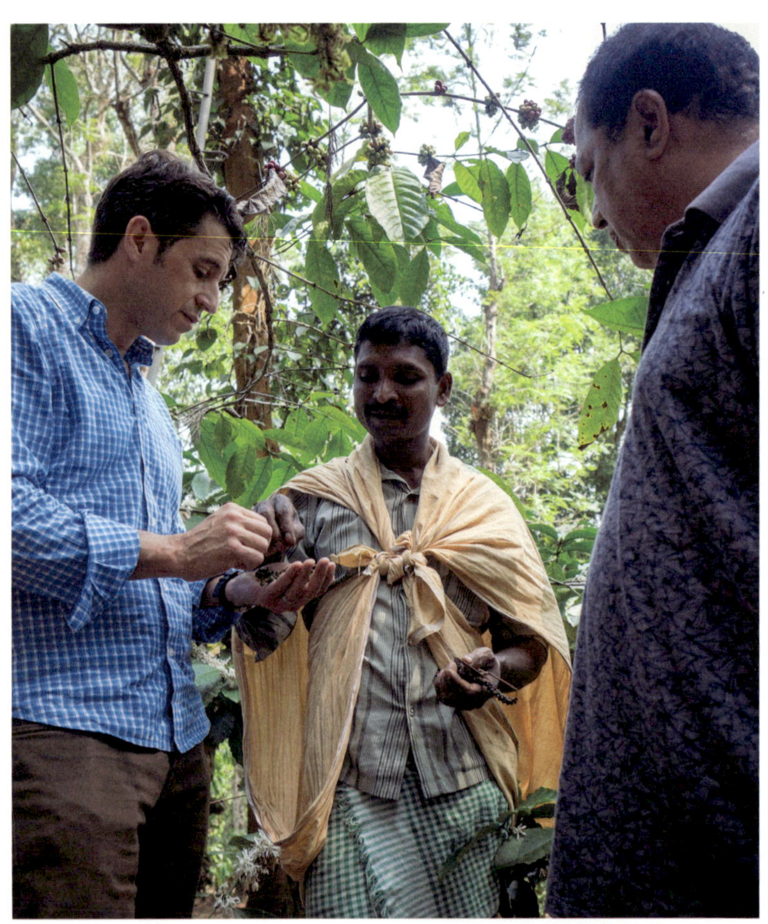

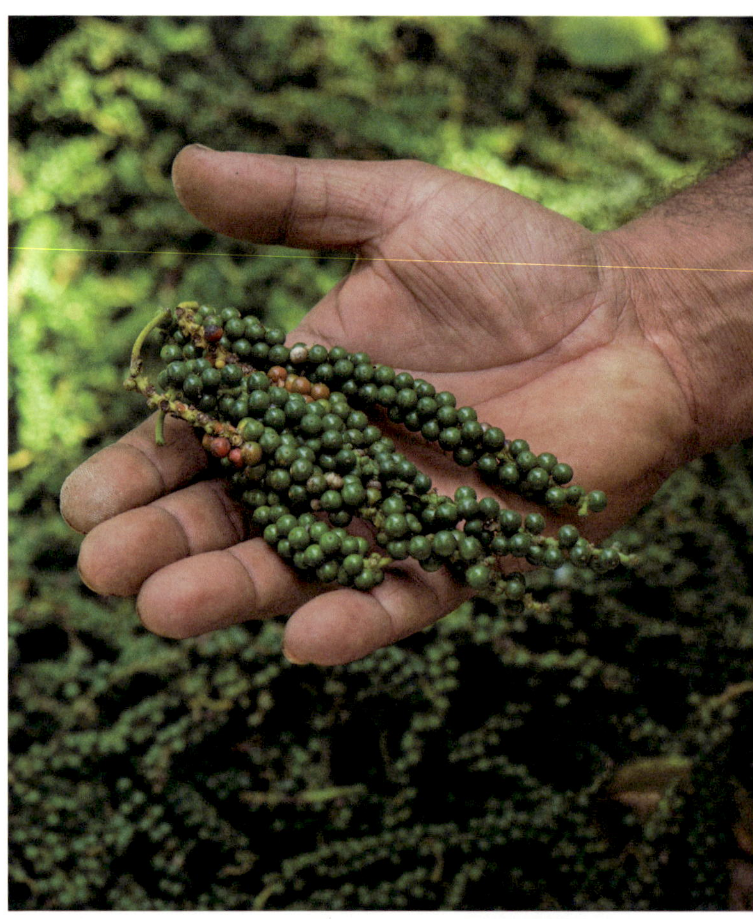

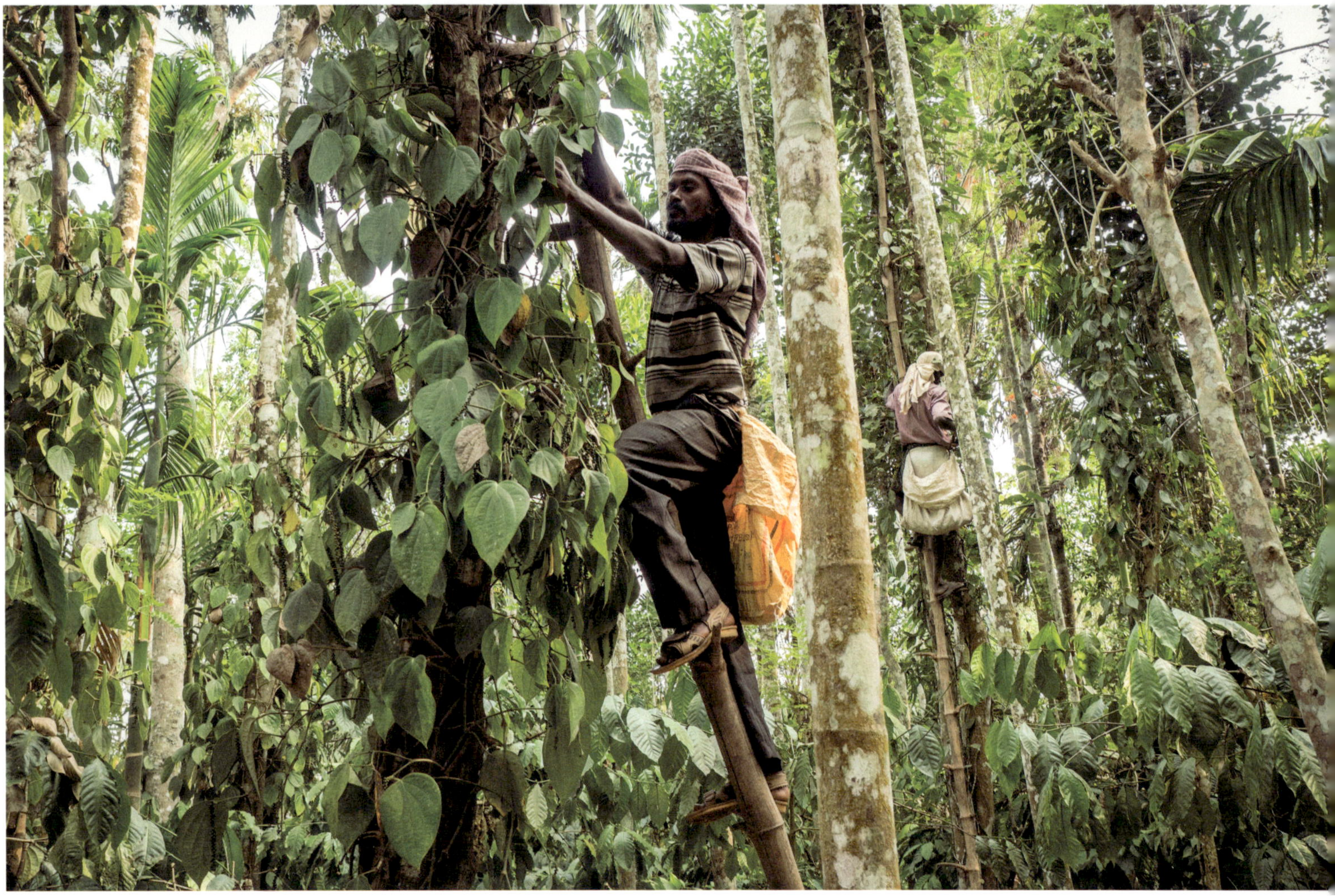

Photos by Alan Shortall

The Reluctant Trading Experiment

Scott Eirinberg
Premium Spice Purveyor
Highland Park, IL

"It's a race for the farmers to pick the peppercorns from the vines before the birds and monkeys get to them," the pepper farmer told me. "In India, the early bird gets the pepper instead of the worm."

It was my 12th trip to India, but first time to see the pepper harvest.

Just a few years ago, I actually had no interest in spices. In fact, when my friend Divakar approached me to start a business selling some "amazing peppercorns" he had found growing near his home in India, I thought he had gone a little paagal. (That's Hindi for crazy.)

Why would anyone want to sell pepper? I was Reluctant. Divakar, he was relentless. So, I let him ship me some samples.

I still remember the day the box arrived. I remember grinding the pepper. And the striking, beautiful aroma of limes and oranges. Really.

A month later, I imported the peppercorns and launched a spice company called The Reluctant Trading Experiment. That's when my wife thought I had gone paagal.

In Kerala, I watched men in leather sandals climb bamboo ladders 40' high. The men plucked the pepper drupes from the vines and dropped the fruit into their capes.

Once a picker had gathered a full load, he'd come back to earth and empty his haul onto a tarp. Eventually, the peppercorns would be taken to an open area to dry in the sun, where the green fruit would shrivel and turn black.

All day long, the pickers climbed up and down, cleaning the trees. By late afternoon, several overflowing bags of peppercorns leaned against each other in the shade as the hot Indian sun dropped below the lush tree line.

A group of tired pickers sat down cross-legged to relax and celebrate a hard day's work. Instead of a six-pack, they shared a fresh pot of chai.

It had been an exceptional day for everyone. Except of course, the birds and the monkeys.

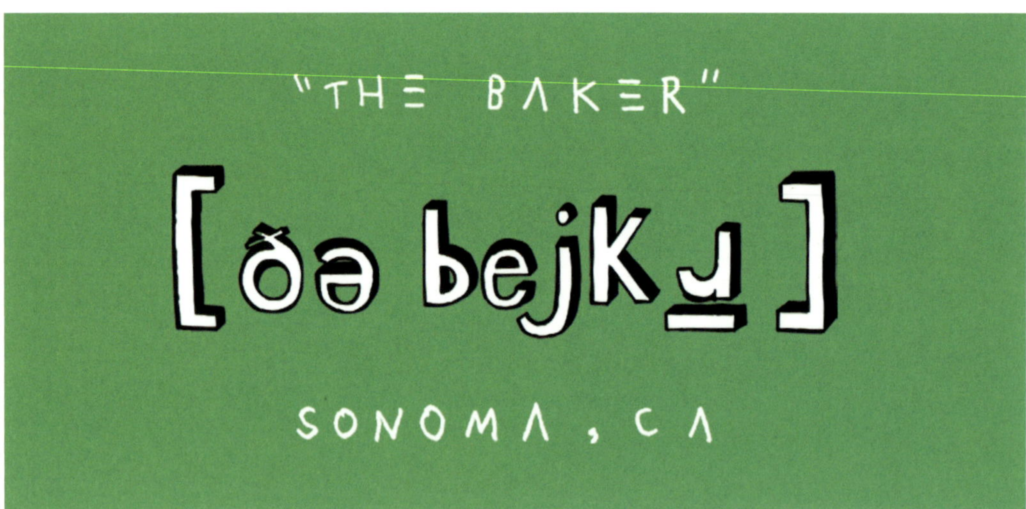

mike zakowski

the bejkr
sonoma, california

art by patrick sean gibson

It takes a special person to get pumped about an overnight bake. Mike Zakowski is one of them. After hearing so many great things about Mike, I was excited to meet up with him to watch his work. They say it takes 10,000 hours to truly master a skill. Watching Mike work, you soon realize, he has more than mastered his craft. His motions were methodic and slightly entrancing, and I was amazed and inspired by his non-stop baking schedule. Once he started baking, the flow of bread coming out of the oven seemed impossible for one person to be producing.

Mike has taken bread baking and brought it to a whole new level of difficulty. He only uses natural yeasts, stone mills his flour out of locally sourced grains, bakes in wood-fired ovens, and doesn't use any white flour. You would assume a baker this skilled would be running a massive operation, and after talking with him, I learned he used to do just that. But now, he'd rather work by himself, making his loaves of bread by hand, embracing the "old ways" of baking, and selling straight to his neighbors at the Sonoma Farmer's Market. At the market, there is a constant line of at least fifteen people waiting to buy their weekly supply of bread or one of his pretzels as they come straight out of the live-fire oven.

Mike's thoughts on a few questions:

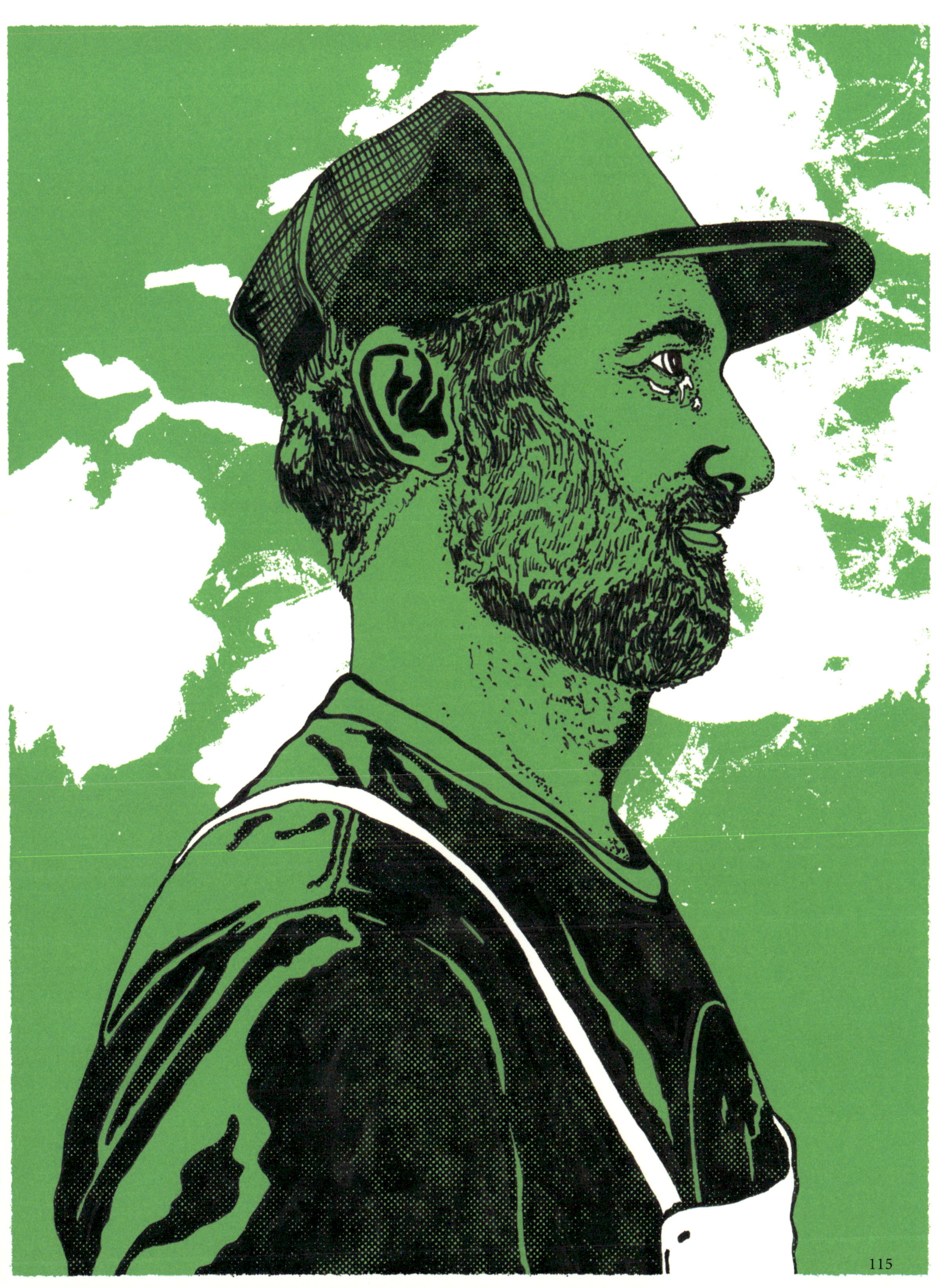

TELL US A LITTLE BIT ABOUT YOUR BACKGROUND. HOW DID YOU GET STARTED COOKING?

I HAVE BEEN ~~BEEN~~ AROUND BAKING + COOKING FROM MY EARLIEST CHILDHOOD MEMORIES. FROM PLANTING + PICKING THE WEEDS IN THE GARDEN TO HARVESTING + CANNING OUR ABUNDANCE FROM THE SEASON. DURING THE HOLIDAYS WE WOULD TRAVEL TO MY GRANDMOTHERS HOUSE AND DO SOME HOLIDAY BAKING + SAUSAGE MAKING TO SHARE WITH THE EXTENDED FAMILY. I HAVE BEEN WORKING IN RESTAURANTS SINCE MY TEENS, THEN TO CULINARY SCHOOL WHERE DURING MY EXTERNSHIP I WORKED IN A BAKERY, THAT WAS 1993.

HOW WAS BREAD BAKING DIFFERENT DIFFERENT WHEN YOU FIRST STARTED OUT?

THE DIFFERENCE FROM WHEN I STARTED BAKING AND TODAY IS THE AVAILABILITY OF GRAINS + FLOURS. MAINLY JUST WHITE, WHEAT, + RYE WAS AVAILABLE AND TODAY THERE IS SO MUCH MORE VARIETY OF GRAINS LIKE EINKORN, EMMER, KHORASAN, SPELT, + COUNTLESS OTHER RED + WHITE ~~wh~~ HEIRLOOM WHEATS SUCH AS RED FIFE, CHIDDAM BLANC DE MARS, SONORAN, ROUGE DE BORDEAUX, FOISY, SEASHORE BLACK RYE.....

WHY DID YOU CHOOSE TO BAKE THE WAY THAT YOU DO?

I DID NOT CHOSE HOW I BAKE, FOR ME THE SPACE, EQUIPMENT, AVAILABILITY OF GRAINS + SEASONAL INGREDIENTS INSPIRE ME + DICTATE HOW I BAKE. MY STYLE IS EVER EVOLVING BASED ON WHAT IS AVAILABLE YEAR TO YEAR SEASONALLY.

WHY DO YOU THINK ITS IMPORTANT TO USE LOCAL GRAINS, SEEDS, AND INGREDIENTS IN YOUR BREAD?

TO SUPPORT LOCAL FARMS, KEEP THE CARBON IMPACT LOW AND THE MILES AS SHORT AS POSSIBLE.

HOW MUCH OF THE FLOUR IN YOUR BREAD DO YOU MILL YOURSELF?

CURRENTLY I MILL 40% OF THE TOTAL FLOUR I USE

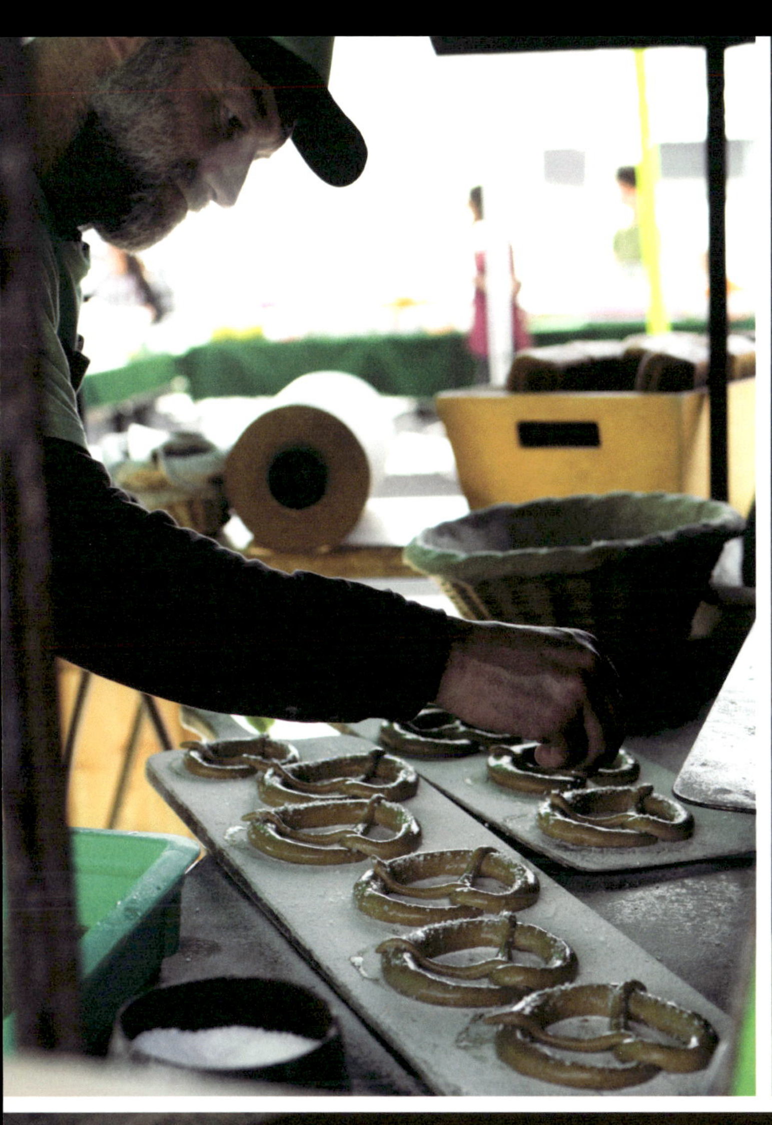

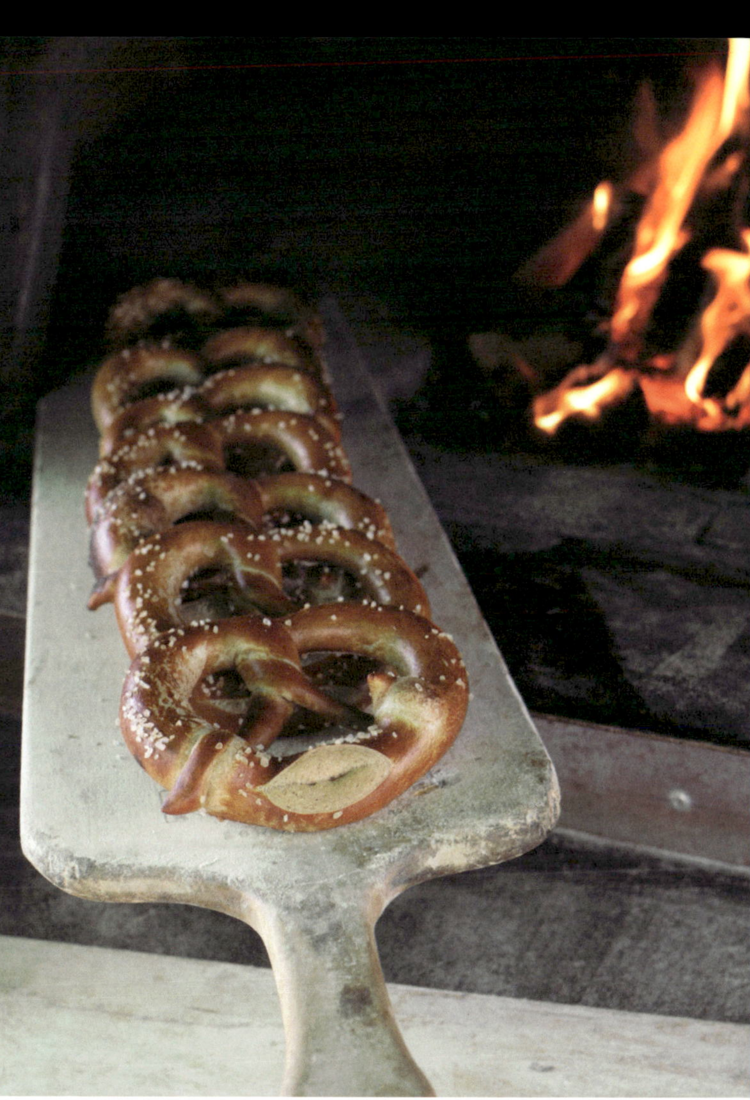

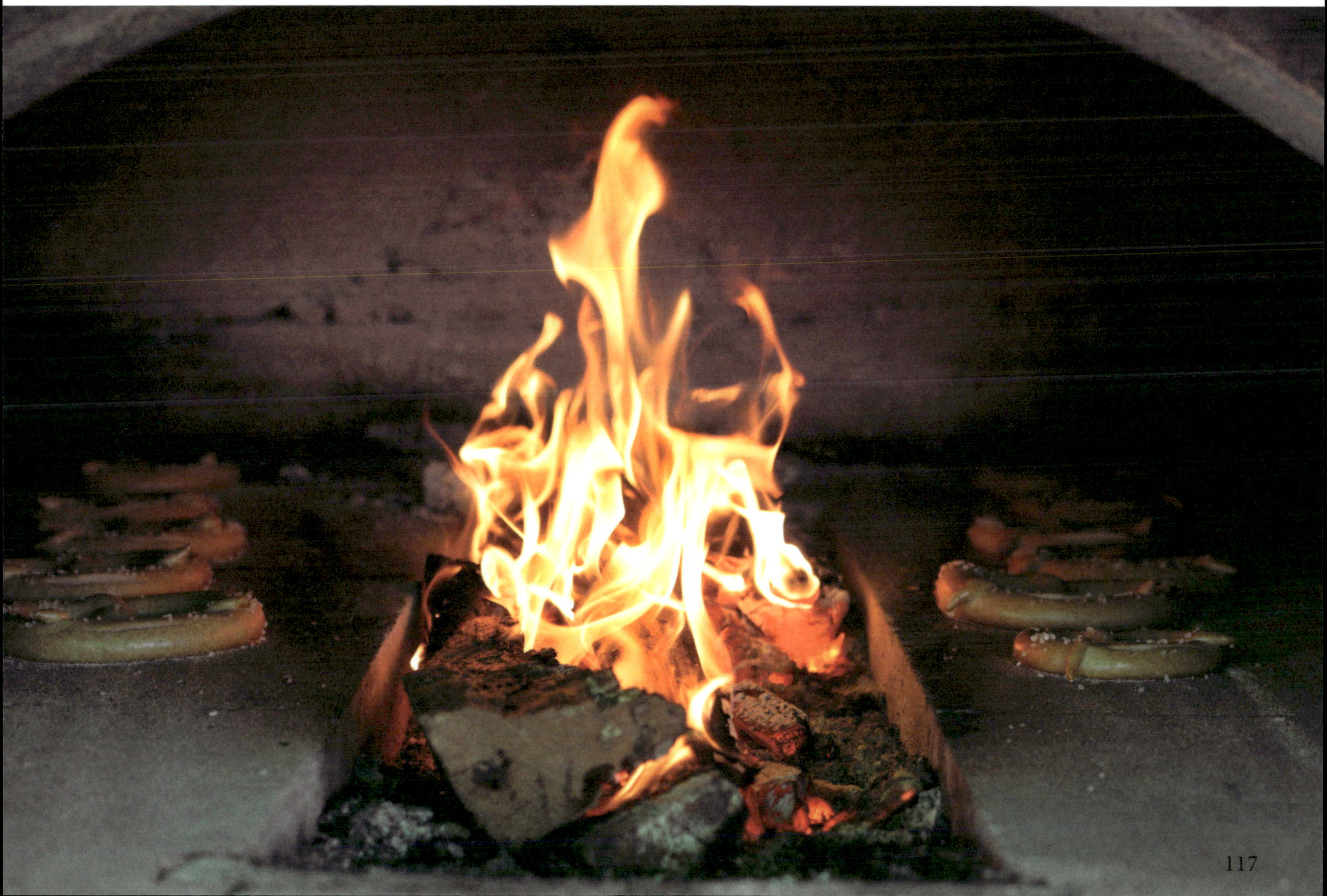

DOES FLOUR ACT ANY DIFFERENTLY WHEN IT IS MILLED FRESH?

FRESH IS BEST, THE AROMA + FLAVOR DON'T COMPARE, AS FOR THE PERFORMANCE ITS ~~VERY~~ HAS LOTS OF ENZYMATIC ACTIVITY AND COULD TAKE MORE WATER. DEPENDING ON THE GRIND OF THE FLOUR AND HOW DRY THE GRAIN WAS FROM HARVEST.

WHAT IS IT ABOUT THE EINKORN WHEAT THAT YOU LIKE SO MUCH?

EINKORN IS WHERE IT ALL STARTED, OLDEST CULTIVATED GRAIN, THE MOST NUTRITIOUS, AND FLAVOR UNLIKE ANY OTHER. IT IS DIFFUCULT TO WORK WITH BUT THAT IS THE CHALLENGE, THE AROMA OF THE FRESHLY MILLED FLOUR + BAKED LOAF ARE TRULY UNIQUE. ITS MY FAVORITE LOAF AS IT IS FOR MANY OF MY CUSTOMERS AS WELL.

WHAT DO YOU THINK THE MOST PROMINENT MISTAKE THAT YOU SEE BAKERS MAKING?

THE MOST PROMINENT MISTAKE I SEE IS OVER OR UNDER FERMENTING THE BREAD WHICH IS EASY TO DO. I DON'T KNOW IF I WOULD CALL THEM MISTAKES BUT LEARNING OPPORTUNITIES. HAVING SAID THAT LACK OF EXPERIENCE OBSERVING + UNDERSTANDING FERMENTATION IS A LIFELONG PURSUIT.

WHAT ARE YOU CURRENTLY WORKING ON THAT EXCITES YOU?

EVERYTIME I BAKE IT EXCITES ME AS ITS ALWAYS A CHALLENGE. BAKING BREAD IS ALWAYS A CHALLENGE AND IM CONSTANTLY CHALLENGED BY EACH NEW SEASONS LOCAL GRAINS, COMBINATION OF FLOURS, + FERMENTED GRAIN COMBINATIONS. IN ADDITION OTHER FERMENTED THING EXCITE ME LIKE PASTA DI GRANI FERMENTATI WHOLE GRAIN CRACKERS, APPLE CIDER, + KOMBUCHA.

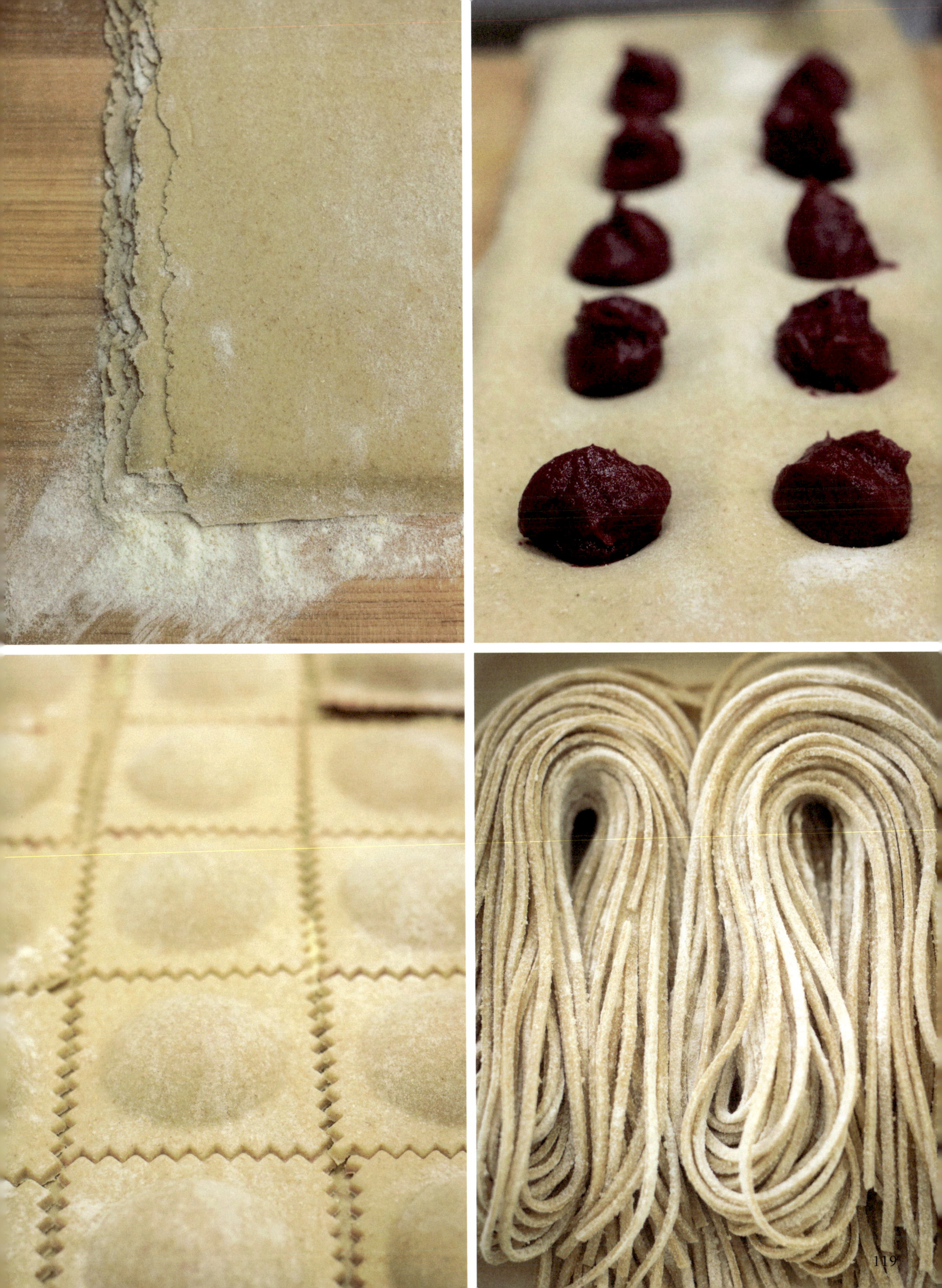

WHY DID YOU DECIDE TO COMPETE IN THE COUP DU MONDE DE LA BOULANGERIE IN FRANCE?

THE COUPE DU MONDE DE LA BOULANGERIE, THE PROCESS FOR ME WAS A STUDY + MASTERY IN BREAD. IT WAS A 10 YEAR JOURNEY FROM WHEN I FIRST VIEWED THE COUPE IN PARIS IN 2002 (THE US TEAM GOT SILVER) TO MY COMPETING ON THE TEAM IN 2012 AND BRINGING HOME THE SILVER WITH MY TEAMATES

HOW DID THE FERMENTED PASTA COME TO BE?

THE PASTA DI GRANI FERMENTATI (FERMENTED WHOLE GRAIN PASTA) HAS BEEN AN IDEA FOR MANY YEARS AND CAME ABOUT FOR REASON OF NUTRITION + DIGESTABILITY. IT LIKE BREAD FERMENTATION IS A CONTINUAL PURSUIT OF CONTROL, FINESSE, + CREATIVITY. I GREW UP MAKING PASTA WITH MY GRANDMA + MOTHER SO FOR ME ITS AN EVOLUTION OF FERMENTATION IN BREAD WITH WHOLE GRAIN MILLING TO MAKE THIS PASTA.

WHEN YOU'RE FORMULATING A NEW BREAD, DOES THE FORMULA MATH ALWAYS WORK OUT? HOW MUCH TRIAL AND ERROR IS THERE IN NEW BREAD DEVELOPMENT?

THE FORMULATING OF BREAD FORMULAS FOR ME IS A PRECISE THING WITH BAKERS MATH. FOR ME IT'S EASY TO CREATE A NEW FORMULA IN WHICH TO TWEAK + PLAY WITH CONSTANTLY.

WHERE DO YOU SEE THE FUTURE OF BREAD BAKING GOING IN THE USA?

I SEE THE FUTURE OF BAKING CONTINUING TO RETRO-INNOVATE ITSELF BY GOING BACK TO THE WAY GOOD BREAD HAS ALWAYS BEEN MADE, LONG NATURAL FERMENTATION WITH A MODERN TWIST BEING A MYRIAD OF GRAINS AVAILABLE + SEASONAL INGREDIENTS. ALONG WITH THIS WOULD BE MORE STONE MILL MAKERS + WOOD FIRED OVEN MAKERS KEEPING A HAND IN THE PAST.

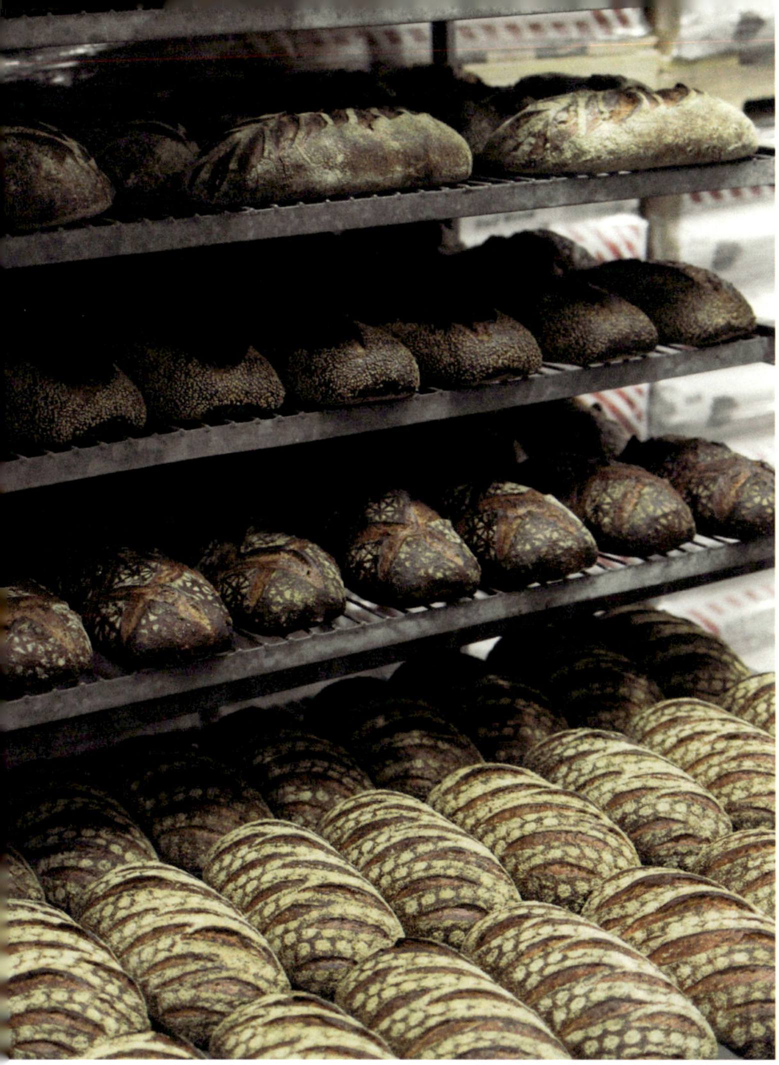

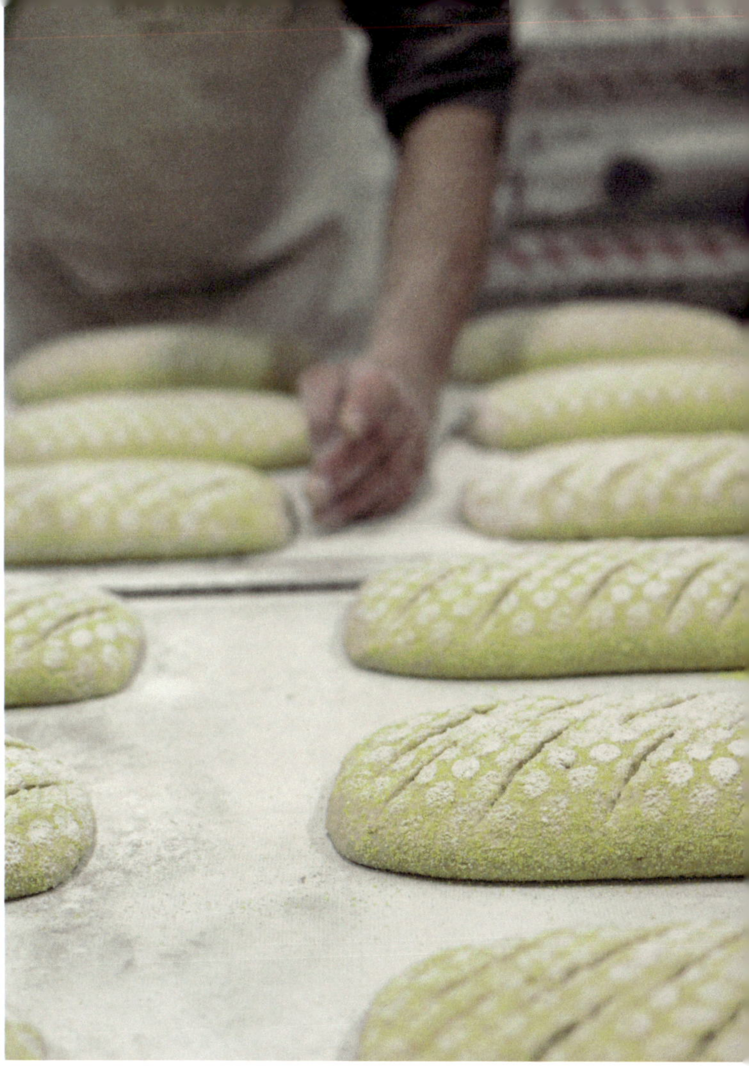

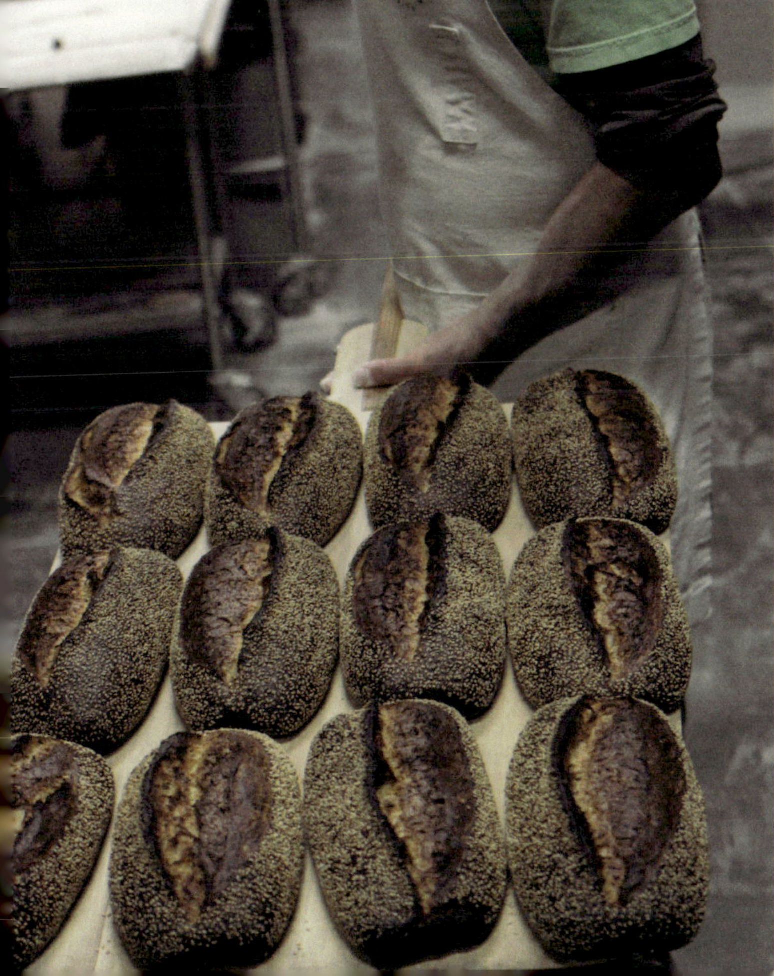

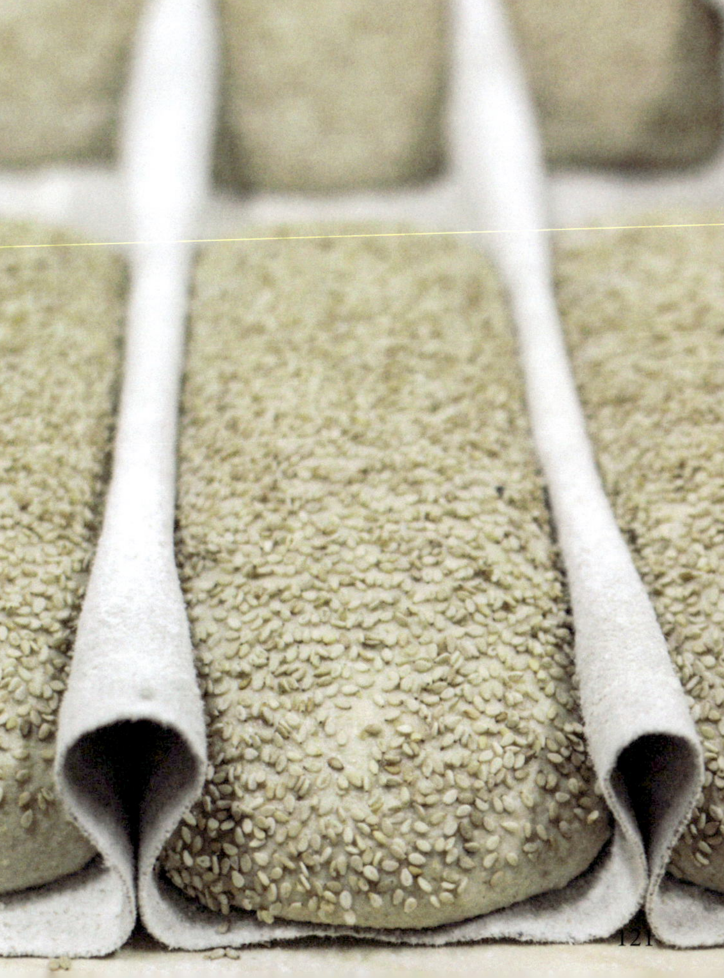

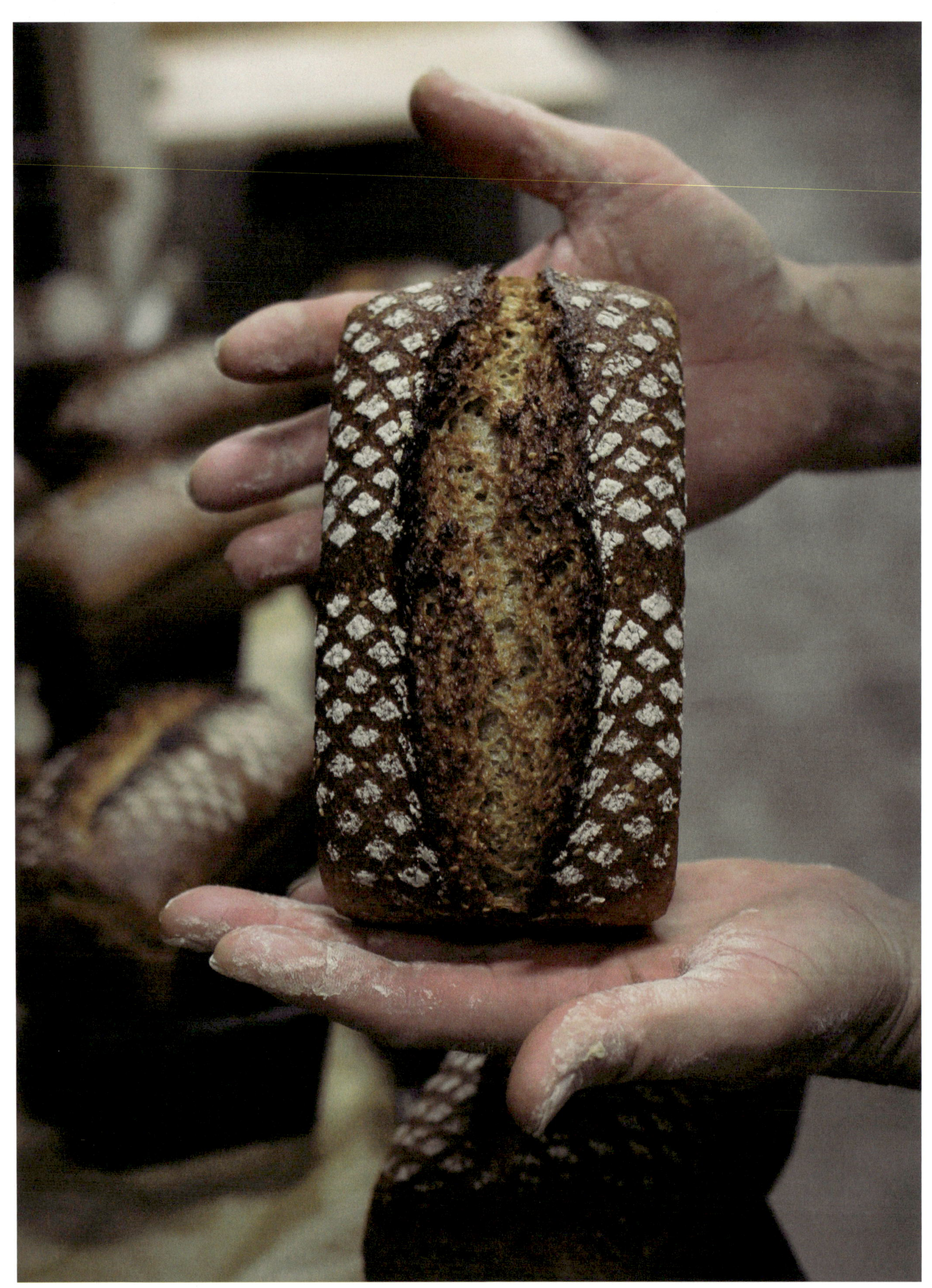

STONE MILLED EINKORN

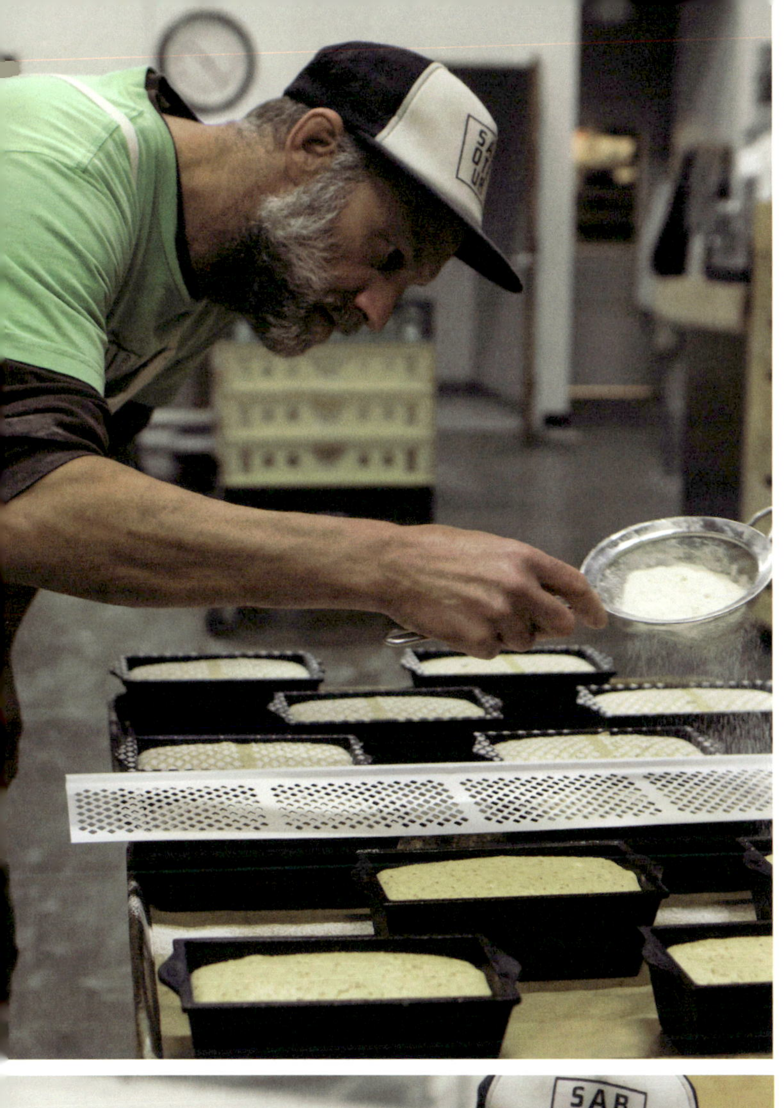

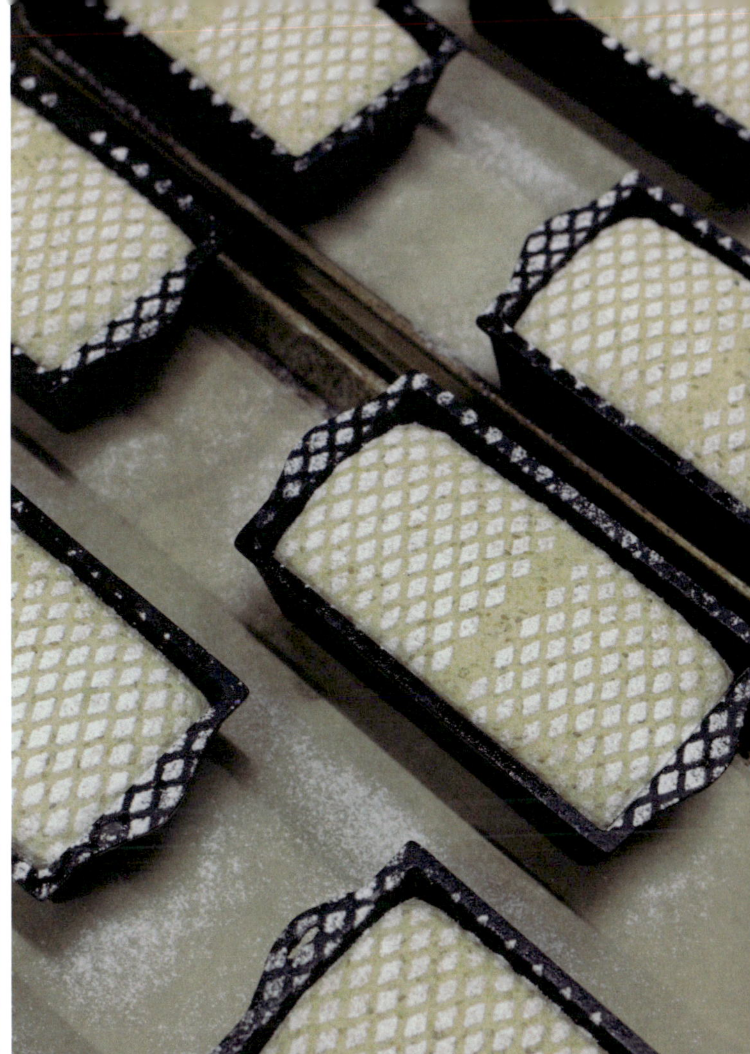

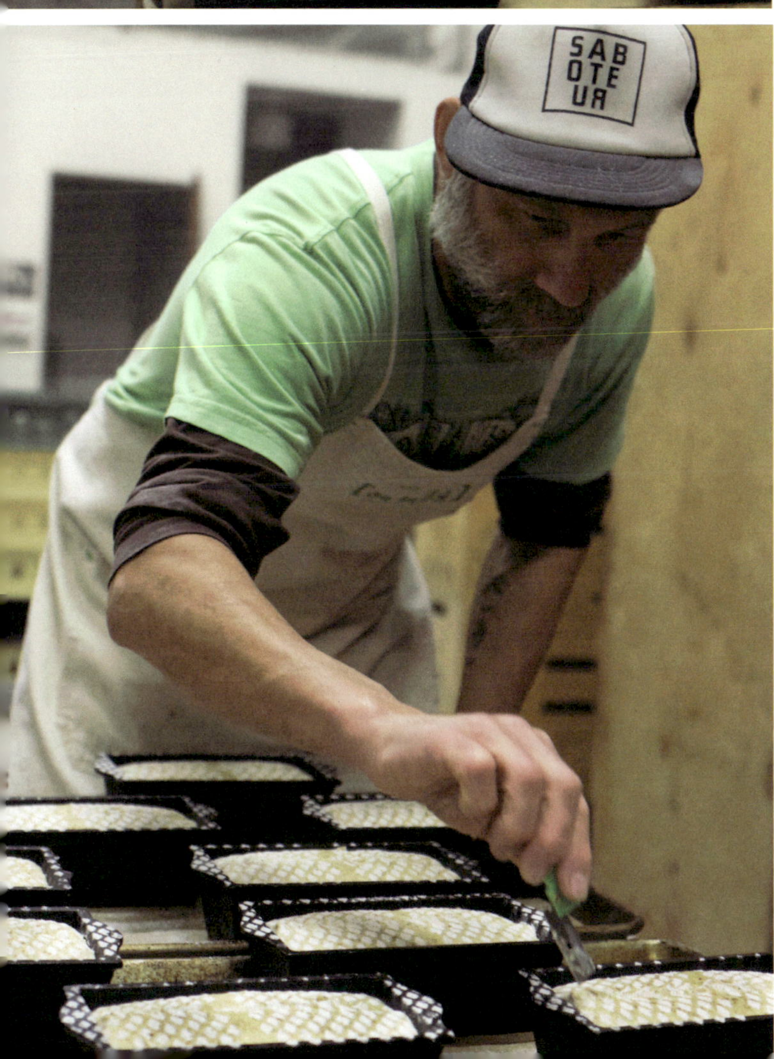
SAB
OTE
UR

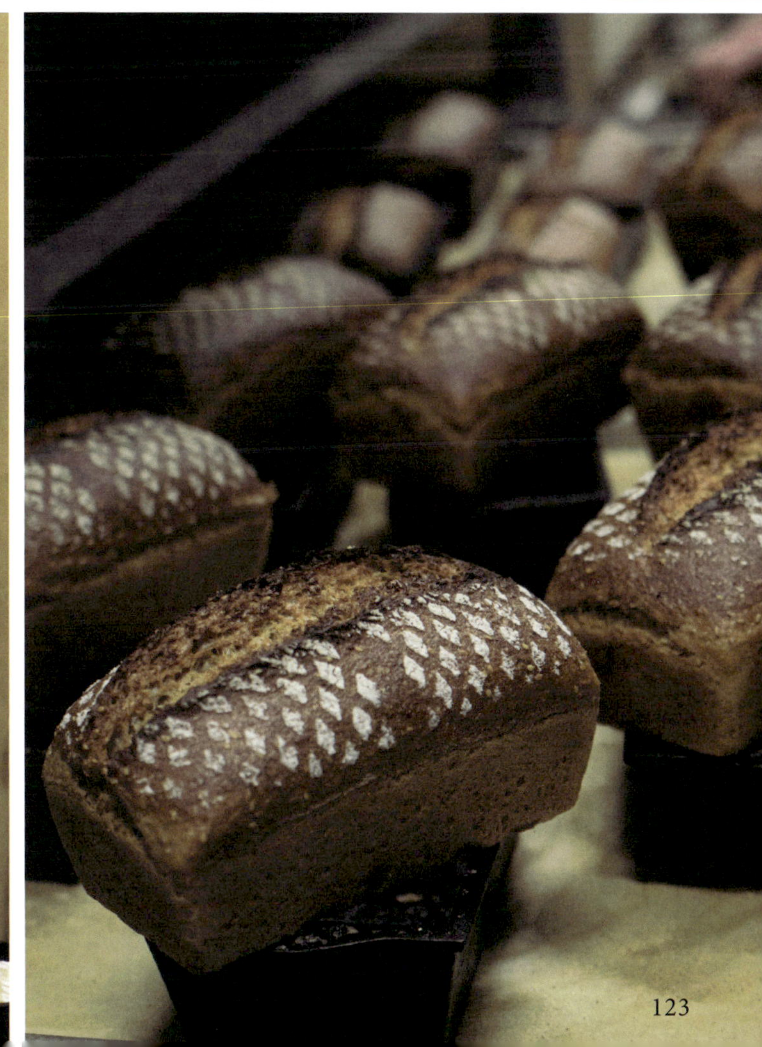

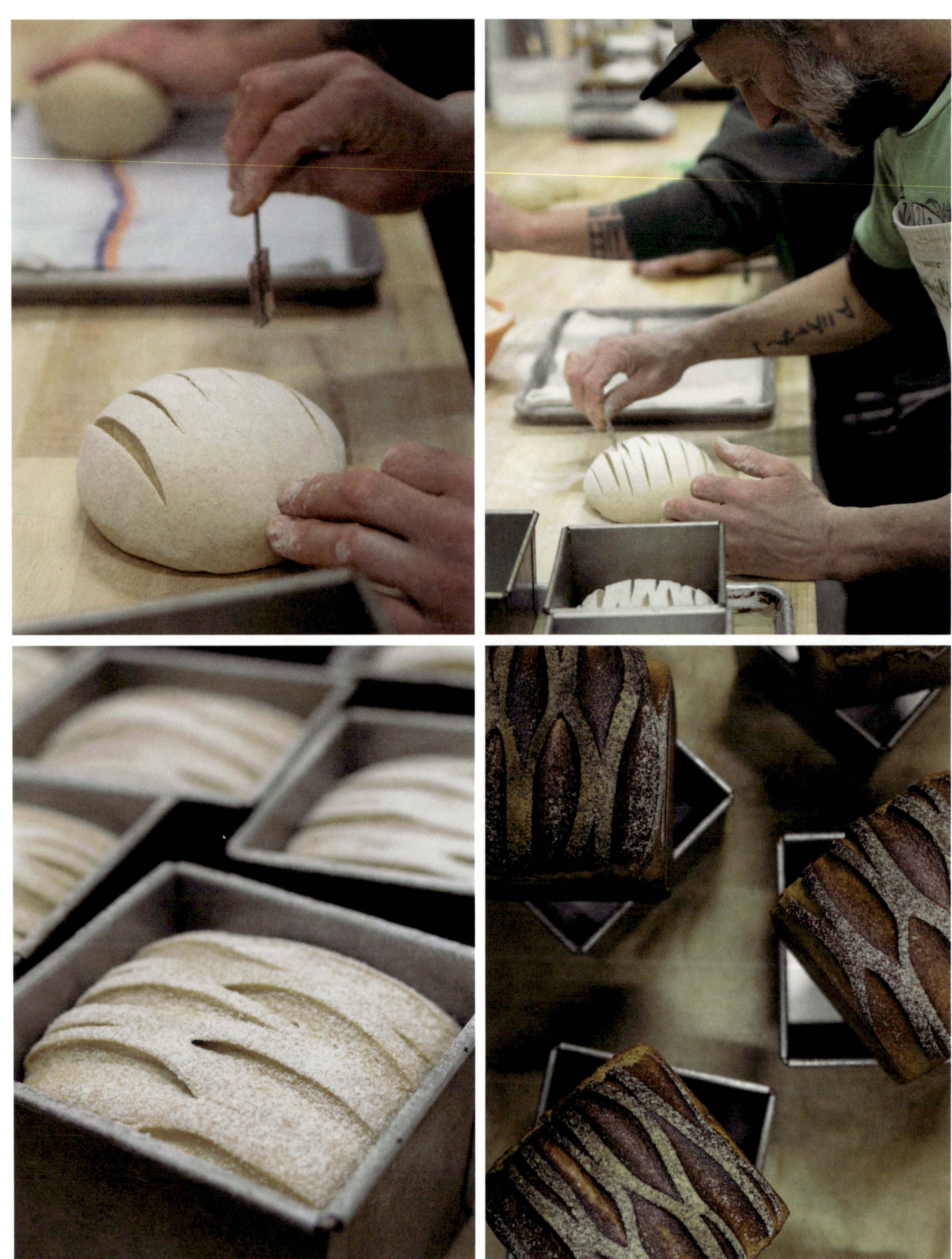

PAIN DE MIE

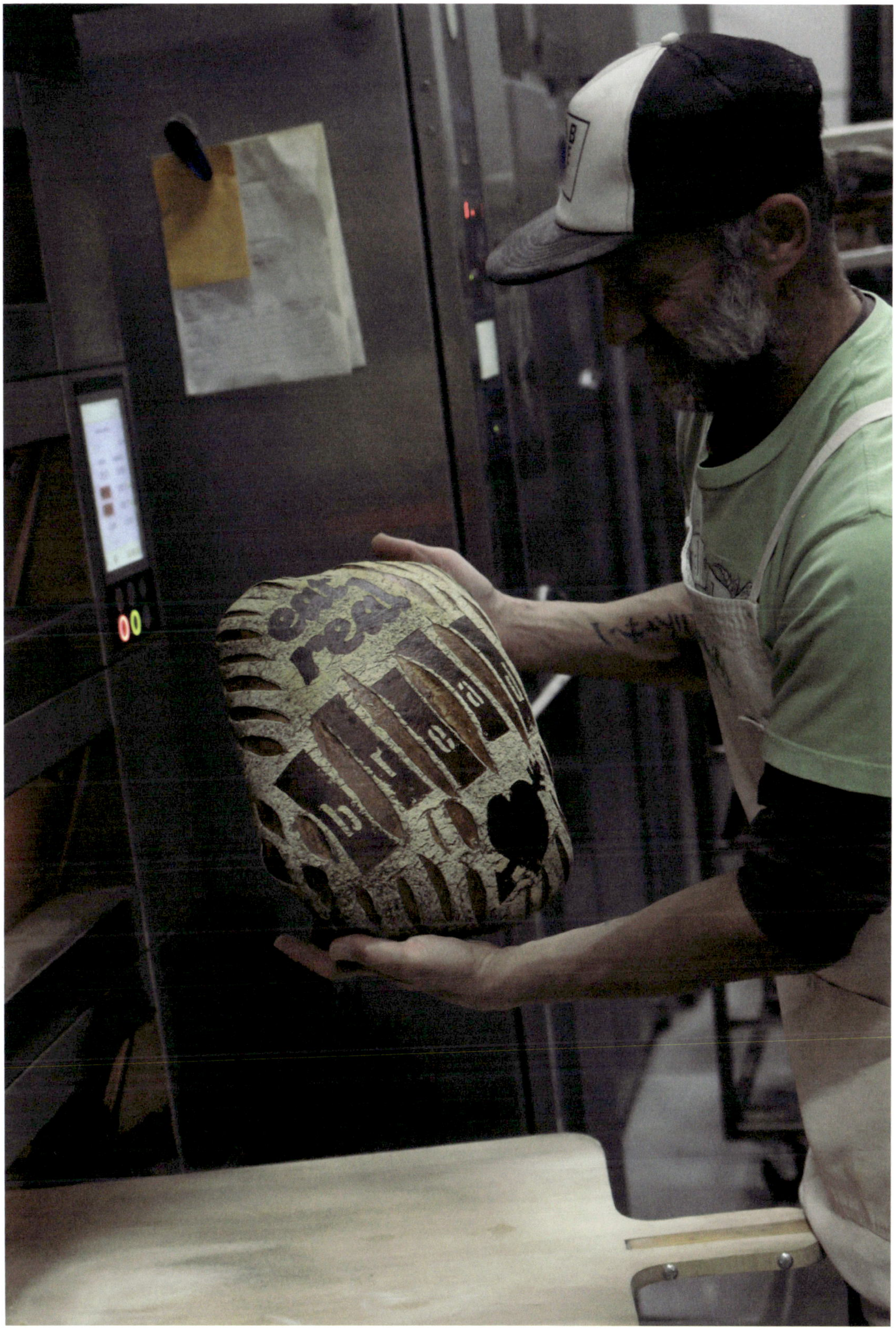

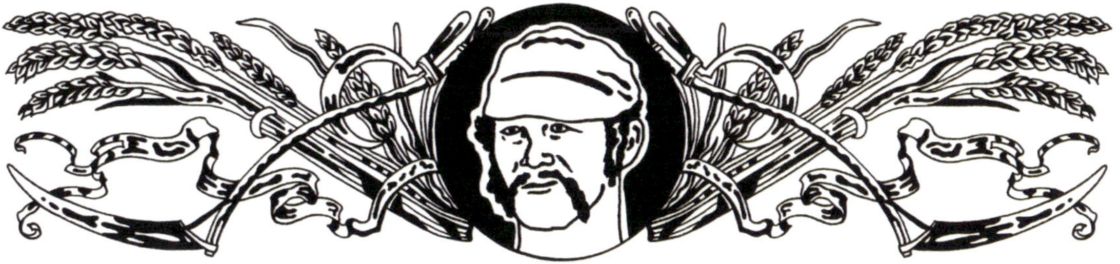

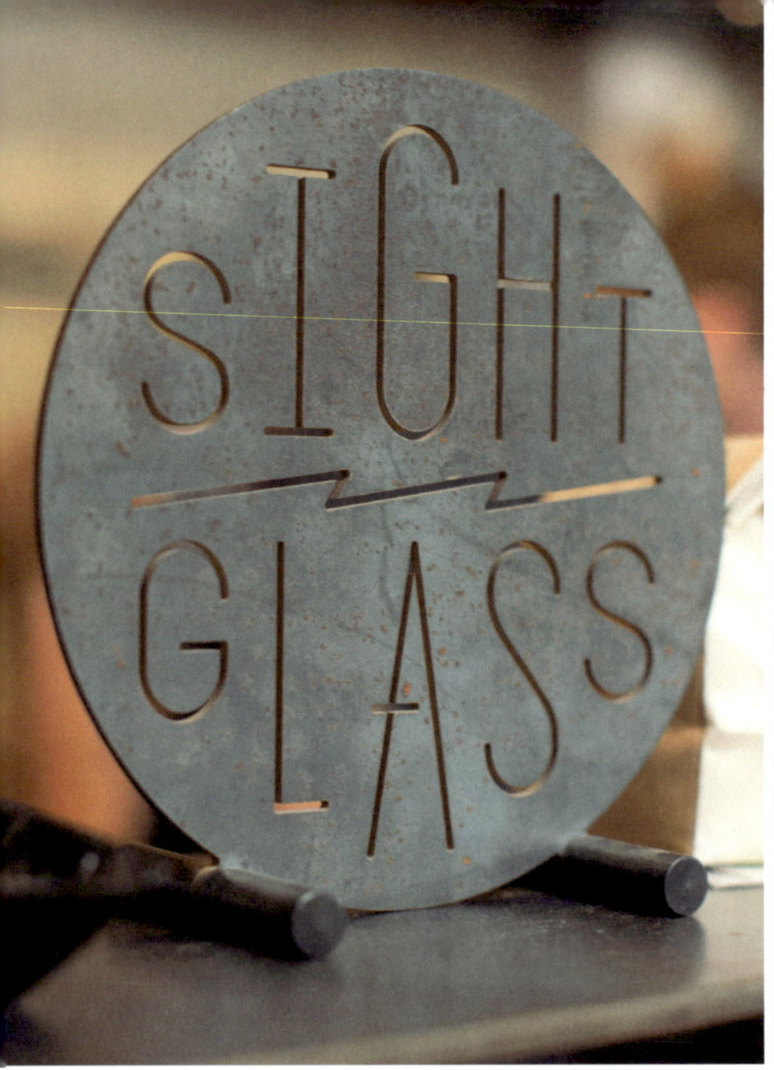

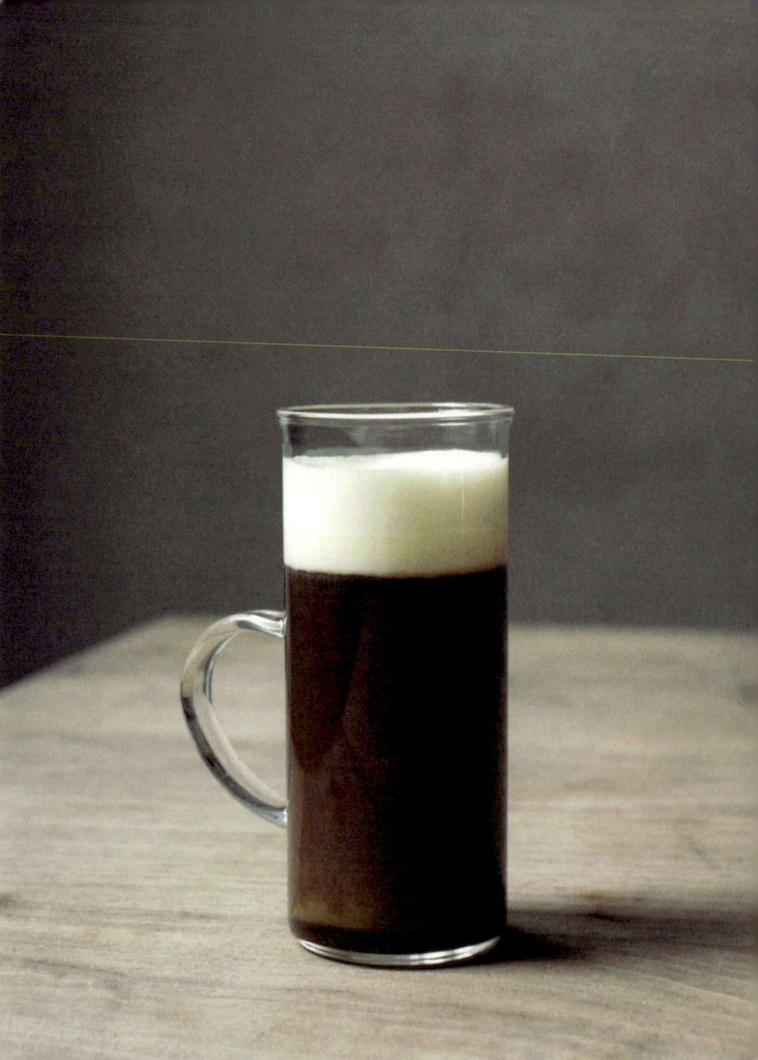

The perfect cup is all about relationships—between soil and climate, producers and roasters, the person pulling a shot of espresso and the one drinking it. To us, the most interesting relationships produce the best coffees; complex and surprising, but grounded in the simple enjoyment of a well-crafted cup.

As a sibling-owned coffee company started in San Francisco, we love working with our friends and peers. We carefully source coffees from producers in Latin America, Africa and the Pacific; help with training and support; and take a thoughtful approach to working with your menu.

Interested in partnering with us? We can help you plan a program, discuss our single origin coffees or blends, or run over the logistics of equipment and service. We genuinely love this stuff.

We'd love to chat! Contact us at hello@sightglasscoffee.com or (415) 861-1313.

Trou Normand

Some relationships bring out our sharper edges. "A young Armagnac has an interesting angularity," according to Eric Johnson, part owner at Trou Normand. The coffee they use in the Cafe Gascogne has the right combination of acidity and body to express the special qualities of a brandy described as "feisty." The traditional luxury of an aged Armagnac is an easy pleasure, but sometimes a great drink is about the challenge.

Cafe Gascogne

Ingredients:

1 bar spoon	Raw Sugar
1.5 oz	Young Armagnac
6 oz	Hot Sightglass Coffee
	Fresh Whipped Cream

Method:

In a preheated glass or mug, stir together raw sugar and young Armagnac. Add the hot coffee. Stir to dissolve the sugar, and finish with a half inch of whipped cream on top.

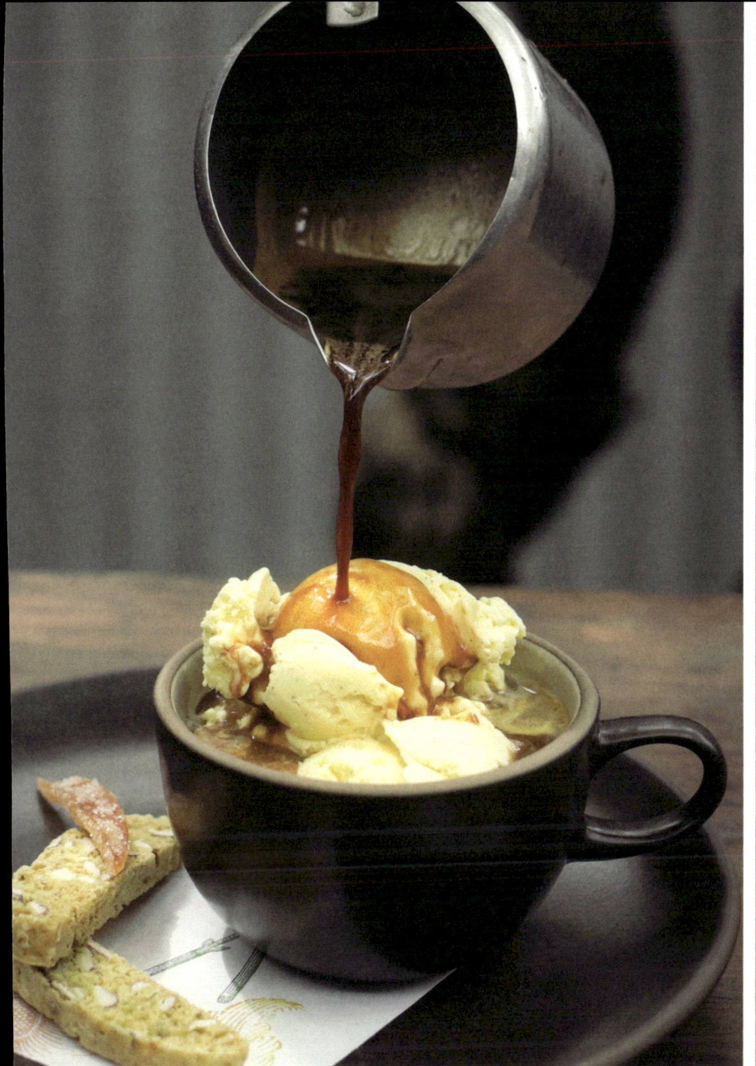

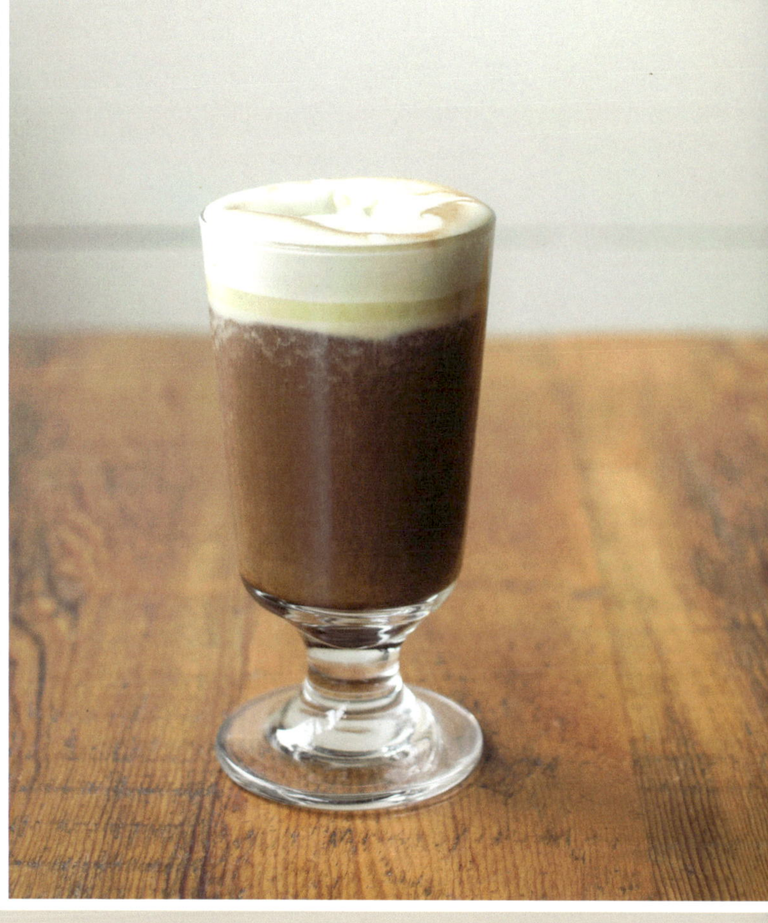

Chez Panisse

Some relationships run hot and cold. The classic affogato—a scoop of ice cream topped by a shot of espresso—is an iconic part of the menu at Chez Panisse. Coffee that's balanced and fruity without stealing the show is key to this dessert, a complement to the ice cream, candied peel, and biscotti, all carefully made in-house at Chez Panisse. The result is, according to pastry chef Carrie Lewis, "beautiful, but also austere."

Affogato

Ingredients:

2 ea	Vanilla Ice Cream Scoops
2 shots	Sightglass Espresso
2 ea	Mazzini Biscotti
1 ea	Candied Valencia Orange Peel

Method:

Pull two shots of espresso. In a cup, place two scoops of vanilla ice cream. At the table, gently pour the espresso over the ice cream and serve with two pieces of biscotti and a piece of candied orange peel.

Rich Table

Some relationships are like old friends. Coffee and chocolate have been comfortable around each other for a very long time, but they still have something interesting to say in this drink made by Tommy Quimby, bar manager at Rich Table. The Fernet helps. (As it usually does.) This drink, like a lasting friendship, "looks very simple, but the complexity is why you enjoy it."

Rich Coffee

Ingredients:

1 oz	Tempus Fugit Creme de Cacao
.5 oz	Fernet Branca
4 oz	Sightglass Coffee
	Pistachio Whipped Cream

Method:

For the pistachio whipped cream, combine pistachio paste with sugar and heavy cream (to taste). Whip. Pour the creme de cacao and fernet into the bottom of a glass. Pour freshly brewed coffee over the top and top with pistachio whipped cream.